The Barbirollis

Other works by the same authors

Harold Atkins
Beecham Stories (with Archie Newman)

Peter Cotes
No Star Nonsense
The Little Fellow (with Thelma Niklaus)
A Handbook of Amateur Theatre
George Robey
Trial of Elvira Barney
Circus (with Rupert Croft-Cooke)
Origin of a Thriller
JP: The Man Called Mitch
Misfit Midget
Portrait of an Actor

The Barbirollis
a Musical Marriage

Harold Atkins
& Peter Cotes

Robson Books

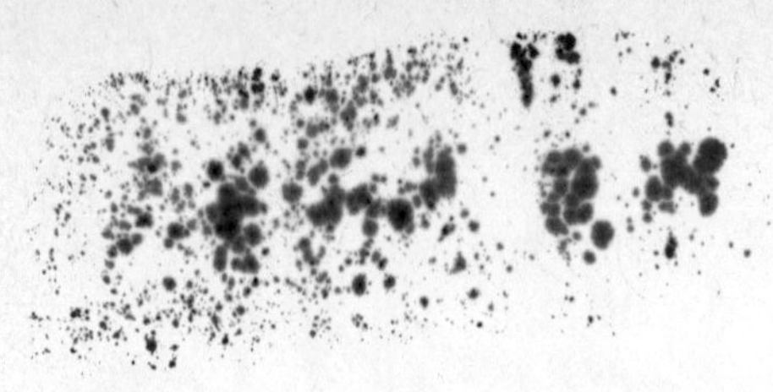

FIRST PUBLISHED IN GREAT BRITAIN IN 1983 BY ROBSON BOOKS LTD., BOLSOVER HOUSE, 5-6 CLIPSTONE STREET, LONDON W1P 7EB.

Atkins, Harold
The Barbirollis.
1. Barbirolli, *Sir* John 2. Rothwell, and Evelyn 3. Conductors (Music)—Biography
4. Oboe music—Biography
I. Title II. Cotes, Peter
785'.092'4 ML419.R/

ISBN 0-86051-211-8

Printed in Hungary

Contents

Foreword

It is rare to find partnerships which work superbly on different levels, particularly in the world of show business. John and Evelyn Barbirolli, exceptional in so many ways, were exceptional in this also. Solo performers lead very lonely lives; when one's partner shares this loneliness the relationship between the two people cannot help but develop in a most special way. The Barbirollis achieved, as a pair, a wonderful marriage, at the same time somehow preserving their independence as individual musicians, and so brought to the marriage a double beauty.

Much has been said and written about John; Evelyn has had a different sort of exposure. As an instrumentalist of the finest quality and as a teacher of the first rank, her marvellous gifts have influenced both the public and the profession in ways which are impossible at this time to evaluate.

John's and Evelyn's devotion to their profession was equalled by one thing, the profession's devotion to them, inspired above all by their human qualities. Loved as musicians, but also loved as people.

To those of us who were lucky enough to know them both, the memory of their partnership warms and gladdens the heart, and a book which brings the story of such a marriage is welcome indeed. Glorious John! Yes, and Glorious Evelyn too!

JANET BAKER, D.B.E.

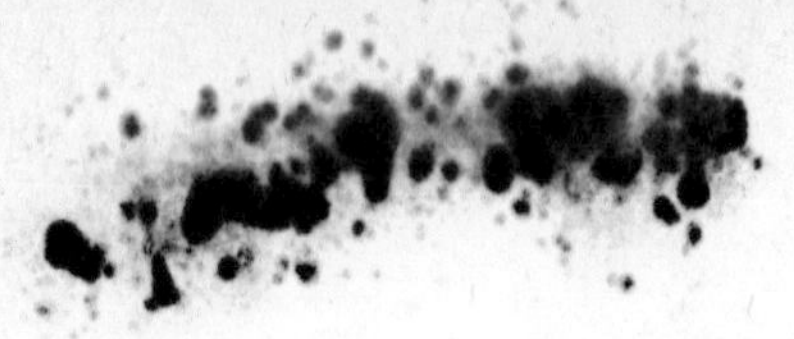

Preface

The lives of John Barbirolli and his wife Evelyn Rothwell formed a duality of deep affection and rare understanding. Both were consummate musicians who loved music-making, both enjoyed the itinerant world of orchestras and concert-providers, both travelled far and wide in many countries. They were received with acclaim and their artistry was rewarded with plaudits, distinguished friendships and public honours. But they clung firmly to a simple private life of their own. And their story has its principal setting not in one of the world's capitals but in the rugged northern industrial city of Manchester, from which the Hallé Orchestra has been an inspired outward-going artistic force for over a hundred and twenty years.

Evelyn has been good enough to give us the benefit of many memories of her dynamic partner and we are grateful for her co-operation in this account of their life together from their first meeting at Covent Garden Opera House. During thirty-one years of marriage she showed constant understanding of the conductor's complex temperament, with its triumphs, exhaltations, depressions and eccentricities. Her balance of commonsense and humour reinforced his energies and tempered his strenuous life. Since his death in 1970 she has carried on her own busy career playing and teaching the oboe, of which she is an international exponent.

The many who knew and admired the music of both in many lands would, we felt, like to know more of their life together and its artistic joys and thrills, and of the affection and high opinion in which they were held by their friends and contemporaries.

H.A.& P.C.

1 *His Beginnings*

Sir John Barbirolli died on July 28, 1970, at the age of seventy. And it was one of those rare events: the passing of an artist which left in ordinary people a sense of loss, so that the tributes which poured in and the reminiscences which poured out were inspired by a genuine sense of grief. But during his lifetime the odds must often have seemed stacked against his being mourned so widely . . .

Giovanni Battista, as John Barbirolli was christened, was born on 2 December 1899, above a baker's shop in Southampton Row, Holborn, in central London. Both his father, Lorenzo Barbirolli, and his grandfather Antonio had emigrated to England from Italy early in that decade.

Lorenzo was a native of Padua and one of his ancestors was organist of the church of Il Santo there. Antonio was born in Rovigo, a small town in the Veneto south of Padua, and both had devoted their lives to music as part-itinerant violinists, playing in all sorts of orchestras of varying sizes and importance. They were even playing together at La Scala, Milan, on the night that Verdi's opera *Otello* had its première in 1887. Among the cellists, too, that night, his conducting still ahead of him, was their friend the young Arturo Toscanini.

Lorenzo, a talented violinist, had just finished his training as an accountant when he suffered a long, apparently serious, illness. To recuperate he went on tour with Antonio, who was leading a touring opera orchestra. They travelled around Italy and Lorenzo was co-opted into the violin section. He loved it, forgot accountancy and continued his life as a musician. Some years later he and his father were in the renowned Scala Opera Orchestra. The year 1890 saw them both touring France with an Italian opera company and Lorenzo was soon tempted to try his luck in Paris.

At 26 he was a tall, handsome man with a prominent moustache, of a courteous and gentle disposition, normally quiet but like most Italians of a volatile temperament. He and his father always enjoyed a diversity of jobs—from café orchestras and small theatre pits to opera houses—and music in those days had a wide variety to offer. He soon found work in Paris in a 'Hungarian' café band, more Hungarian in uniform than in anything else—in fact polynational—which performed in the Café Anglais on the Rue de la Paix. It was in Paris too that he met his future wife, John's mother, a girl of twenty.

He had turned one evening into a modest little eating place in the Faubourg St Honoré for supper, and it was there he saw her. Louise Marie Ribèyrol was an apprentice milliner who lived with her uncle and aunt, owners of the restaurant. She had been born in 1870 at Arcachon, a fishing village noted for its oysters in the Bay of Biscay, 35 miles south-west of Bordeaux. She had come to Paris when about thirteen, on the death of her father, who was of Basque blood. The evening that Lorenzo strolled in she was helping out with the serving.

As he looked up from the menu he had been studying when she came to take his order their eyes met, and stayed met. The friendship that followed ripened quickly into love. Soon he was taking her out and telling her the same story that lovers have told from long ago, as well as of his unconventional musical life and travels and his plans to go on with the Hungarian band to London, where they had been engaged at an opulent hotel in the Strand. He would soon get better pay, put a little money by, find somewhere to live, send for her to join him and then they would be married in London.

In 1892 Lorenzo crossed the Channel with his colleagues for what they all hoped would be a profitable venture. But very soon the leader of the orchestra was found to have become involved in an affair with the impressionable young wife of the hotel manager, and the whole band was sacked.

Lorenzo, left wretched without a job in a strange country where he knew hardly a word of the language, was nevertheless lucky in having a few friends in the Italian colony. But being without money he delayed keeping his promise to send for Louise.

She, growing frantic at the inexplicable silence and thinking he had forgotten her, impetuously decided to come to London on her own. This was typical of her—she would throw aside all caution when her emotions were aroused. She found him part of an Italian coterie, and they faced reverses together. Later she was to tell how for the first six weeks they were so poverty-stricken that they lived on nothing but potatoes, bringing back at every chance a sack of them from the market on a barrow. It was Lorenzo's good fortune that Louise was a splendidly inventive cook, even making of the potatoes something of a speciality. It was in remembrance of this period of penury that she would cook occasionally in after years what she called '*Patate alla miseria*'—a delicious dish garnished with butter and garlic.

Not only was cooking one of Louise's strong points—she also helped out with a dressmaking job during this lean time, being expertly nimble with her hands. Soon Lorenzo had found his feet and was again set up in work. Together they settled down to married life.

From the start the pair were attracted by Victorian London, this fascinating and somewhat ferocious great city of luxury and squalor from which the imperturbable British ruled a large portion of the world. The Latin temperament of the Barbirollis adapted to the English, though at a certain cautious distance. They lived cheerfully and modestly in the smoky immensity of glimmering gas-lamps and glittering theatre signs, hansom cabs and horse-buses, top hats and bowlers, large flowered hats and corseted waists, ragged crossing-sweepers, flower-girls with kerbstone trays and complacent 'bobbies'. In the summer sunny picnics in the parks and in the winter impenetrable yellowish fogs, and plenty of the theatres, hotels and cafés requiring musicians. Irving at the Lyceum, Dan Leno at the Tivoli, Maskelyne and Devant at the Egyptian Hall were in their heyday—aspects of entertainment in Town that little John was never able to forget.

Antonio, attracted as much by family ties as by the prospects of work, also crossed the Channel. He joined the ménage in their Wardour Street lodgings, bringing his wife Rosina and Lorenzo's sister Elisa. He, too, got fixed up with his violin and within a year or two the whole family moved to Holborn, taking six rooms above the shop of a Mr Herbert Harris, confectioner, Southampton Row, near the corner of Cosmo Place, in itself a small Italian outpost leading into Queen Square, where the Italian Hospital still stands.

Father and son busily occupied themselves in the orchestral pits of theatres and on the well-carpeted platforms of restaurants. And at the occasional symphony concert. They had congenial compatriots in this restricted area and when they were settled most of their work appeared to be concentrated in Leicester Square, only half a mile from home. They played in the orchestra of the Moorish-looking Alhambra, on the eastern side of the square, with its Saracenic interior and saucer-dome, dispensing spectacular ballets, acrobatic acts and even—in 1896—a film of the Derby. They alternated this with engagements at the rival house over the square, the Empire Theatre; built in Persian style, it sported a remarkable mixture of Renaissance foyer and Pompeiian staircase, Indian entrance halls, Egyptian pit and notoriously exotic contemporary promenade. Here their music accompanied even more spectacular ballet of the period (Adeline Genée, the distinguished Danish dancer, was première danseuse) and Variety bills composed of jugglers, bell-ringers, conjurors, sensational trapeze artists and trick cyclists. They shared the first violin desk under the conductor Leopold Wenzel, and Lorenzo in due course became leader of the orchestra, which played before the Queen at Windsor Castle in 1897.

Completing the Leicester Square complex was the Queen's Hotel, next to the Empire, a lively, go-ahead establishment with small orchestras in both restaurant and grill room. Lorenzo played in either and sometimes had the distinction of conducting the Sunday evening concerts by the combined players—popular music with a stylish presentation, orchestral excerpts from a widespread choice of operas, and miscellaneous light pieces, often French or Italian and frequently with a vocalist. Lorenzo would conduct not with a baton but with his violin bow, reverting often to his violin while standing—in those days a dashing and romantic way of doing it, with sometimes a swirling gesture, that had appealed to Johann Strauss. His son would later describe him as a musician of great taste—'essentially a café player, I suppose, but of the very first class. He had a most lovely *sound.*'

It was a derivation of this 'sound' that came to be known as the 'Barbirolli Sound' when John conducted in the years to come.

Giovanni (or John, as he was later to call himself, or Tita, the family diminutive of his second name, Battista) first saw the light of day in the very last weeks of the nineteenth century. He came a few years after his sister Rosa, who also showed early musical gifts. Almost from birth the two of them were initiated into an emotionally charged, highly articulate atmosphere of music and a household heavily slanted towards Italy. Mémé (as they called their mother) was a woman of dominant personality but with four voluble Italians the centre of gravity was not French but Italian. Tiny Tita was soon, as he started to talk, picking up three languages: the family Venetian—more of a language in itself than a dialect of Italian—French from his mother, and Cockney English from outside. Venetian won hands down at first. Later he was to be dubbed by many fellow-Londoners 'Cockney John'; never did a scion of London's Little Italy sound so Cockney as John did when he wished to do so.

Streams of musical talk poured over him. He grew up accustomed to vociferous Italian discussions, with snatches of French and bursts of home-grown slang, accompanied by illustrative off-duty sounds of violins.

Tita was only four years old when his father and grandfather introduced him to the mysteries of the Empire rehearsals. Sitting in the stalls or even low down in the orchestra, he made early acquaintance with the fantasy world of ballet and its swirling figures. He was soon treating violins as cossetted toys and soon after that being taught to play one by Grandfather. His sister Rosa had already started the piano. Their younger brother Peter, born eleven years after John, in his turn was to adopt the violin and later in life played, and continues to do so, the viola in the Covent Garden Opera Orchestra.

At the Empire rehearsals little John noticed that Leopold Wenzel, the bearded and volatile conductor, wore white gloves and he gained the impression that these went with the job. He was fascinated by them. When he was five his grandfather would take him on Sundays to listen to the band among the well-kept lawns in Lincoln's Inn Fields, close to their home. The bandmaster too wore white gloves to conduct the overtures, marches, suites and waltzes. So, as his quick eyes and ears took in the uses of the various instruments, the boy first began to formulate the idea that he would like to be a conductor—with white gloves, of course.

After the departure of the band he would sometimes go up to the conductor's place in the small bandstand and imitate him. And at home he would secretly borrow a pair of his mother's white gloves, shut himself inside her wardrobe, beating time with the gloves on in the small, darkened space.

In his early efforts to make something of the violin he developed the tiresome habit of walking about the flat at 37, Drury Lane, whither the family had now moved, muttering to himself. This his grandfather could not stand. As Barbirolli afterwards described it: 'I used to wander from room to room squealing and scraping in a way that got on my Grandfather's nerves. He took a hansom cab to a stringed instrument shop in Wardour Street and brought back a half-size cello. He put it between my legs, saying "Now you'll *have* to sit down".'

Fortunately Tita, though now anchored to a chair, liked the new instrument instantly and began to take cello lessons.

Louise, though matriarch and president of the kitchen, knew little or nothing of music and could not join in musical discussions. Lorenzo's sweet and gentle sister Elise was also very domesticated, helping her sister-in-law with cooking, washing and ironing and preparing pasta. Grandmother Rosina was a very attractive woman, admired for her pretty face and a twenty-inch waist even when she was old. She hardly ever went out of the flat and never 'connected' with English life.

Good-natured Lorenzo would often tell his interested children about life in the Italy they had never seen, about its many opera houses and, among many things he and his father could remember, how Guiseppe Verdi himself sat at the rehearsals of *Otello* at the Scala; of how he had said little at the back of the theatre but would click very loudly with his fingers if he didn't like the tempo or something else annoyed him. John's father recalled somebody inquiring of Verdi why on one occasion he was asking for four pianissimos—*pppp*. Verdi's retort was, 'Oh well, when I ask for four that's because I hope to get one!'

Lorenzo also told stories of the Boer War excitement in London and how on Mafeking Night in 1900 the crowds at the Lyric Club became so mad with joy that his violin was smashed.

On Sunday mornings the children would be taken by their

father to morning Mass at the Roman Catholic Church of Notre Dame de France in Leicester Place*. They ensconced themselves in the front pew but, as Lorenzo didn't want them to have to endure a half-hour sermon, he rose when it was about to begin and led them on tiptoe out again. They would all go off to nearby Greek Street, in Soho, to a French patisserie, Maison Bertaux†, to partake of hot chocolate and brioches or other dainties. Using meticulous timing, they returned to the church, tiptoed in and stood at the back for the Mass. Lorenzo was still carrying out this ritual over fifteen years afterwards with Rosa's children, his grandchildren.

Lorenzo and Antonio supplemented their incomes by some teaching—Lorenzo violin and mandoline, Antonio piano and violin—while Louise took in a lodger from time to time when the need arose. Grandfather Antonio was a talented teacher, downright and authoritative, soon well known in the district and called 'Professor' by his pupils. In the early 1980s Mrs Annette Hewitt recalled his coming on Sunday mornings to give her mother and Aunt Helene a piano lesson each in the upstairs sitting-room of the 'One O'Clock Shop' in New End Street, off Theobalds Road. This was an old-fashioned little Dickensian neighbourhood (blitzed in the Second World War) and the unusual shop was run by Mrs Hewitt's grandmother, Madame Cardon, after early widowhood and the closing of her restaurant in Soho. Her new shop sold everything from eatables to cheap 'fashion' jewellery and was open till one o'clock in the morning, which explained its name. It was used by residents of nearby Brunswick Square including, it is said, some of the 'Bloomsbury group'.

The violinists Barbirolli, on their way home after the show, sometimes called late at the 'One O'Clock Shop' to buy ham on the bone, one of its most attractive specialities. These transactions led to acquaintance, then music lessons and friendship. Antonio began to teach Helene and her sister the piano.

There was, unfortunately, a pattern of interruptions. It was a fairly frequent occurrence for a barrel-organ to arrive and start up operations just below the sitting-room window on

*Rebuilt after serious bombing during the Second World War.

†It is still there, and still dispensing excellent cakes and coffee.

those Sunday mornings. Antonio, stern and fiery in outward appearance, would then fling open the window, bellowing '*Basta! Basta!*' Sometimes he even dashed down into the street to remonstrate with the barrel-organ man. Madame Cardon often descended, too, to augment the controversy and was sometimes moved to pay the man to go away. Next Sunday he would be back again.

2 *Her Beginnings*

Under 'Marriages' in *The Times* of 7 July 1939, appeared the following:
BARBIROLLI, JOHN TO ROTHWELL, EVELYN on JULY 5TH 1939–In London quietly, John to Evelyn, only daughter of Mr and Mrs R. Rothwell of Cholsey, Wallingford, Berks.

Evelyn, the eldest of three children, was born on 24 January, 1911, to Richard Hornsby and Winifred Rothwell in the little market town of Wallingford-on-Thames, Berkshire. (It is now in Oxfordshire through county boundary changes.) Her father was 'in tea' ('something in the City', as he described himself), and came originally from the North Country, though brought up in the south.

Her grandfather, Evelyn recalled, used to travel about China dealing in tea and the business was inherited. Hornsby Rothwell had a City office and she remembered as a teenaged girl seeing him conducting a little occasional tea-tasting there before he took her to lunch at a chop-house. He spent as much of his time as possible in the country, loved walking and was an excellent shot. Even in his eightieth year he could take three cartridges and bring back a hare, a pheasant and a partridge.

Evelyn's mother, who was 22 years younger, was one of twelve children of Francis and Eleanor Hedges, of Brightwell, Berkshire. She was a descendant of Charles Reade, storyteller, ardent social reformer and eccentric author of that Victorian classic *The Cloister and the Hearth*, the popular, though less well known *Peg Woffington* and the old Lyceum melodrama *The Lyons Mail*, one of Sir Henry Irving's greatest successes in its day. Evelyn's family did not enjoy *The Cloister and the Hearth* much, considering it extremely dull.

She had two younger brothers; Richard, born in 1915, and George (known always as Peter until his marriage), born a year and a half later.

When Evelyn was still only four or less she had lessons in reading and writing from a dearly loved aunt (Violet Hedges, known as Aunt Baelie) who had trained at the Froebel Institute for Kindergarten Teaching. She had a great influence on Evelyn throughout her early life. Auntie Baelie decided to start a kindergarten school and for a time Evelyn *was* the school! But she was soon joined by cousins who lived next door (the two families were close friends and grew up together). The school, St Anthony's, grew rapidly and became well known. It was particularly valuable to parents serving in India in the days of the British Raj and the Empire because their children could be cared for even in the holidays. One of Auntie Baelie's 'children' grew up to be the actress Dulcie Gray.

Winifred, the more dominant member of the married partnership, was a practical woman of character and capability. She played the piano a little, and concerned herself a good deal with gardening and was a reasonable plain cook, but cooking bored her. She did not impart her limited culinary capabilities to her daughter. Cooking and domestic activity were left mainly to maids (in those days a normal part of a middle-class ménage). More apparent were her skills in the garden. Natalie James, Evelyn's friend and fellow music student, remembered: 'Whenever I arrange a flower-pot I think of the careful way I was shown when I went over to Evelyn's and into the garden to receive instruction from dear Mrs Rothwell. And I can never emphasize enough the old-world courtesy that was extended in that house.'

Evelyn's father was a gentle man who preferred to leave decisions to his wife. He was given to murmuring, 'Oh, I don't know, yer know' when faced with some knotty problem or asked for advice, until his voice trailed away; he'd quickly pick up his copy of *The Times* or look out on to the lawn, focus his attention on a patch of grass and change the subject. His manners were exemplary and he was courteous and kind to everyone.

A brief impression of Evelyn's father in the 1940s was

furnished by Sidney Rothwell (no relation of Evelyn's), who worked in the Hallé office and became John's secretary. He said:

'I once had the good fortune, with my wife, of visiting the Rothwell family home in Cholsey. We were on a cycling holiday in the Cotswolds: our route took us through Wallingford and I thought it would be pleasant to visit nearby Cholsey. Only Evelyn's father was at home. We had never met before, but he received us most graciously and, in showing us round the garden, displayed all those lovely characteristics of courtesy and politeness that we find in Evelyn.'

Winifred was a very limited pianist but she and some of her sisters were naturally musical. Aunt Margaret taught the piano and violin to children and was one of the piano teachers at Downe House School, where Evelyn was later to study. Another aunt, Geraldine, studied at the Royal College of Music. In later years, when Evelyn wanted to start a serious musical career and her father put obstacles in her way, it was her mother who encouraged her and said she ought to embark on it if that was her wish. Later still, living long enough* to see his daughter one of the country's leading musicians and arguably one of the most notable oboe players in the world, he calmly took credit for engineering the whole thing!

A reminiscence of early days is contained in a letter to Evelyn from Pamela Saxby who as a child was at St Anthony's, and with her brother Nicholas lived with the Rothwells for a short time. She wrote:

> I remember so well the sojourn which Nicky and I enjoyed with your kind parents, as children in the early 1920s . . . ; how very grown-up you seemed to me in the more distant days. *You* wore stocking and suspenders, while I was fobbed off with white socks forever disappearing into little black boots!
>
> I also remember a walk with your Nannie, with all of us children together, in the direction of Shillingford. Behind the garden railings of a house not far from Elmhurst [the Rothwell's house] we saw a hen's egg. Nannie allowed you, as the mature member of her entourage, to go inside

*He died in 1955 at the age of 91. Winifred died ten years after him, aged 80.

and deliver the egg to its rightful owner.

In you went, to the admiration of all beholders, and back you came with the report that the owners were out, but that you had been into the pantry and left their egg on a dish under a pudding basin. What sophistication! It made such a mark on me that I have never forgotten what I ought to do in the same circumstances!

Richard and his brother Peter went to 'prep' schools before going to Cheltenham College and Evelyn was sent at about thirteen to Downe House, an independent girls' school near Newbury, founded in 1907 by Miss Olive Willis (still at that time its notable head). She was to have a lasting influence on Evelyn, who remained there until she was eighteen. One of her clearest memories was of yearly visits to London with her parents to see certain hardy annuals of Christmas entertainments, most notably the evergreen *Peter Pan*, and its almost as long-running rival *Where the Rainbow Ends*.

As Evelyn always put it, she did not take up the oboe—it took her up. She didn't even know what it looked like when it did this.

It happened that Downe House could boast a good school orchestra—a thing much more rare in those days than now. She sang in the school choir but, apart from playing the piano 'very badly' (her own description), she was conversant with no other instrument. She had reached seventeen and was in her last year at school when the orchestra's two oboists left at the same time, leaving a gap that had to be filled quickly. The music staff, including her aunt, had the idea that Evelyn, the only choir member not in the orchestra, might be enlisted. They advanced on her and asked, 'Why don't you have a go at the oboe?'

'I'd never seen an oboe—didn't know one from a bull's foot,' she said. 'But they got me some dreadful little instrument and a very nice amateur started to give me lessons.'

So, there she was, by force majeure, in the orchestra having a go at the unknown instrument even before she had ever heard an orchestra except on the wireless. There were rehearsals, at which she started to play in some way or other. And in her last term she and the other girls would go over to Newbury sometimes to play in an amateur orchestra there—a bold undertaking, in which she struggled along as second oboe as best as she could.

Gifted and determined, she made quick progress. And after a few months of lessons and hard practice came a remarkable bolt from the blue. A scholarship was going—the Berkshire Scholarship—at the Royal College of Music.

She applied for it. The examining board was headed by the College principal, Sir Hugh Allen. The candidate was all trepidation, not ranking her chances high; she felt she could 'hardly hold the thing'. But they were reasonably impressed; the country girl who had never thought of becoming a musician gained the award for twelve months 'on potential' and then, Sir Hugh said, seriously but encouragingly, it would be renewable for another three years 'if you do what I think you will do'.

So instead of becoming what she anticipated she might be—a secretary, or cog in somebody's office—Evelyn now found the way open to training as a musician under the best auspices in London. There was still a battle to be fought at home with her father but she won. A new career opened up ahead and as she travelled up to London in the train, the girl was full of high spirits and excitement.

At the College in South Kensington she was lucky to be put under the tuition of the distinguished oboist Leon Goossens. Then a handsome man of thirty-one, Goossens was developing a new school of oboe playing and the young people competed for a place in his classes. At that time, women oboe-players were not common but Goossens' fame as a teacher drew a number of ambitious girl students. Natalie James, one of his pupils, said, 'In those days there was not a high average standard of sound with the oboe, apart from Leon Goossens' pupils.'

His first major contribution to Evelyn's musical education was to tell her: 'I'm afraid what you've been taught is all wrong—we'll have to try to *undo* it.'

She was not damped by the stricture but rather spurred on to special initial efforts, and she soon met the challenge of the Goossens technique. At that time piano was an obligatory second subject at the RCM, at least for the first year. Freda Swain, her tutor, was well thought of as a teacher in the 1920s. But later Evelyn diversified—she studied the cello for a short time, and even the timpani, because it released more time to devote to the oboe. Her lessons on the formidable kettle-drums were directed by an old but knowledgeable professor named Wheelhouse. 'I remember practising a side-drum roll on a cane chair,' she said. 'A side-drum roll is extremely difficult.'

A fellow-student at the Royal College recalls the tall, slim, upright figure of the animated young woman who showed a friendly and warm-hearted disposition and a keen sense of humour. She lived in a women's hostel, Queen Alexandra's House, just up the steps to the Albert Hall opposite the College building in Prince Consort Road. It was used not only by young music students but also by RADA students and girls taking secretarial and other courses. Living-in was included in her scholarship arrangements. It was a strictly-run hostel; students had to be in at regular hours and even when attending concerts they needed passes to stay out till the end. But it was a pleasant residential base; they lived one or two to a room and could practise freely. There were sinks, stoves and other equipment on each floor and a gas-ring in each room for cooking snacks, while main meals were available in the dining-room.

Natalie James first met Evelyn coming out of a Goossens lesson when Natalie was going in to her first. Evelyn gave her a friendly greeting, afterwards they had coffee in the canteen and from then on they were firm friends. Soon they were taking lessons together, practising assiduously and playing duets.

Some of the gifted professors of the music colleges were often in demand for outside engagements and it followed that sometimes the most promising of their pupils found themselves drawn in too. Professional playing, at first a taxing ordeal perhaps, provided valuable experience and enlarged self-confidence. After a time, as they became increasingly proficient, engagements began to come the way of Evelyn, now nearly nineteen, and Natalie, two years older. One of Evelyn's earliest jobs had an eccentric aspect, but receiving £10 for it—a considerable sum in those days—made it worth the trouble, despite a minor misadventure.

A rich old lady in Wiltshire was holding a fête in her

grounds, and had the bright idea that the village school-children should not only sing but be led across the sward by the Pied Piper, as in Browning's poem. Evelyn was sent to Willie Clarkson, the celebrated Wardour Street wigmaker, who fitted her up for the part.

'I arrived in Wiltshire, having memorized children's songs of the period. About thirty of them sang in a bunch and I played the oboe. Then I had to lead them in a "crocodile" across the fields out of sight. I was playing 'Three Blind Mice' when, just as we were nearing the hedge at the end of the field, the elastic in my tights broke. It was all very difficult because I couldn't hold the tights up and play the oboe too—awful trying to play and to anchor my tights alternately. However, we finally got to the hedge and disappeared—so all was well!'

Other casual experience-building jobs were more conventional, though sometimes rough-and-ready, as Evelyn found her way by bus and Underground to theatre pits and concert halls. There were regular broadcasts with Reginald King's Salon Orchestra led by Afredo Campoli, oboe solos with Lew Stone's dance-band recordings, engagements in small ensembles for entr'actes during the intervals of Shakespearean and other plays, such as *Autumn Crocus* at the Lyric, and later in the large orchestras needed in such musicals as *The Dubarry* and *The Land of Smiles.*

Evelyn and Natalie travelled out to the Elstree Studios, which were making their first 'talking' films and required recorded musical accompaniments, made by orchestras under such specialist conductors as Muir Matheson and Louis Levy. In those days film-making was often highly frustrating—the musicians would get there at 8.30 in the morning and sit around doing nothing till 2.30 am the next day.

Then there were those other wireless light orchestras they played for, transmitted from Radio Luxemburg and Radio Normandy. These broadcast (with advertising interludes) in rivalry to the BBC.

Evelyn, intelligent and even-tempered (despite so many varied activities in the midst of these comings and goings) was regarded by now as one of the Royal College's most promising oboists, captivating hearers by the tone of her instrument. She found Goossens more of a demonstrator than a teacher in the accepted sense—his own playing was so instinctive and so natural that he found it difficult to explain anything technical, but he often played the oboe to his pupils so that they learnt by precept and imitation. Also, as time went on, they so often joined him in orchestral engagements and again learnt much from his wonderful performances. Under his guidance Evelyn was developing a fine technique.

As soon as they could arrange it, she and Natalie set up together in a small flat, though only after due consultation with the College's lady superintendent, who had a list of suitable lettings. The girls took two rooms with a gas-ring on the top floor of a house in Observatory Gardens, Campden Hill, kept by an easy-going landlady, Mrs Hubble, who included breakfast in the bargain. They could practise their oboes up there as much as they liked. Snacks were cooked on the gas-ring but most of the time they lived out and alternated baked beans on toast along with their college friends and lunches or dinners in Kensington Church Street at 1*s.* 6*d.* a three-course meal with coffee threepence extra.

'We lived and breathed the oboe in our flat together,' said Natalie, 'and talked about nothing else. I think she was the dominant character—it was always "Come on, Natalie, time we were off". I don't remember our ever having a cross word.'

An unexpected one-night stand was an engagement to sing in the Covent Garden Opera chorus. They were in Dr Malcolm Sargent's choral class at the time when a sudden appeal was made for volunteers to swell the chorus in Mussorgsky's *Boris Godunov*. Volunteering, they found there were not enough tenors, so they agreed to sing tenor. They rehearsed parrot-like in Russian and had their costume-call.

That night, shepherded on to the vast stage at Covent Garden, the two friends sang their chorus before being shepherded off. For their services each received £4.10*s.*, a good payment for an extra, fifty years ago. Natalie spent her special payment on a serviceable sewing-machine; Evelyn bought more music with her windfall—all her spare money went to increase her repertoire.

Sometimes they were able to deputize for a few nights at one of the more lavish long-running musical shows with a big orchestra such as *The Dubarry*, by Suppé's protégé Karl

Millöcker at His Majesty's, where the cast included the beautiful Continental star, Anny Ahlers,* and Heddle Nash. The large orchestras for these shows were frequently under the control of Ernest Irving, who was unrivalled as a conductor of this kind of music.

When Lehár's *Land of Smiles* opened at Drury Lane in 1931, with Richard Tauber in full voice in 'You Are My Heart's Delight', Franz Lehár himself conducted for a few nights to launch a wild success and then Ernest Irving took over. Leon Goossens was principal oboe with Helen Gaskell second, while Evelyn was the first deputy oboist. Irving had expressly said that she could not play *first* oboe as she was not experienced enough.

The Fates intervened. Goossens was away for a concert and his second oboe was unexpectedly absent because of the death of her father. Evelyn found herself stepping into the breach and at the first oboe's desk, with some difficult solos to encompass.

It was not an easy evening but she acquitted herself creditably. Peter Barbirolli, a player in the orchestra and a judge of talent, noted her performance. His brother John had told him he was looking for an oboe player for his Royal Opera Touring Orchestra and had asked him 'Have you heard anybody?'.

To which Peter was able to say, when he got home that night, 'Well there's a girl playing first oboe with us—very good—sounds like Goossens. I think you ought to hear her.'

'John wrote a letter to me at the College,' said Evelyn. 'I couldn't read the signature—I thought it was Barkworth. It suggested an audition and invited me to be in the foyer at Covent Garden at 10.30 am on a certain date. I was terribly thrilled.'

She showed the letter to her friends and to Goossens. None of them knew who 'Barkworth' was and supposed him to be some official of the Opera House.

As she entered the foyer, or crush bar, she saw a short, dark-haired young man with intense-looking eyes. He had already

*Anny Ahlers was the rage of London in this successful production. She committed suicide during the run when her lover left her.

seen her. She smiled and he murmured 'Ah, so *this* is the player from *The Land of Smiles.*' It was uttered more as a statement than a question, addressed to an applicant suffering from stage fright because she was still only a student. But the smile and the response to it had broken the ice.

No time was lost by this 'rather foreign-looking man,' as she was later to describe 'Barkworth' in her diary. He wrote down a few notes about her experience and then his rapid scribbling ceased abruptly. The short figure quickly crossed to a grand piano. Evelyn, calm on the surface but inwardly consumed with nerves, took her oboe out of its case.

He sat on a swivelling stool and accompanied her as she played a piece she was to remember all her life—the slow movement of a Handel sonata. She noted that his piano-playing was not very good—'he sort of put the bass in'.

He appeared pleased with her performance. Then he asked her to play from sight one or two excerpts from operas. Evelyn was still nervous about her lack of experience, but he eased her anxiety by explaining that it was the job of the conductor to make a talented musician into a really good player.

The audition ended and as he took her right hand in his two hands he told her that she had been appointed to the second oboe desk in the Touring Company Orchestra. As she walked down the staircase of the Opera House she felt she was walking on air. He waved goodbye to her from the doorway—but only for a time.

3 *Youthful Cellist*

We must now return to an earlier period and continue John's career from the age of seven, when he went to his principal school, when he began to attain some proficiency with the cello and when old Grandfather Antonio died, sorely missed by his family and pupils alike.

The year 1907 marked the height of the Edwardian era, with all its Imperial panoply and grandeur, self-confident ostentation and pomp. Few periods had been so stiffly conservative in social structure or seemed so securely comfortable for the well-to-do. The Barbirollis and most of the millions of other citizens struggled along half-submerged, half-enjoying the rich scene of which they had personally only a small fringe share, and scarcely imagined any other; a certain lush music-hall bombast about it all in London alleviated much of the discomfort and paucity of their lives.

Lorenzo in his modest way was getting his share of the lights of the capital. Now musical director of both small orchestras at the Queen's Hotel, he made his Sunday evening after-dinner concerts there a refreshing attraction. At one of them he had given his first opportunity to an unknown young Irish tenor, soon to be world-famous as a ballad and opera singer—John McCormack, singing 'I Hear You Calling Me', composed by the pianist Charles Marshall. The fee paid was only a guinea but more gramophone records were later made of this famous song than of any other in McCormack's repertoire. ('Mother Machree', 'Roses of Picardy', 'Rose in the Bud', 'Macushla', and 'Kathleen Mavourneen' were all ballads McCormack sang.)

In those days, fifteen years before wireless, a new song destined to please the public fancy took a short time to percolate mysteriously throughout the country before being whistled and sung everywhere, in town, village and hamlet, till it was inevitably succeeded by another favourite. Taken up by travelling shows, concert-parties and after-dinner singers, it was sold as sheet-music to tens of thousands of homes containing pianos and amateur vocalists. And the invention of the gramophone brought it on primitive wax cylinder or disc to the families that had bought the wheezy but swiftly developing instrument. So it was with 'I Hear You Calling Me' and the voice of John McCormack.

Lorenzo, branching out, had also founded a quintet for regular afternoon concerts. Known as 'Barbi', he was kindly and helpful to his fellows in the art, and many retained warm memories of their genial Italian chief. His son liked to regale himself by hearing fresh operatic selections at some of the hotel concerts, presented in his father's best salon manner, with a little of La Scala mixed in. Some new allurement in the galaxy of light music was repeatedly widening his horizon. His early tastes and catholicity never left the boy Tita or, much later, the man John Barbirolli.

Indeed, there was then no special gap, as there is now, between light and serious music—light music of quality was regarded with respect by both professionals and public and a tasteful concert-builder could weld the two to bring general delight.

The family had now gone to live off Guildford Street, Bloomsbury, the boy passing out of the French church's kindergarten and entering St Clement Dane's Grammar School in Houghton Street, off the Strand (where the London School of Economics now stands). This school had a reasonably good all-round standard and John's father paid the necessary small fees for him. He was a serious but restless boy. From the ages of eight to fourteen, when he left, he was in the senior school and though not a conspicuous pupil—music at home was too insistent for that—he benefited from a good general curriculum. He was to recall being rejected for the school choir on the ground that his voice was not good enough.

Also, he suffered at first from a nervous speech defect—he could not start off when called upon to read aloud in class. A sympathetic English master cured the trouble, reading aloud with him for a short while at the start. John later became a most accomplished speaker.

Father early initiated son into the world of great artists by taking him along to hear classical music. He listened to Ysaÿe and Kreisler among the violinists and to such great pianists as Pachmann, Paderewski and Saint-Saëns. Many of these were at the Queen's Hall, Langham Place, where Mr Henry Wood, as he then was, had been conducting Promenade concerts* like a gifted Hercules since 1895, with a tremendous repertoire to which he was constantly adding music hitherto unknown in this country. People stood packed together in the arena and girls made almost a fashion of fainting in the heat.

Wood, who began as an opera conductor and was conducting 'Proms' at twenty-five, was a forceful, eclectic personality of cheerful disposition and enormous confidence.

*When Promenade concerts were first given in London in 1838 by a Mr Pilati at the Colisseum, Regent's Park, people promenaded gently about while listening to the music. 'Proms' had several distinguished proponents, including Edward Eliason at the Crown and Anchor tavern in the Strand and Louis Jullien (1812-60), the French showman-conductor, who used white kid gloves and a bejewelled baton, presented by a minion on a silver salver, to conduct Beethoven, at Drury Lane from 1840.

Players admired him for his clear and efficient baton technique, absolutely secure gesture and careful preparation, and they loved him as a 'character'. Young Barbirolli, by observing his first-class methods, so direct in every kind of music, was able to study the conductor's art at the highest level yet, and at the same time to absorb some of the novelties Wood had picked.

Becoming engrossed in detailed scores at about the age of nine, the highly-strung child was often observed by visitors to be sitting in a corner at home, oblivious of the household talk, head bent over a full score, orchestral or operatic—a spare-time habit that was to stay with him all his life. He had made his earliest first-hand acquaintance with opera on the stage when at five he had been taken to hear Puccini's *Madam Butterfly* at Covent Garden.

But for much of his young life John was not an indoor boy. Since old Antonio's death he enjoyed increasingly roaming among the streets, squares and alleys of London, searching out some of the famous buildings and shopping treasure-houses, discovering new corners and facets of the great city. For years he had trotted alongside his Grandfather—now he walked alone. He was proud in later life to have been always a Cockney, in speech if not in appearance. For much of his life as a distinguished conductor, though his English was normally cultured, when he wished he could affect a Cockney accent that could be cut with a knife.

Happy family holidays were spent on the south coast and he once accompanied his father to Paris. On this trip Lorenzo took to his bed with a broken leg for several weeks and so John was on his own in Paris, exploring that city and acquiring fluency in French.

Annette Hewitt, often at the Barbirollis' home with her brothers, recalled the colourful family occasions. 'They were a devoted and outgoing household,' she said, 'always so friendly and welcoming to visitors and encouraging to young ones. It was so interesting to be there. They "lived" music; whenever you went someone was playing.

'You couldn't call it a luxurious home; they were having a pretty hard time, I think, bringing up the children. It was a plain but comfortable middle-class home, with a marvellous atmosphere.'

In preparing their leisurely and discursive meals, Mémé, who was really a cook of genius, managed to combine Italian and French dishes in her own original way. Cooking came much too naturally for her to be able to teach it—she could never say how much or how long. But it became a pleasurable pastime for John throughout his life and he inherited his mother's natural gift.

His reading also developed—by the time his brother Peter was born in 1911 John had become an admirer of Dickens and Jane Austen.

An educational dual existence began when in September, 1910, he was admitted to the Trinity College of Music, in Mandeville Place, Marylebone, with a scholarship to study the cello even more intensely under Edmund Woolhouse. He worked there part-time, continuing a piecemeal presence at the grammar school, now prepared to accept only intermittent attendance. During this time he produced his first gramophone record of violoncello pieces with his sister at the piano, also making his concert debut at the age of eleven at the Queen's Hall in the College's annual concert, when he wore a sailor suit and played part of Goltermann's Cello Concerto on his half-size cello with the College orchestra. A similar concert followed at the Queen's Hall with the Saint-Saëns Concerto. These well-received performances were encouraging enough for him to try to gain a scholarship at the Royal Academy of Music in 1912. He was successful, to his father's great gratification, and moved there to study the cello with Herbert Walenn, the piano with Bernard Symons and chamber music with Hans Wessely, gifted musicians regarded as first-class teachers in their day. (Walenn founded the famous London Violoncello School, which he directed until his death in his eighties.)

The diminutive cellist who entered the Royal Academy in Marylebone Road was a delicate-looking boy of marked Italian appearance, with a small, serious mouth, rather penetrating eyes and thick black hair, parted in the middle. He wore an Eton collar over his jacket, knickerbocker breeches and stockings (the style for boys then). Gladys Parr, the operatic contralto, who was studying at the Royal Academy at the time, was impressed by his intent and serious air of preoccupation and 'business' as he went about with quick steps from one studio to another. Along with an occasional bout of low spirits he was becoming conscious at this time of that fretting reluctance to rest which was to dog him through life. Rather than relax or waste time he insisted upon practising his cello or reading scores.

Indeed, by the time he was thirteen he had played all the Beethoven quartets and Bach's violoncello suites and, with Winifred Small, violin, and Egerton Tidmarsh, piano, was giving a number of school trio recitals. This fruitful stage marked a blossoming of mature talent and judgment.

Debussy and Ravel were preoccupying him. One day he heard Debussy's *La Mer* and pestered his father until Lorenzo found him a score of it. This he studied ardently for its Impressionist orchestration and it became one of his most admired works. He joined a quartet at the Royal Academy whose members were eager to play the new Ravel Quartet, but this met with the disapproval of the Principal, Sir Alexander Mackenzie, who found little virtue in Impressionism. Recalling the incident years later, Barbirolli said the four were determined to play it nevertheless, so went down to the men's lavatory and practised it there. Each of them occupied a separate cubicle, which did not make ensemble easy, and he found the acoustics 'a bit resonant'.

He went constantly to hear the widely diversified programmes at the Queen's Hall, enjoying Wood's innovations, such as Debussy's *Children's Corner*, Ravel's *Valses Nobles et Sentimentales*, Fauré's *Pelléas et Mélisande* and Stravinsky's *Firebird*. Also there was Thomas Beecham, in his thirties, not only giving remarkable concerts with his Beecham Symphony Orchestra but continuing his bold ventures into new fields of opera at Covent Garden and Drury Lane. Young Barbirolli, fascinated by all he saw and heard, sometimes queued for gallery seats and usually took scores up to the 'gods'.

Meanwhile Lorenzo, always encouraging his family in their musical advances, was enlistng the services of his daughter Rosa, now about eighteen and a competent pianist, in his concerts. She played at the Queen's Hotel in his small salon orchestras, even sang sometimes at *thés dansants* and played the piano when Lorenzo and his band performed at Gatti's

Restaurant in the Strand on Sunday evenings. Her brother often proved an appreciative audience for Lorenzo and for Rosa.

Heavy clouds were lowering. The Great War had broken out. Khaki appeared in all the streets, men everywhere volunteering, later being conscripted. London was soon plunged with the rest of the country into black-out, evening workers groping about with flashlamps and electric torches. The Barbirollis, who had moved house to 46 Marchmont Street, another Italianized road in Bloomsbury, fitted, like everyone else, black or dark green opaque blinds to all their windows. The Zeppelins were on their way.

Perceiving that if the war went on he might in a year or two be in it himself, John left school at fourteen, finding one of his first jobs in the orchestra pit at the Duke of York's Theatre.* He also earned some money with spells in a cinema orchestra and even made an occasional appearance with Rosa at the Queen's, playing in a trio with his father.

But for one more year his studies continued at the Royal Academy and in 1916 he partnered Ethel Bartlett in a series of performances of contemporary cello sonatas, both playing from memory—quite a feat—works by Bax, Delius, Debussy, Ireland and Eugene Goossens.

He had been getting in some practice at boxing also and though he was of very light weight he managed to put up a fairly good show in the flyweight class of the 'noble art'. (A heavy blow on the nose in one bout at this time necessitated an operation to straighten the bridge. To the end of his days he carried the scar, his nose looking slightly misshapen.)

Even before leaving the Royal Academy he had put in an application to Sir Henry Wood to be auditioned for a cellist's vacancy in the Queen's Hall Orchestra, which he had so often heard and watched in action. Sir Henry tested him lengthily, finally deciding that he was good enough to become, at sixteen, the orchestra's youngest member. This was a triumphant feather in his cap and delighted Lorenzo, too. It was a great thing to be actually playing now on the platform under the

*It was in the orchestra pit at this theatre that he played the cello during the intermissions of the melodrama *The Thirteenth Chair* in 1917, with Mrs Patrick Campbell in the leading role. JB was never tired of recalling the excitement he felt as he watched the play nightly—the sole member of the orchestra to do so.

baton of Wood—colloquially known as 'Timber'—in Promenade concerts. Eric Coates, later famous for his popular music, then a viola-player in the orchestra at £2.10*s.* a week, recalled Barbirolli among the strings along with Basil Cameron and Eugene Goossens, both destined to be conductors too. And there was Cedric Sharpe the cellist, while Alfred and Aubrey Brain were in the horn section. Though the season lasted for only two months in the year the work was heavy and exacting—six concerts a week and for each only one three-hour rehearsal. But such a gruelling challenge in this professional milieu gave an ambitious youth the experience and resilience he sought.

The war was at its most intense. Zeppelin raids, soon succeeded by German aeroplanes, interrupted some of the concerts, as searchlights probed the skies. Millions of straw-hatted civilians were being called up, trained and marched off in khaki, with their bands, to the stations en route for the front. Casualty lists from France were enormous; mourning blinds were down everywhere for the killed. Long queues at the shops patiently shared the meagre food rations.

During the 'Zepp raids', as they were called, the family, with their little maid from the Foundling Hospital, sometimes ran for shelter to the Russell Square Underground station, the still impressionable Tita later recalling that his grandmother, always a stickler for convention, would refuse to budge from the house until she had her hat and gloves all laid out and ready as if she were going to a party.

When the bombs were falling audiences at the 'Proms' occasionally shrank to two or three dozen but Wood was imperturbable—he was quite oblivious until a crescendo of gunfire coincided with a diminuendo in the music!

Apart from the 'Proms', John's time was spent freelancing now that his student period at the Royal Academy was over. He found a wide assortment of jobs, 'gigs' and 'stands' varying from restaurants, dance halls, hotel lounges and cafés to theatre pits.

Sometimes he deputized in the Carl Rosa Opera orchestra, at others in the Drury Lane orchestra with Beecham conducting in memorable style operas such as *The Marriage of Figaro* and Bizet's *The Fair Maid of Perth*. John could remember how they had to abandon the opera twice here to shelter under the stage and in the adjoining cellars from the air raids. He had already played in a few of Beecham's Shaftesbury and Aldwych Theatre productions. Any engagements under such a master were a fine introduction to brilliant conducting and the stark realities of staging opera.

On a later occasion he played for Beecham in a 106th-season concert of the Royal Philharmonic Society at the Albert Hall, with Arthur de Greef at the piano in Franck's Symphonic Variations, Mozart's Fortieth Symphony and Bantock's *Fifine at the Fair*. A very different type of job was playing with the Christmas pantomime at the old Royal Surrey, in Blackfriars Road, an ancient music hall that had had Sir Arthur Sullivan's Irish father playing the clarinet eighty years earlier.

Lorenzo, Mémé and John welcomed into the family Alfonso Gibilaro, who now married Rosa. This Sicilian pianist and minor composer proved to be a skilled arranger of music. He had first played in a pier orchestra at Weston-super-Mare and was later pianist in de Groot's palm court orchestra at the fashionable Piccadilly Hotel. Their daughter Maria Concetta (Tina) was born in Marchmont Street in 1917 and always considered that Uncle John saved her life in infancy when she incurred a serious haemorrhage and he rushed out in deep snow upon returning from a late-night engagement to secure an essential new prescription from a West End chemist.

To attract the notice of the critics and the cognoscenti, a personal recital at a recognized hall was essential for a young artist. So, on 13 June 1917, John gave his first public cello recital at the Aeolian Hall, New Bond Street, with his friend the pianist Ethel Bartlett.

The Times had this to say:

> Giovanni Barbirolli is a pupil of M. Walenn's and does him credit. His technique is above the average and he played some variations of Locatelli in a masterly manner. But more pleasing is a breadth of style which was shown in Boëllmann's Sonata in A, especially in the last two movements, and though the strings would not always speak as he wanted, there were some well-managed pianissimo effects and excellent intonation.

A little earlier in the day about fifteen German planes had bombed London, killing 97, including 42 women and children, and injuring 439. The Germans bombed an East End school, killing ten children and injuring 50. It was a tense audience that gathered to hear John play after so distracting a day. More credit then that the unsettled atmosphere at the start was soon dispelled by the rapt assurance and promise of the young performer.

He gave a second successful recital in November, playing Brahms, Grieg and Debussy, and then, soon afterwards, exchanged music for another world—that of the Army.

He would be a volunteer, not a conscript.

4 *A Conductor Emerges*

John had little more than a year in the Army, as it turned out, and he was fated to spend it in England. However, it was the Army that introduced him to conducting.

Private Barbirolli was in the First Reserve Garrison Battalion of the Suffolk Regiment stationed on the Isle of Grain, at the confluence of the Thames and the Medway, in Kent. An Irish sergeant-major, finding his name unpronounceable, nicknamed the Italian-French Tommy 'Bob O'Reilly' and 'O'Reilly stand at ease' it was. Heavily engaged in basic training, drilling and fatigues, he was nevertheless on medical grounds (including a heart murmur and slight ear and nasal trouble) not passed for overseas duty.

After he had been in khaki for barely two months the opportunity arose for John to join the regiment's voluntary orchestra, which generally played in the canteen. This had been formed because the colonel was musically inclined, though he proved chary about time to practise. Even more fortuitous, after a few weeks the regular conductor, a Lieutenant Bonham, was 'off sick' one Sunday and 'Bob O'Reilly's' musical comrades, a few professional musicians amongst them, who had observed his proficiency as a principal cellist, suggested that he should 'have a go' instead. He was asked about this when scrubbing the floor of the lavatory and such was his delight at the idea that he excitedly knocked over a pail of dirty water, a good deal of which was spilt on his uniform.

It was a highly successful 'go', the scratch orchestra and John enjoying it in equal measure. The novice conductor instinctively felt, almost from the moment he started off with his baton, that he knew how to control this part of the Army, if no other. His home practising and stick-waving fantasies now stood him in good stead; this baton was, like the platform, real at last. He seemed to take wing and was in full charge. His stick technique was utterly natural. He never thought about, or had difficulty with that side of conducting.

In a few months the Germans had exhaustd their last 1918 offensives on the Western front and at last the great all-out counter-offensives of Haig and Foch, launched in August, defeated them decisively in the field in 'the hundred days' after four years of fighting. John, immersed in anti-gas training in England, had been newly promoted to lance-corporal instructor when the War suddenly, or so it seemed to him, came to an end. Demobilized in April, 1919, 'O'Reilly' became Barbirolli again and started to pick up where he had left off over a year before.

Freelancing once again, he was booked immediately for the Alhambra, accompanying Diaghilev's Russian Ballet: a first-class theatre engagement, with much beautiful and original music, that lasted for three months. He was playing in the orchestra pit at the first appearance of *La Boutique Fantasque* to Rossini's music and *The Three-Cornered Hat* to de Falla's, the great dancers on the stage including Tamara Karsavina, Leonide Massine, Lydia Lopokova and Stanislas Idzikowsky. It was only a year later that a particularly intimate association with ballet presented itself. This was when Anna Pavlova returned to London after six years' absence and John found himself among the cellos at the great prima ballerina's Drury Lane season. One night, through the refusal of the others, he took the absent principal cellist's place. So beautifully did he play the Saint-Saëns solo cello accompaniment to her famous romantic solo dance 'The Dying Swan' that this lone artist of genius, acknowledging the applause on the stage, divided her bouquet of tiger-lilies, throwing down half to him. She sent for him afterwards to thank him, holding his hand within her own beautiful hands with what he discovered to his surprise was a 'steely' grip. And the *Daily Telegraph* reviewer wrote: 'There was a remarkable cellist for "The Swan" dancing, unnamed in the programme.'

As the Twenties dawned, he was plunging into a maelstrom of jobs—cinema turns in which small orchestras played suitable contrasting accompaniments to actions and emotions on the screen; hotel work again, with light music such as Luigini's *Ballet Egyptien* (popularized by Pavlova), Edward German, Percy Fletcher, *The Lilac Domino*, *Chu Chin Chow*; and theatre pits—'I played everywhere except in the street,' he said years afterwards. One of the advantages was that he could be his own master.

Also there were occasional symphony concerts to transport him to the higher reaches and remind him again of his conducting ambitions. He would fondly recall playing as an extra cellist under Sir Edward Elgar in *The Dream of Gerontius* at the first post-war Three Choirs Festival at Worcester and he was the soloist in 1921 in one of the earliest performances of Elgar's Cello Concerto with the Bournemouth Municipal Orchestra under (later Sir) Dan Godfrey—one of two solo appearances with that noted orchestra. It was probably this early acquaintance with the concerto (he was also in the orchestra at the Queen's Hall when Elgar and the LSO were rehearsing and playing its first performance) that developed John's devotion to the music of Elgar.

He had operatic stints at Covent Garden with the Beecham Orchestra. And he had a very lucrative offer to become a music hall conductor, which he refused. He played in the first performance of Gustav Holst's suite *The Planets*, one of the landmarks of English music at the time.* The composer is chronicled as having conducted *The Planets* on 22 November 1919, with the New Queen's Hall Orchestra at the Queen's Hall, the première of the complete suite coming a year later with Albert Coates as conductor in that hall. Dr Adrian Boult had conducted parts of it in 1918 and February, 1919.

Barbirolli of course maintained the most delicate elements in his playing by keeping up his chamber music. In 1922 he joined André Mangeot's International String Quartet, with Mangeot

*Barbirolli declared that Holst wore bright red woollen socks, his trousers were too short and his tailed coat didn't fit him.

as first violin, Boris Pecker second and Harry Berley viola. They played English composers as well as Haydn, Mozart and Beethoven and he had the opportunity of touring in France, Spain, Belgium and Germany.

Mangeot, though French, helped (with Peter Warlock) to keep Purcell on the map through the English Music Society that he formed. His first wife Beatrice, herself a violinist of note, later Lady Hancock, found the Quartet's cellist a cheerful, slightly rotund young man with a quirky, rather Cockney sense of humour who played the cello 'like an angel'. Accompanying him home, she met his mother—'rather fiercely French but looking like an Italian woman'—and, well to the fore in the kitchen, John demonstrated to his visitor how to make a real pasta sauce.

In 1924 he was in the Kutcher Quartet, founded by an old boyhood friend, Samuel Kutcher. Their concerts included very early broadcasts from Savoy Hill, the BBC's first 2LO (London) studios.

In this year he had saved some money and he decided to take a conducting plunge. For a series of concerts at the Chenil Galleries, Chelsea, he launched twelve hand-picked musicians under the title of the Barbirolli String Orchestra. Early audiences soon found that the young conductor, though looking tense and unduly serious, knew what he was about. The little band was musical, well balanced, precise and zestful. At its first concert it impressed its listeners with Bach and Purcell.

Gramophone records had been made of both the International and the Kutcher Quartets and now the new string orchestra broke into recording with subscription series for the National Gramophonic Society. Critics began to recognise it as sensitive and well-drilled. The BBC was soon to put it into its contemporary music series broadcast from the Chenil Galleries. Slightly enlarged, it was unobtrusively making a name for itself when Barbirolli had a stroke of extraordinary luck . . .

Frederic Austin, versatile as baritone, composer and opera director,* was then head of the British National Opera

*He had made a great hit in 1920 by his arrangement of Gay's 'The Beggar's Opera' for Sir Nigel Playfair at the Lyric, Hammersmith, singing Peachum himself. It ran for 1,463 performances.

Company, and had dropped in at the Chenil Galleries once or twice. He came one night in December 1925 to the Wigmore Hall when the Barbirolli String Orchestra was giving a concert of music, including excerpts from an opera by that diversified composer of the time, Bernard Van Dieren. Austin was particularly impressed by the conductor. After the concert he offered him an engagement as an extra conductor for the BNOC.

'Although I'd never conducted a large orchestra I knew I could cope,' Barbirolli recalled, and he accepted without hesitation.

The British National Opera Company was the successor in 1921 of the Beecham Opera Company of 1915-1920, performing in English on tour and founded by a number of the excellent artists from the Beecham Company. Its performances included, besides *The Ring* and other Wagnerian operas, many of the well-known 'touring' Italian ones and a few English works too. The chance it gave to Barbirolli at this juncture marked a great *accelerando* in his career—one that led to further remarkable leaps within a few years.

When he stood in the conductor's place in the pit of the Newcastle Hippodrome on September 22, 1926, inaugurating the BNOC autumn tour, he was acutely conscious not only of handling a large orchestra for the first time but also of conducting opera and directing a chorus for the first time. Before him lay the score of Gounod's *Romeo and Juliet*. It was a daunting moment.

But from the opening the French opera proved a winner. He followed it in the same week with the two Italians, Puccini's *Madam Butterfly* and Verdi's *Aïda*. Both were successful.

Rehearsals for these performances had been very limited, partly through John himself. Austin had warned him that he could have only nine hours' rehearsal for the three operas. But the first six hours of the nine were arranged for a Friday. It is a strong Italian superstition that no new enterprise should ever begin on Friday, for fear of bad luck. After consulting his family, John decided he dare not accept the Friday rehearsals for this vital occasion and told Austin that he had a previous engagement for that day. Austin could not change the rehearsals so John agreed to give the three operas with only three hours' rehearsal for the lot! But it became a week of triumph.

The company travelled on to a succession of other major cities, adding such customary works as *La Bohème* and *The Barber of Seville*, and Barbirolli's first acquaintance with Manchester, later to become an intrinsic part of his life, was made that November. Mancunians at their Opera House first saw him at 26—sleek-haired, with magnetic brown eyes and only his nose a trifle out of proportion. His firm mouth and general air of somewhat introspective determination completed an arresting face and physique.

Samuel Langford, the distinguished music critic of the *Manchester Guardian* (said by Neville Cardus, his successor, to look like a cross between Socrates and Mussorgsky), wrote a memorable piece on the Manchester debut six months before he died:

> Mr Barbirolli made his first appearance in Manchester as a conductor for the performance of *Madam Butterfly* yesterday afternoon. He is quite a young man of slight build and refined physique and sensitive bearing, and it was soon apparent that a nature highly sensitive to music inhabits his frame. In him Puccini appears to have found an interpreter who should give his music a new life among us. Certainly he should make Puccini more acceptable to the musician than any conductor we have had. He treated Puccini's music yesterday for what it is—rhapsodic music in the original sense of the term—stitched together in short snatches of strictly dramatic application.
>
> The music lived in a perpetual change, and always on the instant Mr Barbirolli had the transition informed with meaning and an exquisitely appropriate style. To these ends he was armed with a resource of eloquent gesture which everywhere passed admiration. The performers, singers and players, everywhere followed him gladly and dullness became for everyone an impossibility.
>
> What Mr Barbirolli will do with other masters remains to be proved. In Puccini at least he is an absolute master. With such a conductor Miss Miriam Licette as Madam Butterfly seemed perfectly happy . . . The music once

> more took on a freshness that for us at least was considerably worn away.

In January 1927, when the company reached the popular Golders Green Hippodrome in London, John shared the conducting with Aylmer Buesst, the Australian conductor. John's *Romeo and Juliet* now came before the London critics. The *Daily Telegraph* wrote 'The performance would have done credit to any opera house', adding that the opera's grace and eloquence were faithfully reflected in the singing of Miriam Licette and Tudor Davies. Excellent too were Parry Jones' Tybalt and Robert Radford's Friar Lawrence.

> The performance was immensely helped by Mr John Barbirolli, whose first London appearance this is in control of the BNOC's forces. The playing of the orchestra showed perfect responsiveness to the wishes of the conductor, who very evidently knew exactly what he wanted, and how to get it, so that there was not any detail in the orchestral score that was not treated with care and finish. The singers, moreover, were not a little indebted to Mr Barbirolli for the always alert and sympathetic accompanying.

Others in the talented company were Norman Allin, Dennis Noble, Gladys Parr and Frank Mullings.

John had come to opera as an Italian fascinated with the sound and the tense drama, yet steeped minutely in the scores—the result of long years of study. He had never needed to learn baton technique and the fluid nature of his conducting gave operas a continuous style. With an inborn sense of the verve and excitement of the theatre, he was showing that he could bring out all the nuances of string tone, particularly in Italian opera.

He was exhilarated by the ebullience of Rossini's *Barber of Seville* and decided to produce it himself as an 'off-season' summer experiment at the King's, Hammersmith, and the Wimbledon Theatre. He had met J. B. Mulholland, whose family owned these successful suburban theatres and whose daughter Joan, a cellist too, was an old friend. Mulholland supported the venture and the BNOC granted permission as well as supplying singers and orchestra.

It ran for a fortnight with Barbirolli as impresario, conductor and producer, even looking after the lighting. Miriam Licette was Rosina, Dennis Noble the Barber and Heddle Nash Almaviva, with Percy Heming as Dr Bartolo, Gladys Parr and Robert Radford, and the theatres were crowded for performances very highly valued by the critics.

But the British National Opera Company itself was running into financial breakers, paying heavy entertainment tax and incurring debts. Its members, however good, could not hope for any real permanence or a long career for it without aid. This was not forthcoming.

5 *The Elgar Break-Through*

At about the time that Evelyn at school was taking her first steps with the oboe, John Barbirolli, eleven years ahead of her, broke into the symphony concert firmament, as into the world of opera, with an equally startling impetus and an equally unexpected piece of luck.

On 12 December 1927, two years after Frederic Austin attended that momentous concert at the Wigmore Hall, Sir Thomas Beecham was prevented through illness from conducting another momentous concert. This was a Monday night concert by the London Symphony Orchestra in the Queen's Hall including Elgar's Symphony No. 2. Beecham's indisposition caused a harassed search round for a substitute, only 48 hours before the event. One or two members of the orchestra suggested the name of John Barbirolli. He was telephoned. Could he do it?

John had played the cello in the symphony but had never seen the full score. He was just replying that unfortunately he didn't know it and couldn't possibly do it when . . .

Lorenzo, who had been listening just behind him in the hall, interrupted in no uncertain manner. He put his hand over the telephone mouthpiece and told his son, volubly and in Italian, that he'd be the world's biggest coward and idiot if he didn't accept. 'While I was saying no, he exclaimed, "Don't be a fool! It's not every day that you'll get an opportunity like this!" I capitulated—and learnt the symphony between Friday night and Sunday morning.'

John went to the first rehearsal and worked hard at it that Sunday morning. The second was on Monday morning. The rest of the programme he knew well—Haydn's Symphony No. 104, the 'London', and Haydn's Cello Concerto with Pau Casals as soloist. No problem there.

No problem about the whole concert. No hitches in the symphony, which was heartily appreciated by the audience. He and Lorenzo were delighted to read in the *Daily Telegraph* the next morning:

> Mr Barbirolli has won golden opinions in his work with the BNOC and everyone was anxious to see how he would command the more august forces now placed under his baton. That expectancy turned in the course of the evening to enthusiasm.
>
> The Elgar Symphony is a long work, heavily laden with what one may call emotion . . . a conductor has to keep a tight hand on the orchestra and on himself. Mr Barbirolli came through the ordeal successfully, moments of special beauty being the brilliant climax of the first movement and the diminuendo which marks the coda of the finale. His skill in keeping his forces in control also showed up well in the third movement, where the emphatic rhythms were admirably brought out. Mr Barbirolli has few personal idiosyncracies and his beat is always indicated in a straightforward way.'

Not all the other critics were so encouraging, but the concert put Barbirolli on the map. He had proved himself with a great orchestra at an awkward moment and was soon offered further guest engagements with the LSO, while that august body the Royal Philharmonic Society began to take an interest in the rising young conductor. Sir Edward Elgar, too, sent him a note of thanks for what he had heard was a splendid performance.

Moreover—and no mean thing—the concert had galvanized

Fred Gaisberg, the dynamic bowler-hatted talent-scout and impresario of the Gramophone Company who had been making *His Master's Voice* celebrity records from their Maiden Lane Studios since 1898. He had rushed backstage to book Enrico Caruso in Milan in 1902—now he rushed backstage again. A small man with an intense manner, he cried 'Don't sign any contract! See you in the morning!', then vanished.

He was as good as his word and John began to conduct in a series of world-distributed operatic records, accompanying a stream of renowned 'red-label' artists such as Chaliapin, Melchior, Frida Leider, Florence Austral, Backhaus, Suggia, Gigli, Heifetz, Kreisler and Rubinstein. He managed to include before long several recordings by the Barbirolli String Orchestra, having already recorded on disc his own arrangements of a Purcell Suite for Strings and a Marcello Allegretto.

Before the BNOC's autumn tour began in 1928 John had gained another exceptional distinction. He was appointed a guest conductor in the international season at Covent Garden. He shared part of the Italian side with Vincenzo Bellezza, who had directed the first *Turandot* in England the previous year. How much John's foreign name helped it is difficult to gauge—there had been precious few English ones in the list over the years. But a special merit in opera was the key that unlocked the door. Barbirolli had been demonstrating not only exuberance and warmth, but also an intuition almost as if he were inside the characters while concerned also with the whole spectacle.

His first appearance before the curtain at Covent Garden was on 30 June with *Madame Butterfly* in a short popular English season. He conducted *Butterfly* and *La Bohème* several times that summer in the international season and continued to make Covent Garden appearances, mainly in Italian works and Wagner, until 1934.

A Delius concert that he broadcast was picked up on his radio by Frederick Delius, living near Paris, and the composer wrote saying, 'I felt you were entirely in sympathy with my music'.

In further provincial towns John added *Falstaff* to the repertoire. His old friend, Gladys Parr, who after the Carl

Rosa Opera secured a three-year contract with BNOC from 1926, took part in the long *Falstaff* preparation, with six weeks of rehearsals.

The Twenties, drawing to a close, had been a good decade as decades went, according to Rose Macaulay—merry, decorative, intelligent, cultured. The cheerful age of jazz reached its zenith and half the population were in the grip of the dancing craze. Salon orchestras of Lorenzo's kind were going out, replaced by dance bands. It was the epoch of the Savoy Orpheans, Jack Hylton's, Harry Roy's and all the other crack 'big' bands in the hotels and night clubs—millions listened nightly on the wireless, mostly with headphones and crystal sets with cats'-whiskers. This optimistic gaiety was, however, soon to be met with a huge rebuff—the world financial crisis and depression.

Barbirolli was too preoccupied and serious to have time for these light-hearted trends, though he had a secret predilection for Duke Ellington and loved Jerome Kern's 'Smoke Gets in Your Eyes'. As for dancing, women said decisively that he was not good at it.

Leading off in 1929 came a further distinction—that of conducting, on 17 January, at the Albert Hall a Royal Philharmonic Society concert in its 117th season. He chose Debussy's *La Mer* in a programme that included Haydn's 'Oxford' Symphony (No. 92) and Delius' Cello Concerto, with Alexandre Barjansky as soloist. There was an unusual happening in this. Aiming at a very high pitch of excellence in the strings in *La Mer*, he found he was permitted no more than two rehearsals. So he made the grand gesture—he would pay for the extra rehearsal himself (having computed that the cost would about equal his fee). In this way he better satisfied his perfectionist ear. He went on to conduct RPS concerts twice again—in 1930 and 1931.

The spring of 1929 was saddened by the sudden death of kind and hard-working Lorenzo Barbirolli. Over-excited at John's return from a tour, he had a stroke on 31 March. So ended, at 64, the life of this man of parts and integrity whose violin had sweetened his son's imagination and taught him so early to appreciate the beauties of instrumental tone. If he had lived another two months he would have heard him conduct Mozart's *Don Giovanni* at Covent Garden with a distinguished cast that included Mariano Stabile and Elisabeth Schumann. He would have been proud to read the *Times* account, declaring that much of the orchestral playing was very fine and complimenting the conductor on the difficult task of combining with such ability so heterogeneous a team, whilst the *Daily Telegraph* said the performance was wholly admirable and remarked that the young 'Anglo-Italian' conductor was formerly a member of the orchestra.

Also in 1929 came the last days of the BNOC, beset with more financial trouble, which went into liquidation. But the Covent Garden powers acted quickly, salvaging many of the singers to form a new Covent Garden Touring Company, to sing opera in English throughout the country, and John was the obvious choice for musical director and chief conductor. His performances in the Opera House had been admired. The His Master's Voice company also made some claim to have exerted influence at Covent Garden on his behalf.

He was soon busy getting together an orchestra of about fifty good players that would preclude casual 'takings-on' in various towns, as the BNOC had done to augment its numbers while touring. The new company emerged on the stage of the Opera House itself in a fortnight's 'fill-in' season. John's niece Tina, then about eleven, was there when he conducted *The Mastersingers*. She had not heard him do opera before. 'I'm afraid I just dozed off,' she said, 'But my uncle said afterwards that he didn't blame me at all'.

When the tour began in Halifax the first performance in English of Puccini's *Turandot* was given. Also the Eva in *The Mastersingers* was a young soprano who was later to figure in Barbirolli's life, Marjorie Parry. A former Royal Academy student, she had come up from the BNOC chorus to larger roles such as Elizabeth in *Tannhäuser*. As the company travelled on in a repertoire including *Lohengrin*, *Falstaff* and *The Barber*, Marjorie Parry sang Musetta in *La Bohème* and Lola in Mascagni's *Cavalleria Rusticana*.

Sometimes John suffered moods of deep depression and Gladys Parr would be asked to go for a walk with him after the performance. In gaunt streets of strange towns they would crunch through snow while she told him all the funny stories she could think of to cheer him up, and often succeeded.

She rated him highly as an operatic conductor. 'He gave out

something that greatly helped the singer,' she said. 'For an *Aïda* in Halifax they suddenly told me, "You'll have to go on tonight." I said, "I haven't sung that part for twelve years." There was no time for rehearsal and they sent the score round to my lodgings.

'Before each act John came to my room and explained some of the things we would do—such points as "I take this in four, and this in two". That was all. But I didn't make a single mistake that night—and at the end there he was, standing down in the pit applauding with the audience.'

Gladys was sometimes invited to John's Boxing Day parties to be among his family, when Mémé cooked remarkably good pheasant and the assembly included Rosa and Peter, with his wife Pat. Later she went on to secondary parts in the Covent Garden grand season, such as Magdalena in *Die Meistersinger*. Still later, as a character actress, she had numerous roles in Benjamin Britten operas.

The following year, in his next Royal Philharmonic Society concert, John introduced Vaughan Williams' *Fantasia on a Sussex Folk-Song* and also played Debussy's *Rondes de Printemps*, of which he was very fond. Once again he conducted at Covent Garden, with Eva Turner in *Aïda*. Gladys was to spend another six weeks of rehearsal for Johann Strauss's *Die Fledermaus* before the touring started again. When it was introduced in Glasgow she sang Prince Orlofsky and Marjorie Parry was a charming Rosalinde.

John dreamed of more concert appearances but, despite his occasional successes, engagements were still not easy to come by at the top in competitive London. Glasgow, however, where some of his best operatic work was being performed, provided one opportunity at the end of the year, when he was invited to conduct the Scottish Orchestra, which had been going through a bad patch.

His first concert of a series with this orchestra was at the St Andrews Hall on 8 November 1930. Percy Gordon, the *Glasgow Herald* critic, said of it: 'He showed how quickly he and his players have arrived at a high degree of mutual understanding.' But the César Franck Symphony, added the critic, was 'too reserved in expression . . . Mr Barbirolli's scheme of interpretation, if raised to a higher emotional temperature, would have been very satisfactory'. Brahms'

Second Symphony on 11 November pleased the critic better, but he yet wanted 'more subtlety of expression' and more lyrical quality.

It has to be remembered that the orchestra John was suddenly called upon to deal with was in rather poor shape, as will be seen later, and he could not work miracles. But the canny Glaswegians were impressed by the new man's wrestlings and they bore him carefully in mind, as they went their homeward ways, for the future.

6 *In Scotland*

When John first met Evelyn, auditioning her in the Opera House that day in July, 1931, and engaging her for its Touring Company's orchestra, she was greatly thrilled by her good fortune. She did not linger at the Royal College even to take her diploma. Also she was impressed by the warmth and cordiality at the interview, surprised to find that Barbirolli was shorter than she had judged from seeing him on the concert platform. Being English she was glad to notice that though he looked foreign he did not act like a foreigner . . .

It was respect at first sight. In the pit of the Opera House, where she first played with her new companions as second oboe, next to an old Italian first oboe, her admiration of the dynamic young conductor deepened. The bond between them, she felt, was music. But she did not know him well and at this time John had a deep affection for Marjorie Parry.

That summer he was partnering Tullio Serafin, the distinguished Italian conductor, in the Italian part of the grand season. John's operas included Puccini's comic work *Gianni Schicchi* as well as *Turandot*. In the autumn came a six-weeks English season by the Touring Company on the stage of Covent Garden before it started to travel. The first rehearsal Evelyn attended was of Smetana's *The Bartered Bride*, sung for the first time in English. Also she watched Barbirolli coping with the trying task of rehearsing a revival of *The Wreckers* with the formidable Dame Ethel Smyth, its larger than life composer, in the offing.

Dame Ethel, with her plain-cut country clothes, man's hat and racy wit with incisive articulation, had been a respected phenomenon for many decades. It was not insignificant that her father had been an artillery general. An able composer, she lived with her sheepdog, Pan, in a cottage at Woking. Her most notable extra-musical activity had been to be locked away in Holloway for two months in 1911 in the Suffragette cause, conducting her 'March of the Women' through the bars of her cell window with a toothbrush.

Born in 1858, she ran away in her youth to study music in Leipzig, and her six operas combined English bluffness with German romanticism. The first was *Fantasio*; the second *The Forest*, produced in Dresden in 1901 and at Covent Garden in 1902 and 1903. Then came her most successful, *The Wreckers* (Berlin 1906, London 1909), inspired by her love of the sea and ships. *Boatswain's Mate*, a comic opera from a W. W. Jacobs story, made its London debut in 1916, *Fête Galante* in Birmingham in 1923 and *Entente Cordiale* at Bristol in 1925. She also wrote a Mass, first performed at the Albert Hall in 1893, a violin and horn concerto and two choral works, *The Prison* and *Hey Nonny No*, which she is said to have sung weirdly on occasion to suffragettes to her own piano accompaniment.

Sir Henry Wood told in his delightful *My Life of Music* of how he found one day at his home what he thought was a mechanic in breeches awaiting him. He said 'I want you to repair my bicycle'. The figure turned and said, 'Bicycle? I am Ethel Smyth!'

The Wreckers, which had been conducted by Beecham (not to her liking) and was to be later revived in 1939 at Sadler's Wells, was a highly dramatic opera about Cornish ship saboteurs, tumultuous and romantic—a goodish opera though not a 'draw'. But now, what with preparing *The Bartered Bride* and steering the orchestra round the reefs and shoals of Dame Ethel's rehearsal vagaries at the age of 73 (she would want to dictate tempo, method and even new notes) John found his work cut out.

Dame Ethel would send him detailed page-by-page suggestions, couched as 'remarks', such as '146 to end of Scene, sempre *pp*' or '152, flowing tempo'. She would write: 'I want a small rehearsal of all principals to be called and have a list of the things I want to rehearse. *With you* I chiefly want to go through 'The Cliffs' with the score (you haven't quite got that) . . . Rehearse the *whole* Finale Act II after the lovers fly (that is all wrong and ineffective).' And 'Could you fix up say 1½ hours (with someone to play piano) for me to put in the colour required? You know: the exact look, and sound, and gesture.'

She even pursued him to his home, writing 'I am telling Goodwin and Tabb (Mr Stooks) to deliver Act III at 2, Woburn Court tomorrow instead of the stage door and unless I hear from you to the contrary I will be there on Friday myself at 11.30 am.'

Tina, staying with her grandmother, heard an imperious knocking and 'there was this vision'.

'Ethel Smyth here,' said the vision. 'Mr Barbirolli, please.' And when told he was not at home, 'There, then,' said Dame Ethel unsmilingly, producing a large wad of papers from some receptacle, 'give these to him when he comes back.'

Calling for an extra week of chorus rehearsal, Dame Ethel said in a letter to John: 'I have written to Colonel Blois [the Covent Garden managing director] that I utterly understand the need of economy but that at the same time I could not possibly run the risk of *another* half baked performance [like Beecham's, presumably]. I therefore told him I would gladly pay for the other week myself—50 singers at 10*s*. means £25 and this is preferable to under-rehearsal and fiasco! . . . I also told him that I mean to take Avis's part in the ensemble rehearsals (and duet rehearsals with Mark and Jack too), which will help the others (and indeed all of you).'

Evelyn took part in the many rehearsals for *The Wreckers*. She was one of those who shared in the Dame's benignant approbation at one of them, which she demonstrated by offering to give the whole orchestra tea. There was a Lyons café very near and they all trooped off after her to it. When they had all joyfully had their poached eggs, baked beans and so on she collected all the bills and made her way to the cash desk. But producing the money proved a problem for the eccentric old lady.

'She had several long skirts,' said Evelyn, 'rather voluminous and almost trailing on the ground. She started gathering up her skirts and also gathered up what appeared to be about six petticoats underneath. She held them all high up in the air, groping beneath them until she came to a sort of money belt round her waist. She then took a purse out of the belt and paid, the while holding everything up, and then she put the purse back and let everything drop down again.'

All this provided the orchestra with enormous delight and amusement. They stifled their laughter in a state of near-collapse.

The short season at the Opera House was not well attended, opera in English by a touring company failing to attract sufficiently the sophisticated 'regulars'. The company took to the 'road' with the same productions, and Evelyn found herself travelling round the number one dates. From city to city she went, living in 'digs' and encountering a variegated collection of often draughty theatres—a fortnight at Glasgow, Edinburgh, Manchester, Liverpool and for the less important towns a week.

She played sturdily under the lights as John and the singers tackled *The Valkyries* and *The Mastersingers* or Richard Strauss's *Der Rosenkavalier* when that opera first made its appearance in English during the tour. The Octavian was Marjorie Parry. She looked stunning in a white satin costume and red satin shoes. Evelyn recognized that she was a very good artist on the stage, pretty and very musical though vocally limited. Among her other roles were Liu in *Turandot*, Mistress Ford in *Falstaff* and Leonora in *Il Trovatore.*

Trade was plummeting everywhere, with the country gripped in the world depression. The company suffered badly at the box office, despite good notices, struggling grimly on into 1932. In that year even the chances of opera at Covent Garden were thrown into jeopardy but Sir Thomas Beecham saved the situation by reappearing as conductor, soon becoming artistic director. John was invited to direct one performance of *Die Meistersinger*, Beecham handling the other three. The two conductors also shared *Tristan* on tour.

John married Marjorie in June, 1932. A few months later the Touring Company ended its short career.

Even before the winding-up occurred John had made a decision. This was to accept an invitation to conduct in

January and February the second half of the Scottish Orchestra's short winter season of concerts in Glasgow and Edinburgh. The conductor of the first half was to be Albert van Raalte.

It might have been regarded as rash to leave London for an out-of-the-way orchestra. But his desire was to be also a concert conductor, to handle the greatest music; his flair for opera, he considered, could pull him a little off orbit. Here was a chance of six weeks on the concert platform, to gain more experience in a wider repertoire and control his own symphony orchestra for a while. The demise of the Touring Company had at any rate opened the way to this.

The forty-year old Scottish Orchestra was the creation of the Choral and Orchestral Union of Glasgow and served Edinburgh too. Its guest conductors had included Sergei Koussevitsky, Albert Coates and Felix Weingartner. But it was at present somewhat in the doldrums, losing some of its best players to more lucrative posts, and the Union was looking round for someone to infuse more life, improve the attendances and attract more munificence from patrons. Its leaders had seen and heard Barbirolli in opera; they decided to try out the exuberant young conductor in a fairly cautious set of programmes.

He gave his first concert in St Andrew's Hall on the last evening of 1932. Percy Gordon, a critic not given to flattery, wrote in the *Glasgow Herald* that the opening Purcell Suite (arranged by Barbirolli) contained a wide variety of style and was well played with fine finish. The Brahms Second Symphony 'might have gone a little deeper in the first and second movements', but 'the lovely Allegretto was finely played and the Finale was brilliant'.

A good start—and other much-enjoyed music during the six weeks included Sibelius' Second Symphony, Beethoven's Eighth, Dvorak's Fourth (now numbered Eight), Elgar's Introduction and Allegro for Strings and Vaughan Williams' 'Job' Suite, played on a night when Marjorie Parry was the vocalist in some Wagner and Haydn. Two concerts were held in Glasgow each week—on Tuesday and Saturday nights—and one in Edinburgh on Mondays.

Even in the midst of these John took a few outside engagements and in Manchester on 12 January he conducted the Hallé Orchestra for the first time, giving the César Franck Symphony and Mozart's Symphony No. 40.

At the last Scottish concert of the half-season on 11 February he declared that he had completed six of the happiest weeks of his career and he was cheered to the strains of 'Will ye no' come back again?' The half-season must have been what the organizers hoped for. When June arrived it was announced that John was to take over in the following season as permanent conductor.

Four hundred attended a reception for the new conductor, graced by the Lord Provost of Glasgow, in October before the 1933-34 concerts opened. John amused his audience by describing how some people could only imagine an orchestra as something they had heard on the wireless. On the prevalent hobby of dial-searching for stations he went on: 'Ask them about music and they say, "But you haven't heard my set!". Their listening takes the form of a Jules Verne fantasia—"Round the World in Eighty Seconds".'

He was urging Glasgow people to dispel apathy and come to the concerts and in the event they did, attracted partly by lower prices. He had been authorized by the Union to overhaul the orchestra and he made about a score of changes in personnel. One of them was to bring in Evelyn as first oboe. The previous one, Leon Dandois, left because John disliked his tone quality and his awkward personality, both of which were hindering the achievement of a blended woodwind ensemble.

She recalled that he required another audition before deciding—then she was asked if she would like to come. 'I didn't know him particularly well then, but I accepted with alacrity.' Where a local appointment could not be made new players came from such orchestras as the London Symphony, the Royal Opera House and the Hallé.

The Committee and John had also come to a working agreement about the programmes. They dared not be too adventurous for fear of scaring off audiences. He naturally desired to go forward. A balance was struck. There was the usual intense Barbirolli preparation, with five hours a day rehearsing, except when they had nine-hour sectional sessions—the strings for three hours, the wind and brass for three and then the full orchestra for three.

Evelyn found comfortable lodgings only a few minutes' walk from St Andrew's Hall and shared them with Eileen Grainger, the viola player John had imported from his Touring Opera orchestra. They had a sitting-room together and a bedroom each, and a kindly landlady looked after them well.

At the opening concert there were queues at the box offices and every seat was full. An insufficient issue of programmes had been printed for the packed house. The Scottish Orchestra was being rediscovered by people who had not heard it for years. The *Mastersingers* Overture started off the music and the critics were delighted to find a 'highly sensitive and brilliant' performance of Tchaikovsky's Fourth Syumphony. To quote a musical onlooker, Hugh Marshall, Barbirolli 'seemed to be bursting with a talent and an enthusiasm which he could scarcely control and which spilled over generously on those who worked with him'. He was invigorated by crowded halls from the start. Ronald Kinloch Anderson, the musician and gramophone record producer (who, many years later, was to produce all John's last recordings), said: 'The Scottish Orchestra was a good second-class orchestra when he came. J.B. vitalized and galvanized it. Suddenly under his hands it became a much better orchestra and gained some standing. There was an air of excitement when he conducted.'

He blended the familiar and the unfamiliar. Music, as the season progressed, included Delius' *Song Before Sunrise*, Bax's *The Tale the Pine Trees Knew*, Sibelius' First and Second Symphonies, Chaminade's Flute Concerto and Elgar's 'Enigma' Variations. Percy Gordon wrote in the *Herald*: 'The fine quality of this year's Scottish Orchestra is notable—it is the best we have had for a long time.'

It wasn't long before Evelyn had some special work to do. As early as January she was the soloist in a Handel oboe concerto; at a later stage came concertos by Marcello and Pergolesi (the latter arranged for her by John).

He did not confine himself only to Glasgow and Edinburgh but took his forces to other towns. A select band of twenty-six, for instance, gave a Mozart concert in a church hall at Greenock, with a short lecture on the composer by a wealthy Glasgow enthusiast. Then, as well as travelling to London to make gramophone recordings, he managed to fit in a short season with the Leeds Symphony Orchestra, an enterprising though undistinguished body that needed a transfusion of energy. And he was invited to take the opera class at the Royal Academy of Music when he was able. All seemed promising for the future.

But things were not well in his domestic life. Marjorie had spent some part of the season with him in his Glasgow lodgings but they were proving temperamentally incompatible. One trouble was that she seemed unable to develop any easy, or intimate, association with the closely-knit Barbirolli family. John, unable to give up his family, enjoyed the nearness of his Woburn Place flat to his mother's home in Marchmont Street. Marjorie did not.

When she was in Glasgow Evelyn and Eileen Grainger were occasionally invited to meals with them. But it became apparent that John and Marjorie, close together on the concert platform, were drifting apart.

During the summer of 1934, when John was conducting the London Symphony Orchestra at the Welsh Eisteddfod, making occasional conducting jaunts to recognised seaside orchestras, Evelyn returned to London. She had kept on her flat with Natalie James, finding further freelance engagements, chief of which was the first season of the Glyndebourne Opera.

She had signed a contract with the Scarborough Orchestra, which entertained holiday-makers in a decorative Winter Garden overlooking the sea, when Fritz Busch, who with Carl Ebert was about to launch Glyndebourne under its founder John Christie, was looking for oboe players. He consulted his brother Adolf Busch the violinist, who was performing a concerto in the provinces with Barbirolli conducting, and passed on the query. Just as Peter Barbirolli had done three years earlier, John replied, 'Well, why not hear Evelyn?' Natalie was also mentioned, so it was not long before both were auditioned and became first and second oboes at Glyndebourne's début. Scarborough generously released Evelyn from her contract.

For the first two or three nights in the country opera house, said Evelyn, there were only a few of Christie's friends present for *Figaro* and *Cosí Fan Tutte* and the special train came down from London nearly empty. 'We didn't take long to pick up, though, for the critics soon let the public know the kind of opera that had been created down in Sussex.'

This led to something equally rewarding. Immediately after the first Glyndebourne season Gordon Walker of the London Symphony Orchestra (whose players comprised a good deal of the Glyndebourne body) turned to them and said, 'You two girls have really made history—we're very pleased with you.' And they were then invited to take part with the LSO in a broadcast performance. It was held in the big 'No. 10', the cavernous studio rented by the BBC under Waterloo Bridge.

'A stunned silence greeted us when we two walked into the studio,' said Natalie. 'We were the first women ever to play in the LSO. Someone said to us, "We don't have *women* in this orchestra . . ." But we were in, though we had to be very careful not to offend any of the men musicians. Conductors would be captivated by Evelyn's playing—her tone had piquancy and they'd smile at us. It was embarrassing—we didn't want the men to think that this was just because we were women. It was very difficult.'

Evelyn recalled playing in the studio with Sir Hamilton Harty conducting. 'It was very primitive and infested with rats.'

At home in their flat they would happily practise away. 'We weren't interested in anything else—it was so fascinating,' said Natalie. Then, when the winter season approached, they shut up the flat, Evelyn took the train from Euston to Scotland and Natalie went back to live with a Kensington family she knew. This routine went on for several years, until Natalie's marriage.

7 *To Loch Lomond*

By the time he had begun his second full season with the Scottish Orchestra towards the end of 1934, John had developed concert conducting into a full-fledged technique, had raised the level of the orchestra and was once more arousing the admiration of Glasgow for bringing sparkle and zest into the programmes.

He had an acute Italian ear for beauty of sound in string instruments. He concentrated on this, trying to develop a pure singing tone in the strings, caressing and shaping with warmth the rich quality, extending this care to the rest of the orchestra, being particularly concerned with correct bowing and marking the scores in detail accordingly. From this developed what became widely known as the 'Barbirolli Sound', a distinctive tone which emerged with the Scottish Orchestra.

If his Italian father bequeathed to him emotional intensity and love of beauty in sound, he inherited from his French mother his physical vitality, a tough and determined strain. It has been said that a Frenchman has the inborn logic to stop just where the Italian starts. There is some sense in this sententious observation. John was flexing his powers of control in evoking the emotional depths of music through this amalgam of Italian and French.

Yet he was also proud of having been brought up in England. He would say 'I am very English and very Italian' (thinking no doubt of his home life) and sometimes boasted of being 'more English than the English', playing down the Frenchness that was probably more important than he reckoned. The English side of his nature was ingrained since early days—cricket, school in Holborn, the Edwardian theatre—and with it had come a powerful love of Elgar's music.

He had called on the composer at Worcester in the summer of 1933 and listened to the Master's own recording of the tone poem *Falstaff.* He played both Elgar symphonies in the Glasgow concerts (without much response) and regarded him with veneration. In November, 1934, after his first two concerts, which contained Sibelius' First Symphony and Arnold Bax's tone-poem *The Tale The Pine Trees Knew* (dedicated to Barbirolli), he made his next appearance in an 'In Memoriam' tribute to Elgar, who had died in February, a few months after their meeting. David M'Callum, the leader of the orchestra, was soloist in the Violin Concerto, the second part of the programme being in memory of Delius (*Eventyr*) and Holst (parts of *The Planets*).

The management were pleased with the increasingly large audiences that Barbirolli's presence drew to these early events and at the large upturn in subscribers and guarantors, which helped in subsequently engaging such distinguished soloists as

Artur Schnabel and Vladimir Horowitz, the pianists, and Bronislav Hubermann, the violinist.

So much for the public face. The private one had for some while been a different matter. John had ceased living with Marjorie during the summer. By the end of the year his friendship with Evelyn was beginning to develop more deeply. She was receiving from him occasional lessons in the cello, her second instrument at the Royal College. By January he was writing 'Evelyn dear'.

As a musician he had been fascinated by the sound of her oboe playing. Beatrice Hancock, years later, declared that 'Evelyn's oboe had the Barbirolli sound; she's a beautiful player—her phrasing, her sensitiveness to whatever she's playing.' They came together as musicians. But he soon appreciated the warmth of her character, her candour and intelligence and her powers of critical judgment.

They began to go for long walks, talking animatedly, chiefly about music. He confided to her his plans for the orchestra and a score of ambitious ideas for airing more music yet unheard in Glasgow. He had found a responsive ear and a constructive tongue. A tenderness and an affinity arose between them and they fell in love. 'It was fairly gradual, after he and Marjorie had parted, when he was living alone,' remembered Evelyn.

Glasgow was the scene of their courting and they would sometimes travel out to Loch Lomond for these long rambles. 'We went on the tram,' Evelyn said. 'It cost us twopence and the Loch began where the tram finished.' Both of them liked to dine on juicy steaks in a quiet restaurant—at that time John was a more rotund figure than he was later to become. His eccentric eating habits had not hardened. A mutual appreciation of claret—Evelyn had been allowed by her father, a knowledgeable judge, to taste wine from an early age of three—was one of the pointers to their discovery that many of their ideas blended.

She was twenty-three, with vitality and a keen sense of humour, matching his broad Cockney jokes with her own lightsome approaches to problems. They soon found themselves complementary—the cool Englishwoman of self-effacing thoughtfulness and the very Latin, introspective young conductor.

When the season ended in February, Evelyn returned to London and John carried out his first foreign assignments with two orchestras—the Helsinki State and the Leningrad Radio. The Russians greatly enjoyed his Tchaikovsky and his general choice of Russian music. Also he had begun to be heard of in the United States, where his gramophone records were known. The praise accorded him by celebrity artists he had partnered for HMV like Fritz Kreisler and Pablo Casals the cellist (or engaged to 'draw the house' in Scotland, such as Artur Rubinstein and Alfred Cortot the pianists and Jascha Heifetz, the violinist) was attracting attention.

These international artists were not only adding to John's prestige in Glasgow but earnestly talking about him elsewhere. There was curiosity about the new name and Arthur Judson, the far-sighted manager of the New York Philharmonic Orchestra, began to bear him in mind.

Evelyn now started her second summer season at Glyndebourne Opera. 'She had five years there,' related Natalie James. 'I was always in her shadow but we made a very good department.' John had begun his habit of taking a house in Sussex in the summer, not far from the sea, to give the family a change, and Evelyn and Natalie, staying in Lewes, convenient for Glyndebourne, would spend some time with them all. Evelyn found herself greatly drawn to the lively Barbirolli ensemble and was soon treated as one of the family.

More work with the London Symphony Orchestra came along. There were stints, many and varied, with Herbert Menges at the Old Vic and with studio orchestras, such as once-a-week turns with Fred Hartley and his Quintet for Radio Luxembourg. She also had the good fortune to be engaged as first oboe in the new Queen's Hall Orchestra, re-formed by Sir Henry Wood in that year with two purposes—to make a documentary film about the history of the gramophone and (mainly) to record for Decca. Later it was to give a series of Sunday afternoon concerts. Sir Henry considered his wood-wind section remarkably fine.

Evelyn was once again among a number of freelancing LSO colleagues. No trouble about women in the orchestra this time—Wood was no stranger to them, having pioneered the introduction of six into his Queen's Hall Orchestra, from 137 women applicants, as long ago as 1913!

'Sir Henry was extremely kind and helpful,' recalled Evelyn. 'We were to do a recording of Vaughan Williams' "London" Symphony and I'd never played in it. You didn't rehearse at a recording session—you just *made* the record. He asked me to come along a little early and he took me through everything—told me exactly what parts were important, what he was going to beat, and he really looked after me.

'He was a marvellous rehearser—we all adored him. I know you could say he wasn't the greatest conductor who ever lived—he was perhaps a bit routine—but he would use every moment of rehearsal so as to get together a performance in a remarkably short space of time. It might not have been a great performance but it was all jolly efficient—and we loved him!'

John had been making occasional appearances at Sadler's Wells Opera, conducting *The Barber of Seville* with E. J. Dent's new translation and *Madam Butterfly*, as well as further afield in *Tristan* with the travelling Carl Rosa and with Covent Garden Opera's current tour.

Peter Barbirolli and his viola were in the Sadler's Wells pit. The family were forever converging. A couple of years before, when Peter was engaged at the Alhambra for Colonel De Basil's Ballets Russes de Monte Carlo, a famous season, the theatre's treasurer, distributing the pay packets to the orchestra on a Friday night, remarked, 'I've paid out for your grandfather, your father, your brother and now you!'

Europe was beginning to darken with the sinister rise of Adolf Hitler. Already there was a faint and ominous shadow of the conflict to come, but the uneasy epoch was cheered by the knowledge that the 'slump' seemed over. There was more money about, people were spending again and everyone supporting the re-formed Scottish Orchestra foregathered once more in Glasgow. There was, for the third time, an admitted upsurge in the playing and the prestige of the orchestra. And it was paying its way. Many years later a resumé of the period published by the orchestra said: 'Barbirolli's genius as a conductor, his charm, his dynamic personality and his innate musicianship attracted many newcomers. In 1935 interest in the concerts was still increasing.'

Sibelius' Fifth Symphony was presented, also Berlioz'

'Fantastic' Symphony, Debussy's *La Mer*, Delius' Violin Concerto, Stravinsky's *Pulcinella* and *Petrouchka*, Walton's Viola Concerto. Artists included Alexander Kipnis, Russian operatic bass, Benno Moiseiwitsch and Walter Gieseking, the pianists, and Adolf Busch and Albert Sammons, violinists.

During the season John's mother paid a visit, amusing her family by telling how she, who knew nothing about music, was looking on at a St Andrew's Hall rehearsal when some courteous official handed her a full score of the complex choral work under way to help her to follow what was going on!

His interest in chamber music extended John's Glasgow friendships. He joined in with musical families through his cello, or simply talked about music with them at their homes until the small hours. 'It was our good fortune,' wrote Hugh Marshall, 'to have him amongst us when his youthful genius was in full flood. He was a completely dedicated artist.'

These were days when he was lionized in the city. His wry humour and volatile temperament appealed to the Scots. There were a few detractors—some people, resenting the original style, criticized his dramatic entrances, short quick steps to the rostrum, stick held downwards before him. They charged him with showmanship. But as one of his best players said, 'He knew all about how to walk on but I wouldn't say it was acting. He simply had an Italian's inborn sense of theatre.'

A few others held it against him that he was a 'foreign' conductor. After one concert, as he was acknowledging applause, a woman in the audience asked her husband, 'Do you think he'll make a speech?' Her spouse replied, 'No, I don't think so—he probably can't speak English.' (Sir Henry Wood considered that the Scots actually preferred a conductor with a foreign name—they had had so many.)

John would stroll in the quiet streets with Evelyn after the concerts. 'Those were golden years for us both,' she once said, 'among the happiest of my life. Meeting John was the best thing that came to me through playing the oboe.'

There were more visits to other Scottish towns with a smaller orchestra, as well as series of concerts for children. John had just ended his season and Beecham's provincial tour by the Covent Garden Opera reached Edinburgh and Glasgow early in 1936. Beecham had invited him to conduct *Tristan*, with Walter Widdop and the highly acclaimed Eva Turner,

Britain's first international prima donna, as Isolde, when suddenly, on 3 April, came a bolt from the blue.

John received a cable offering him a limited ten-weeks season conducting the New Philharmonic Orchestra, beginning the following November.

8 *Applause, Applause . . .*

To his great surprise John was being invited to take up the ten-weeks season at the moment that Arturo Toscanini, generally regarded at that time as the world's supreme conductor, had relinquished the chief conductorship of the New York Philharmonic. It was apparently an extensive try-out—it did not follow that John would inherit the mantle but at any rate he would be given an adequate chance of showing what he could do.

The unexpectedness of the offer also astonished the musical public. Little was known about Barbirolli in America except for his gramophone records. But, as Evelyn said later, Arthur Judson, the manager, impressed by so many glowing reports from distinguished artists who had played and recorded with him, took a chance with the 'new broom' and engaged him. The half-season offer represented a much-coveted accolade and when the news of it was announced the Scottish Orchestra were magnanimous—they granted their conductor the necessary release for him to accept. Music-loving Glaswegians were thrilled by the news.

The New York Philharmonic Orchestra, America's oldest, had been founded in 1842—a month after the Vienna Philharmonic—as a players' self-governing co-operative. It had experienced a chequered history, with traumatic periods. In 1909 it abandoned the co-operative system and Gustav Mahler was appointed as conductor for a short, vigorous and stormy time. Later, Joseph Stransky was permanent conductor for a while and it carried on sturdily, though out-classed by the Philadelphia and Boston Orchestras. In 1929, after merging with the New York Symphony Orchestra, it was injected wth a double-dose of adrenalin by the appointment of Toscanini, who had left Italy disgusted with Mussolini's Fascist regime.

The New Yorkers adulated the fiery Italian, who succeeded in obtaining, with his strong discipline, forthright attack and literal approach, such precision and lucidity from the orchestra and such fidelity to the music. There was an undertow of criticism that he emphasized structure and technique at the expense of poetry and mood, that his tension was too aggressive, particularly in Beethoven, and that his musical choice was too conventional. But he drew the crowds and the management, exultant at the results, vainly attempted to persuade him not to resign in 1936, when, after disagreements, he said he wanted a change and to be free.

The best orchestra in the world was (and probably still is) the Berlin Philharmonic, then conducted by the great Wilhelm Furtwängler—any connoisseur who heard it, even in 1931, would probably have admitted that it had no equal—and the Vienna Philharmonic, also directed by Furtwängler, ran it pretty close. The New York management first invited Furtwängler (who had earlier made guest appearances) to take Toscanini's place.

This shy and spiritual German was, however, trying to tiptoe his way through the turmoil of the Nazi revolution. He rejected Nazi dogmas and stoutly defended those of his musicians who were Jewish, but he essayed tact in dealing with Hitler and his minions. He had refused to be a 'political' conductor in Germany and to hold permanent appointments. There was even a story of a violent scene with Hitler at Winifred Wagner's Bayreuth house in which Hitler threatened him with a concentration camp. Furtwängler replied, 'In that case I'll be in good company.'

New York might have been a way out. But his caution was interpreted abroad as tepid ideological deviousness and there were hostile gestures in the United States when his appointment to the first half of the coming New York season was announced. What with the clamour in America and Goering deliberately complicating his position at home, the disgusted Furtwängler declined the invitation, cabling: 'I have an aversion to political controversies, I am not a politician but an exponent of German music.'

Leopold Stokowsi and Bruno Walter, both of whom were approached, had other commitments, and the choice fell unexpectedly on Barbirolli (said to have been suggested by

Toscanini), with guest conductors such as Igor Stravinsky, Artur Rodzinski and Georges Enesco for the second part of the season. Judson's idea was that a youthful conductor might build towards the orchestra's future—some critics hinted that the ensemble had not always been greatly helped by the imperious ways of Toscanini.

But he had given it an unparalleled success and much prestige and the next conductor would naturally have to face an exaggerated backlash of comparison. Accepting the offer (and no doubt thinking that Lorenzo would have advised just that), John nevertheless saw that the task might prove thankless and unenviable. He certainly did not underestimate his vulnerable situation and, indeed, during the summer was a prey to extreme nerves. Apart from a few broadcast concerts, he passed most of his time studying scores to prepare for the ordeal. Sometimes he was with Evelyn in London, with evenings at the flat she shared with Natalie, or taking walking excursions when she visited the Barbirolli family at whatever house they took in Sussex.

At a Glasgow reception in his honour, just before he left, he said he was continuing as musical adviser to the Scottish Orchestra and would be with it again in January. In the mean time Georg Szell was brought in. In London, to speed him on his way, musical friends gave John a supper at Pagani's, the Edwardian restaurant in Great Portland Street (a famous haunt of musicians, destroyed in the Second World War).

When he embarked for New York in October (he afterwards related) he willed himself to forget he was supposed to be succeeding Toscanini. 'I said to myself, "You've been hired to do a job. Do it as well as you can."'

Meanwhile, Sir Thomas Beecham had been taking extraordinary action in New York. A guest conductor of the New York Philharmonic in January, he evidently coveted Toscanini's post for himself. At any rate he was furious when John was appointed and set about firing off letters to the committee and management denigrating him and declaring that he could not understand why they were appointing this 'young upstart'. Evelyn, who later saw the letter sent to Judson, was of the opinion that the jealousy evinced had a fortifying effect on the committee, who recognized that such a virulent attack was a fair sign that Barbirolli was good. John's anger when he heard of it knew no bounds; he never forgave Beecham for this insufferable behaviour.

On arrival in New York John was tactful with the Press, declaring that he was a very simple person and hoped that Americans would like him, and that he did not intend to follow in the footsteps of the Maestro, who was unique . . . At his first rehearsal he was liked by the orchestra—a body that contained only about a dozen British-sounding names out of a hundred of mainly mixed European origin. They immediately noted his meticulousness and his geniality—the latter quality had not been conspicuous with Toscanini. And John was initiated into the ways of handling the committees—including the women's committee, headed by the redoubtable Mrs Ruth Pratt, a rich and influential social group that swayed many a decision and moved many a mountain by its likes and dislikes.

The first concert, at the Carnegie hall on 5 November, was gratifyingly successful. It included Mozart's 'Linz' Symphony (No. 36), Bax's *The Tale the Pine Trees Knew* and Brahms' Fourth Symphony. The critics admired the tension and vitality. Lawrence Gilman, music critic of the *New York Herald Tribune*, wrote: 'He had mastered that first and last secret of the fine interpreter's ability to lead us to the heart of music: the ability to discover and to realize the melodic impulse that gives it life and direction and coherence.'

Olin Downes, the *New York Times* critic, wrote of the Brahms: Exceptional virility, grip, lyrical opulence . . . In general a red-blooded, dramatic and grandly constructed reading.'

The Orchestra was so delighted that its members fired off a cable to the Glasgow Choral and Orchestral Union which said 'Thanks for Barbirolli'. Immediately the convenor of the Union replied: 'We have learnt to value him in Scotland not only for his outstanding musical personality and enthusiasm but also for his sane and practical outlook on the business side and for his own social charm. Our best wishes for the success of his period as your conductor'.

John followed up with his Purcell-Barbirolli Suite, Elgar's 'Enigma' Variations, Bach and Haydn, Beethoven and Wagner (which particularly impressed—'The veritable authentic

KING'S THEATRE, Hammersmith

WEEK COMMENCING MONDAY, JULY 25th, 1927

EVENINGS at 8 MATINEE: THURSDAY at 2.30 Box Office Open 10 to 10

JOHN BARBIROLLI PRESENTS

THE

BRITISH NATIONAL OPERA COMPANY'S

PRODUCTION

THE BARBER OF SEVILLE

(ROSSINI)

IN THE VERSION BY FREDERICK AUSTIN

MIRIAM LICETTE GLADYS PARR DENNIS NOBLE ROBERT RADFORD

PERCY HEMING PARRY JONES HERBERT LANGLEY HEDDLE NASH

MARGUERITE ANDERSON ERIC GRAIE SYDNEY RUSSELL

Conductor - JOHN BARBIROLLI

DAVID ALLEN & SONS, LTD.

…othwell

Sidney Rothwell

A play bill from 1927, and a more enduring record of John Barbirolli – his name is now part of his beloved Manchester (though perhaps not on the style of architecture he would have preferred).

A musical marriage: the young Evelyn with her oboe, a photograph taken in Scotland in 1934, and (opposite) John with his cello at home in Manchester in the 1960s.

On tour: Evelyn and John in St Andrews in 1937, and (below) about to leave for Australia in 1955. John's hats got wider over the years!

John and Evelyn in California in 1942. Evelyn says that she cannot now remember what they were looking at so eagerly. (Below) J.B., brother Peter and Mémé: a family gathering in Greenwich Park in the late 1950s.

Pat Barbirolli

BBC Hulton Picture

J.B. and Mémé, after the first performance of Vaughan Williams' Sinfonia Antartica, *given in the Free Trade Hall, Manchester, on 14 January 1953.*

An affectionate greeting between friends: Lionel Tertis, the great viola player, and J.B. Audrey Napier-Smith looks on. (Below) J.B. greatly enjoyed working with Peter Cotes. Here they are in the television studio when the Hallé made its ITV debut in 1958, its centenary year, from the Free Trade Hall, Manchester.

TV Times

The opening concert of the Hallé Centenary Season was on 16 October 1957. Here Evelyn, Artur Rubinstein, J.B., Mémé and Nela Rubinstein look at congratulatory messages. (Below left) J.B. 'playing' a cello of flowers, when he was presented with the Freedom of the City of Manchester on 21 March 1958 and (right) making prints for the 'Pavement of Fame' at Belle Vue in 1959.

Wagner', said Gilman). Vaughan Williams was soon in the picture and so was Sibelius. Of Richard Strauss's *Don Quixote* Gilman wrote: 'One of the most moving, lucid and eloquently faithful performances that New York has ever heard.' According to Gilman, John's programmes were 'among the most skilful, interesting and provocative that have ever engaged the activities of the orchestra'.

At one rehearsal he was said to have shed such an original light on Beethoven's Second Symphony that the whole orchestra cried out 'Bravo, maestro!' The concerts were crowded, the critics were for the most part complimentary, the management were happy with the takings and John seemed to have succeeded gracefully in following Toscanini without a tumble.

Cordial relations with his musicians were soon established. They got to appreciate his sincerity, energy and serious devotion to music. His confidence was enhanced by the new people he worked with. Though short, he gave the effect of stature on the conductor's stand and looked an imposing figure.

He was as detailed in rehearsal with them as with the Scottish Orchestra, emphasizing the importance of true tempo and of discovering the form and shape of a work. He studied the psychology of players and adapted gestures to them: 'Sometimes you pull it out of them; sometimes you let it emerge.' He devoted the usual attention to clear string articulation and tone. With audiences he had the power of evoking suspense, exhilaration and that intangible thing, the shiver of the spine that comes rarely and at peak moments of music.

Olin Downes noted approvingly that he conducted from a score and not from memory 'in the ridiculous and unnecessary way in which certain celebrated conductors find it necessary to imitate Toscanini.' John never, in fact, would conduct from memory. Evelyn explained: 'He was going to do so when he first started. But then he decided that if he'd memorized a score he *must* be able to write it out in every detail. Otherwise it wasn't fair to the orchestra and particularly to the soloist. He *could* conduct from memory—he did so with the whole of

The Mastersingers at a rehearsal but he never felt justified in doing so at a performance.'*

In a month John had been accepted—by December he was offered the post of permanent conductor for the next three years at a salary of £15,000 a year.

Evelyn, who had been receiving letters full of increasing confidence and happiness, welcomed him back in good time for both to be in Glasgow on 18 January 1937, for the second half of the Scottish season. He was also able to fit in a Hallé concert and to conduct the London Philharmonic Orchestra at the Colston Hall, Bristol, when the *Bristol Evening Post* critic wrote: 'He took the audience by storm. His restless activity and his original mannerisms—among them a curious circular beat—fascinated the audience, who at the close of Elgar's Second Symphony gave him a most enthusiastic ovation.'

John had Florence Austral to sing in Wagner at his first Glasgow concert and performed Beethoven's 'Choral' Symphony at one of the last. He also took the orchestra on a three-weeks tour of Scotland before saying farewell to all his many good friends in Glasgow, who were loth to see him go after such an unexpectedly short while.

Again he was at Covent Garden, conducting in the Coronation season *Tosca* and *Turandot* with Eva Turner and Martinelli. In the autumn he returned in triumph to New York, where he was to take 26 out of the 28 weeks. He was now, however, to meet the unexpected competition of Toscanini himself, heading a reconstituted National Broadcasting Corporation Orchestra. This did not affect a very rewarding season, in which the music included Delius' Dance Rhapsody No. 1, Bax's Third Symphony, more Elgar, some Poulenc and Bartok, plenty of Haydn and Wagner. Kirsten Flagstad made her first American appearance with the orchestra in excerpts from *Götterdämmerung*. Artists included

*Toscanini, who always conducted from memory, once told John: 'I would never have done so had my sight permitted me to use a score. I am fortunate in having a naturally good memory, which makes conducting possible.' He could see a score only by lifting it up till it almost touched his eyes. He said he could never wear spectacles because any strong enough to see a score on his desk would preclude him from seeing the orchestra and keeping contact with it.

Sergei Rachmaninov, Rubinstein, Schnabel and Mischa Elman.

Purcell was then little-known in America and of his *Fairy Queen* dances, arranged by John, Gilman declared: 'Mr Barbirolli is evidently a connoisseur of Purcell. His selection was an admirable choice . . . The dances (scored for strings alone) are not only captivating in their grace, freshness, vitality, melodic and rhythmic distinction, but they served to inspire Mr Barbirolli and the glowing string section of the orchestra to show themselves at their best.'

Of a performance of Walton's 'Façade' Suite he said: 'It is scarcely a common occurrence for the great and august Philharmonic-Symphony Orchestra to turn itself into a kind of super-jazz ensemble and incite its audience to hearty mirth. Yet precisely this happened, with Mr Barbirolli aiding and abetting, and incidentally making Mr Paul Whiteman seem, by comparison, a very staid and conservative old gentleman indeed'.

It was one of the most successful seasons in the Orchestra's history, with an average concert attendance of nearly two and a half thousand. John's reception throughout was enthusiastic —Downes wrote of one February concert: 'Nearly every performance of the evening, good or bad, was applauded with practically equal fervour and tumult.'

In the summer John and Evelyn took a motoring holiday in France, with Evelyn at the wheel. They made Rouen their centre for delightful excursions and then travelled down the Normandy coast into Brittany. She again spent part of her time with the Barbirolli family in Sussex when she could get away from Glyndebourne.

John's return to New York in the autumn of 1938 was at the time of the Munich crisis, when Chamberlain was assenting to Hitler's part-occupation of Czechoslovakia. During the new season, the last before the European War, he conducted for 26 weeks, introducing Elgar's Second Symphony, Stravinsky's *Rossignol*, Rossini's *Petite Messe Solennelle* and music from Debussy's *Pelléas et Mélisande*. He slightly enlarged the repertoire of American composers and it was estimated that the British music provided six per cent of his programme time. He also took the orchestra to visit other cities.

Rivalry with Toscanini's orchestra, chiefly on the radio, was a mild irritant (the two men at this time got on well personally) and they were even neck-and-neck one week-end with Beethoven's Fifth Symphony. Barbirolli held his own, was praised, lived alone and cooked for his visitors. At Christmas time as usual he sent off to England boxes of assorted chocolates for Peter's daughter and Rosa's younger son. And he gave a party for the children of members of the orchestra.

9 *Together*

While John had been directing what some people afterwards described as the most brilliant programmes of his New York tenure, Evelyn in England had been playing as a member of the orchestra at the 170-year old Sadler's Wells Theatre in both opera and ballet. She had an open contract that allowed her freedom to freelance. So she was able to be with the London Symphony Orchestra for its concerts and to make records with Sir Henry Wood's new Queen's Hall Orchestra.

Opera at Lilian Baylis' theatre (she had died a year before) was conducted chiefly by Warwick Braithwaite (conductor of the Scottish Orchestra two years later) and Lawrance Collingwood, with occasionally Sir Adrian Boult as guest conductor; ballet often by the distinguished composer Constant Lambert. In this particular season Ethel Smyth's *The Wreckers* surfaced again. On the ballet side the rising young dancer Margot Fonteyn, just twenty, was for the first time the Swan Princess in *Swan Lake* and Aurora in Ninette de Valois' production of *The Sleeping Princess.*

When John returned to London in the early summer the divorce between him and Marjorie was being finalized. In a few weeks a date could be fixed for his marriage with Evelyn, who had finished at Glyndebourne after five years. They were quietly married on 5 July at the Holborn Register Office, not far from where John was born. He gave his name as Giovanni Battista and she as Evelyn Alice. They were 39 and 28. The witnesses were Tom Cheetham, a Lancastrian colleague from the Scottish Orchestra, Alfonso Gibilaro, John's brother-in-law, and Evelyn's two bothers Richard and Peter.

Lady Hancock, formerly Beatrice Mangeot, said years later: 'He married Evelyn because she was jolly nice and pretty, but I'm sure he also married the Sound—because her oboe had got the Barbirolli Sound—she's a beautiful player.'

The marriage did not come about without some difficult moments with Evelyn's father. 'He didn't much like my becoming a musician but he got used to that,' she said. 'But when he heard that I was to marry a man who was a Roman Catholic, divorced *and* a foreigner it was a shock, and the whole thing was anathema to him. He was extremely Victorian—22 years older than Mother, who was much more ready to accept a musician.

'The good thing was that he did get used to it, and he became frightfully fond of John, who was very good with him. The rest of my family accepted John immediately.'

For their honeymoon, in an unsettled atmosphere with risk of war, they went again to Normandy and Brittany, touring in Evelyn's car. Italy had been settled on earlier, but the war threat altered their plans. If John had been in Mussolini's country and war broke out he would, as the son of an Italian father who was never a naturalized Briton, have been liable for conscription under Italian law.

They started their honeymoon at Newhaven, crossing the next day. Another night was spent in Rouen before moving to Honfleur and down the coast to a charming little hotel at Arromanches. They pottered about to Bayeux, Caen and Mont St Michel. In Brittany a couple of nights at St Malo, a trip up-river from Dinard to explore the delightful little market town of Dinan . . . then on to Vitré, near Rennes.

This blissful and refreshing interlude lasted less than three weeks. On their return, John found himself summoned urgently back to New York by a management anxious to have their main asset with them before war broke out. But there was an inescapable delay in procuring an American visa for Evelyn as the State Department closed its visa section when war was declared, and John had to sail alone towards the end of August—she was to follow soon.

Evelyn waited with her family for a visa. There was a great bustle of evacuation of children from the cities and towns and she joined in the task of welcoming some of them at local country stations and driving them to their new homes in farms, cottages and country houses.

Four days after Barbirolli had sailed, Hitler's war began.

The momentous events on the other side of the Atlantic did not mute the musical scene in New York. The Philharmonic season started as usual in Carnegie Hall. One of the early Barbirolli novelties was the première of the Czech composer Jaromir Weinberger's 'Under the Spreading Chestnut Tree' Variations and Fugue. Another was Castelnuovo-Tedesco's Second Piano Concerto with the composer as soloist. There was also a revised version of Tchaikovsky's Violin Concerto by Fritz Kreisler, soloist after an absence of seventeen years.

Weinberger's Variations were inspired by seeing a cinema newsreel of George VI at a young people's camp in England, dressed like them in sweater and shorts and laughing as he sang with them this community 'action' song.

The October number of the *Philharmonic-Symphony League Bulletin*, organ of the 'friends' of the orchestra, had a picture of the new Mrs Barbirolli, showing a brown-haired, rather pensive-looking young woman with thoughtful eyes, wearing a simple dress. The *Bulletin* said it was hoped she would soon be in New York to meet League members at the October lunch. In fact Evelyn missed the lunch—she had to wait until 21 October for her visa and sailed on the 25th in an American ship.

'I had a very warm welcome,' she said, 'and thought New York very beautiful. We had a flat at the top of Hampshire House, looking out on to Central Park South. It was on the 28th floor—we shared the lift with Yehudi Menuhin, who had the other flat on that floor.' In the twilight, when all the lights went up, Evelyn thought the effect was wonderful. Skyscrapers tapered to various shapes and made an extraordinarily lovely scene.

'We went back many times in later years when John guest-conducted but the city was never quite the same and I don't think it was only because of our being younger and the personal circumstances. I think New York has very much changed, more perhaps than many other cities, and very much for the worse.'

They lived in a white-painted flat containing a spacious

living-room, a good-sized bedroom, a bathroom and a small 'bar' kitchen off the living-room. The new life was very exciting for the new bride. She was stimulated by the vitality around her. 'I liked the Americans—very friendly and hospitable.'

She gave up her professional playing to be at John's side and soon found that his job entailed a certain amount of 'socializing', in which she was expected to share, since the orchestra was largely subsidized by the rich and socially-conscious. In turn she encountered leading members of the various committees and some social events were almost obligatory. Evelyn, hitherto rather shy, at first found it both difficult and demanding but she was soon aware of the currents and, for John's sake, 'in the swim'. As a musician she was able to talk on knowledgeable terms with players in the orchestra and to make friends there, too.

Except when touring, he was usually at home when off-duty, often busy with scores or reading a good deal, usually biography (his main love) or thrillers. They had a small private room at an exceptionally cosy little Italian restaurant nearby; run by the family Bronzo, and used by the orchestra, it offered home cooking and moderate prices.

Evelyn was drawn into a particularly interesting private chamber music session. Benjamin Britten, who was then in New York, suggested to her that they should tackle some Mozart string quintets and said 'You can have a bash on the oboe.' This led to a glorious time for five musicians including Evelyn, attempting the first violin parts on her oboe, and Britten playing the viola.

Interesting music that entered that season into the Philharmonic Orchestra's programmes included Debussy's Rhapsody for Orchestra and Saxophone, Ibert's Chamber Concertino, Paganini's Violin Concerto in D, with Zino Francescatti as soloist, Elgar's Introduction and Allegro, and the première of Benjamin Britten's Violin Concerto, the soloist being Antonio Brosa.

Evelyn accompanied her husband on what was for her an exciting trip—the orchestra's concert tour of fourteen cities in America and Canada, which began in November. The American cities included Washington, Chicago and Pittsburgh and in Canada they played in Ottawa, Toronto and Hamilton.

During the Ottawa visit John and Evelyn were entertained by Lord Tweedsmuir*, the Governor-General of Canada.

John always wore his large broad-brimmed Verdi-style black hat and in the winter a black overcoat with astrakhan collar (which he had acquired for the trip to Russia and Finland in 1935). It was noted that some members of the orchestra during this tour were themselves following something like this fashion! John's theatrical idol, Sir Henry Irving, had been largely imitated by his Lyceum company of actors in much the same way in the early years of the century.

There was fun at rehearsals. One story tells of diminutive Labate, the principal oboist, who was of Italian extraction and spoke broken English, shortening words. Mozart to him, for instance, was 'Motz'. Wanting to know at rehearsal whether he would be required to play in the Schubert Symphony or wasn't wanted in the Mozart, he went up and said 'Good morn'. What we play? Motz?' 'No, Schub,' responded John, to a roar of laughter.

In Ottawa John glared at late-comers when the National Anthem had been played and held up the concert until they were settled and quiet. This was to become a regular habit in the future when audiences failed to behave with the respect he felt they owed the music.

But in New York, despite the robust excellence of the concerts that season, there was becoming manifest a gradual swing of Press criticism against Barbirolli's conducting. There had been for some time the intensive rivalry of Toscanini and the NBC concerts and the undercurrents of unrest were said to have been partly inspired by the Toscanini faction—though Toscanini himself was on ostensibly friendly terms with John.

Whispers began to be heard that the younger Italian was not wearing very well, that some of his performance were looking a little thin, that he was unduly impetuous or lacked a firm rhythm, that his energies were not sufficiently controlled.

Wolfgang Stresemann, for many years Intendant of the Berlin Philharmonic Orchestra, said years later: 'When America's leading music critic, Olin Downes of the *New York Times*, became anti-J.B., it did seem that he was fighting

*Lord Tweedsmuir was John Buchan, noted novelist in his day.

impregnable forces, solidly lined up against him from past memories of Toscanini.'

Evelyn described the circumstances, as she saw them, thus:

'Lawrance Gilman, the *Herald Tribune* critic who had given John wonderful notices, died. Downes had always been the commentator of the regular Sunday evening coast-to-coast broadcasts by the Orchestra that everybody listened to. Then Arthur Judson, the Philharmonic's manager and head of Columbia Concerts, did a very silly thing—he sacked Downes from that job. Downes was furious with Judson and from that time wrote badly about the Orchestra.

'It was nothing to do with John—he was the unfortunate person in between. Other critics began to follow suit—it was all very hurtful and left its scars on the whole of John's life.'

John would occasionally dine at Bronzo's with Toscanini, who could tell many entertaining stories about Puccini and other composers. They would also have Sunday morning pre-lunch drinks, when gossip would be exchanged between wives of various musicians, with Toscanini often capping what the others had said with unflattering comments about his colleagues. One day he turned his malicious tongue against Bruno Walter. This enraged John so much that he got up and said, 'I'm sorry. He's a good friend of mine and a great man and I don't agree with you,' walked off and never returned to the group. This hardly helped an already delicate situation.

But at any rate the Orchestra and most of the public remained faithful to the name of Barbirolli. The women's committee, too, was loyal. In February 1940, his contract was formally renewed for two more seasons.

10 *The Hallé Beckons*

John and Evelyn travelled widely in the New World from the spring of 1940 onwards. In Philadelphia his orchestra performed excellent Wagner to discriminating audiences that boasted a famous orchestra of their own. An invitation to conduct the Vancouver Symphony Orchestra in a charity concert entailed a wonderful and lengthy journey by train through the Rocky Mountains. Then on to California to conduct at the Hollywood Bowl during the summer.

The train journey to Vancouver gave Evelyn and John the pleasure of a drawing-room carriage suite with double berths and days of relaxation with wonderful scenery. This change from the bustle and clamour of New York was a great solace for their nerves, with well-served meals and no intrusive telephone. The beautiful little house they rented was built half-way up a mountain and they delighted in the splendid view over the sea, the mountains and Vancouver itself. Very near was a small and unfrequented nature reserve to which they often drove. It was glorious 'escapism', to which they returned several times in other summers before leaving America.

Evelyn could recall a wonderful pool where they bathed in the cold water. Here they watched the leaping salmon, and in its surrounds beavers building dams could be observed at their labours from a suspension bridge which the pair had to cross. 'The business of crossing would terrify me,' she remembered, 'but John was wicked, waiting till I was on it and then swinging it!'

For the next three early summers they returned to the same house in Vancouver, so greatly were they attached to this beautifully situated city where strangers were received with so much charm and cordiality—not that they permitted the word 'stranger' to apply to either of them for long. But though regarding Vancouver as finely situated, Evelyn believed that in building their cities the Canadians resembled the Australians —'They could have made Vancouver, as the Australians could have made Sydney, one of the world's most beautiful cities; but they didn't quite do it!'

These Canadian visits brought John some relaxation, although he rarely took time to rest, as well as opportunities to be amongst Canadians of British stock. The Hollywood Bowl outdoor concerts, on the other hand, meant activity in a purely American scene. In that series (then very prestigious, with classical concert performances) he conducted the Los Angeles Philharmonic Orchestra before audiences of many thousands.

For the later summer months they rented a house in California where, said Evelyn, they played quartets privately with fellow professionals including Francescatti the violinist and the violist William Primrose. At Heifetz's home they had 'marathon' chamber music. José Iturbi sometimes played four-handed Mozart at his house with Vladimir Horowitz, the Russian-born pianist who had the reputation of being the world's finest. They used two pianos, saying that otherwise they got in each other's way!

It was at a party at Horowitz's house in Beverly Hills that John had his first encounter with Charlie Chaplin. The famous comedian seemed 'up-stage' at first and conversation was difficult. Then John, a propos of something, said in a Cockney voice 'D'ye remember the Mile End Road?' Immediately Chaplin thawed and they got on splendidly. They were soon exchanging memories of Kennington and Lambeth (where Chaplin spent his impoverished boyhood), as well as Islington and Stepney. Chaplin asked John what part of London he sprang from and the discussion turned to Holborn and Bloomsbury, where Cockney slang is indistinguishable from that within sound of Bow Bells.

The two men animatedly chatted away—and those close enough could pick up talk of Albert Chevalier, Harry Champion, George Robey and Gus Elen among others—all famous London music hall comedians when J.B. and Charlie were children.

John went on one summer to Chicago to conduct the Symphony Orchestra at its festival at Ravinia, riveting the audience (said the Press) with Rossini and making pulses throb with excitement over Sibelius. His return to Vancouver for a Canadian Red Cross concert marked the solo appearance of Evelyn in the Pergolesi Oboe concerto that he had arranged. This performance inspired Arthur Benjamin to write for her his Cimarosa Concerto.

In New York the pair enjoyed visiting the homes of a small circle of friends, but although good mixers they did not claim to be 'sociable' people—they cherished their simple privacy, John especially not caring for social gatherings. He said of smart restaurants: 'They give me the willies.' They treated themselves to the theatre occasionally, to the cinema very rarely.

A poor sleeper, John had come to terms with insomnia years before by working at night, when he found he could cover twice as much ground. He worked incessantly throughout the day also, without relaxation. His day might begin with toast and coffee for an invariably early breakfast, never later than eight o'clock, and go on till three or four the next morning, and he would never eat properly till work was done after the evening concert or after his rehearsals were finished.

This intensive activity and concentration stemmed partly from childhood habits of industry—his mother had said that no child had worked harder. Youthful overwork as well as heredity may also have been a contributing cause of his occasional deep depressions and obsessive need to turn to more work to drive them away. 'He would work his way out of them,' said Evelyn. 'His fits of depression became more frequent as he grew older. They made him reluctant to stop work. He had enormous energy and activity of mind. He never needed a lot of sleep—he liked to work at night undisturbed, when others were asleep.'

Part of this nocturnal labour was in studying scores new and old, or putting the bowing marks into string parts. Evelyn wisely made no attempt to change the habits of a lifetime—certainly of long before their marriage. And she resigned herself to accepting that if dinner was ready and he desired to spend another hour on a score he would do so. 'I understood,' she said, 'because, in a way, I was made a bit like that myself.'

She developed her cooking skills alongside his in the small 'bar' kitchen. 'I hadn't learnt to cook at all, either at home or at school. So we had to experiment. He was a very talented and keen cook—I don't think I was particularly gifted though I had a certain aptitude. I used to watch John and mostly assist. Certainly I always did the sauces and mayonnaise and cooked the pasta.'

Often they would prepare the main meal of the day well after midnight. John enjoyed this repast and took a long time over it. His propensity for hot plates for each course was due to his habit of eating very slowly and talking a lot. And the hot plates were often cold by the time he had got round to finishing his course.

A 75th anniversary concert in honour of Sibelius; the Barbirolli version of a Purcell Chaconne; Britten's Sinfonia da Requiem; Bizet's Symphony, discovered only seven years before;

Rachmaninov playing his Rhapsody on a Theme of Paganini and Benny Goodman as soloist in Mozart's Clarinet Concerto—these were some of the highlights of the 1940-41 New York season, which throve despite the strictures and animosity of some of the critics.

The kind of rough 'Press' to which John was sometimes subject in New York can be typified in a passage by Gilman's successor, Virgil Thomson (*Herald Tribune*, 24 November 1941):

> 'The Brahms was routine Barbirolli. That is not to say that the conducting was inefficient but that the musical conception was derived from the work of inferior masters like Stokowski and Toscanini. Stokowski himself used to do a better job of the Brahms Second than this, but Mr Barbirolli's tendency to alternate soft passages with ton-of-bricks *fortissimi* is a vice that has been spread around America chiefly by Leopold Stokowski . . . His [Barbirolli's] tendency to whip up these same passages into a positive fury is an imitation, I should say, of Mr Toscanini's most serious fault as a musician. The futility of this was measurable by the restlessness of the audience and by the number of quiet sleepers visible.

Others would slightingly extoll his abilities as an orchestral accompanist to solo players at the expense of his symphonic work. It was becoming clear, now that the glamour had rubbed off, that certain influential groups wanted to change course, to drop their star from the permanent conductorship. Evelyn felt that Toscanini had a certain hand in it; at any rate, his competing concerts tended to harden attitudes all round.

When the 1941-42 centenary season arrived the management engaged guest-conductors (ten of them), including such powerful names as Stokowski, Bruno Walter and Dmitri Mitropoulos, the Greek conductor of the Minneapolis Symphony Orchestra—and Toscanini. Here was a means of edging Barbirolli out; he had only a moderate share of the season and filled in his spare time by guest-conducting other American orchestras. Then in 1942, after five years' tenure, his contract was not renewed.

To change conductors is nothing new. Certainly no slur

attached to a non-renewal, for whatever the overnight American re-evaluation, it was a splendid achievement to have battled on for so many years and given such a display of versatility. John stayed longer in New York (known as the 'graveyard of conductors') than anyone else, including Toscanini.

By now, Americans had more basic battles to fight than the warfare of music. In December, 1941, the Japanese attacked Pearl Harbour and after two years the United States was joining lone Britain in the war. John, worried about how his family were faring in the blitzes, decided to pay a visit to England. He thought he might make a small contribution to the war effort by offering to conduct for war charities without fee. The sea passage was arranged by A. V. Alexander, then First Lord of the Admiralty, who obtained Churchill's approval, but John was unable to take Evelyn with him—passages were almost impossible to arrange with the authorities: official transit came first. He set off alone in April in a 3,000-ton Norwegian bacon freighter, part of a convoy of 75 ships which were reduced to 32 by the U-boats!

In war-torn Britain he conducted 32 concerts in a month, including a tour of England with the London Symphony Orchestra and one of England and Scotland with the London Philharmonic. Trains that were crowded with troops took him to concerts in pitch-black cities with no lights to be seen—except where there were blitzes. His mother travelled with him often in blacked-out carriages on the tours. Typical examples of the programmes were those at the Albert Hall, Nottingham, when Beethoven and Wagner were given under his baton by the LSO, as well as Stravinsky's 'Firebird' Suite and Tchaikovsky's Fifth Symphony by the LPO. Everywhere he went there was a great war-time thirst for music. Back in London he conducted in part of Jay Pomeroy's season at the Cambridge Theatre. Of this concert Julian Herbage declared: 'With the rather scratch resources of the present-day LSO it was a really brilliant feat.'

John returned to America in a banana boat and the convoy again lost several ships through meeting a U-boat pack. This transatlantic sortie intensified his already strong desire to get home. He now wanted desperately to be back in England again, though he had to carry on through his contractual time, with plenty of guest engagements, such as with the Seattle and Chicago orchestras and again at the Hollywood Bowl; followed by a three-months autumn spell with the Los Angeles Orchestra in Los Angeles itself.

He introduced Vaughan Williams' 'Pastoral' Symphony at a New York Philharmonic concert in February 1943, and Olin Downes had a change of heart to bid his old *bête noir* farewell; 'For me this symphony is one of abiding poetry, singularly personal and independent in its craftsmanship and unique in its evocation of beauty.' At John's last New York concert on 7 March after Scriabin's *Prometheus* and Debussy's Fantasie for Piano and Orchestra, audience and orchestra united in singing 'For Auld Lang Syne'.

Already he had been approached by the Los Angeles orchestra to become its permanent conductor, but an insuperable obstacle loomed here. Pedrillo, powerful union boss and head of the American Federation of Musicians, was suddenly insisting that all conductors and solo artists should become members of the union—and membership required taking American citizenship. 'I couldn't do that then, or at any other time for that matter, but especially during the war,' John afterwards said.

Providence took a hand. On 25 February came the momentous cable from the Hallé Orchestra in Manchester, signed by R. J. Forbes, Principal of the Royal Manchester College of Music and an occasional guest conductor of the Hallé himself. It said: 'Would you be interested permanent conductorship Hallé Orchestra? Important developments pending.'

'John hadn't been in touch with the Hallé at all,' said Evelyn. 'But we had determined to go back to England, anyway, and this unexpected telegram was a delightful bolt from the blue. It solved all our problems and we had something to go back to.'

It had in fact been sent through the initiative of Philip Godlee, Chairman of the Hallé Concerts Society, who knew that Forbes was acquainted with John. After John had cabled a tentative reply that he was 'always interested' to consider such a distinguished post, Godlee in April offered him the appointment at £3,750 a year for 150 concerts, with full artistic control.

He accepted. He was the Hallé's fourth permanent

conductor since its inception in 1858. He had spent seven years with the New York Philharmonic—the longest period anyone had had.

11 *Restoring an Orchestra*

Acceptance of the Hallé offer meant immediately for both John and Evelyn a perilous gamble with death and a miraculous escape. They sailed for Lisbon in a neutral ship, the Portuguese *Serpa Pinto*, dodging more U-boats. At Lisbon they were booked for seats on a plane for England, flying four days later. As it happened, they switched seats to an earlier flight.

'The authorities,' said Evelyn, 'realizing that John urgently wanted to get back for the Hallé, gave us the two seats booked for Leslie Howard, the film actor, and his manager, because Howard wanted to stay longer in Lisbon to see a preview of one of his films. He flew four days later with our tickets—and his plane was shot down . . . It should have been ours.'

Many and various rumours circulated at the time, and persist to this day, about the reasons for the Luftwaffe's attack on the Dakota. One was that German spies reported that Winston Churchill was on the plane (Howard's manager looked a little like him). Another was that Howard had been singled out because he was carrying out a clandestine mission for Sir William Stephenson, the Canadian secret agent. Still another was that the Nazis were after another Secret Service man in the same plane.

The Barbirollis went straight by train to Manchester, arriving on 2 June 1943. The *Manchester Guardian* reported that there was a 'good crowd' at the station to greet them and that John spent the afternoon discussing outstanding matter with Hallé officials.

These 'outstanding matters' must have been somewhat disconcerting. Evelyn said frankly: 'We expected to find the Hallé Orchestra ready for action and we hadn't perhaps inquired as closely as we might have. We had been rather misled about it. I don't think John would have been so eager to reach Manchester if he'd known what he was coming back to. The Hallé was in such a mess—he found rather less than a third of the necessary personnel.'

But Manchester's famous orchestra had not been in a mess a short time before and the reason for its sudden difficulties will be discussed soon. Harold Atkins, working on the *Manchester Guardian* at the time, attended splendid symphony concerts by an excellent full-scale orchestra in various cinemas after the Free Trade Hall had been destroyed by incendiaries in Hitler's blitz. It was a brilliant and capable orchestra in 1941-43, conducted by such leading men as Dr Malcolm Sargent, Sir Adrian Boult, Leslie Heward and Basil Cameron. A typical notice of one of Sargent's concerts by the perspicacious Granville Hill, music critic of the *Guardian*, said: 'The performances yesterday were extremely fine . . . The playing [of Brahms] was as deep and true in utterance as any of the previous fine performances we have known.'

The *Hallé Magazine* declared a year or two later: 'How much is owed to the old orchestra under Malcolm Sargent in the dark, grim first days of the war . . ! What helped it through those faltering days to the time when it played to new audiences undismayed by the black-out and the bombs was Sargent's vigour and courage and the unconquerable spirit of the man . . . At that time Sargent was the principal conductor of the Hallé and the mainstay of the Liverpool Philharmonic.'

Of the many raids through which he travelled or conducted Sargent considered that the blitz on Manchester on 22 December 1940, immediately following the Hallé's performance of Handel's *Messiah*, was his 'finest specimen', and he assisted in fighting the fire-bombs on the roof of the Midland Hotel.

The Orchestra's peripatetic existence in theatres, cinemas and at the King's Hall, in the Belle Vue amusement park, was eagerly supported by a new young war-time public to whom its music was exhilarating and uplifting. Crowds, many of them in uniform, formed queues all around the Albert Hall in Peter Street. To the Hallé directorate there seemed to be a big opportunity here that had to be grasped. Then, in May 1942, Sargent accepted the principal conductorship of the Liverpool Philharmonic Orchestra and seemed no longer likely to conduct the Hallé. Liverpool, helped by the disbandment of the BBC Salon Orchestra, had ambitions to expand its status. Manchester, of course, had no desire to take a second place and Philip Godlee, the Hallé's chairman and managing director of a successful textile firm, pressed ahead with a bold plan to put it on a full-time basis for the first time, with all-the-year-round contracts and an expansion to 250 concerts annually instead of the usual 40. A new permanent conductor would be needed with the drive, personality and experience to put all this through.

About half the leading players were also members of the BBC Northern Orchestra, which could offer employment for four days a week. Godlee and his friends expected considerable changes of personnel with their plans, as a number of regular players could not undertake full-time jobs because of other commitments. But what they did not expect was that most of the 'dual-purpose' players would prefer the BBC to the Hallé. Only four out of 35 stayed. As one official later put it: 'Up to that moment we had a good orchestra but when we said "Either sign for us or for them" most of them decided for the BBC.'

'When John arrived,' said Evelyn, 'we found no money and few players; something like a third had gone to the BBC because they wanted safe jobs. There was only a nucleus left, including Laurance Turner, the very loyal and excellent leader.'

With the huge gap, the Society advertised for players and according to T. E. Bean, appointed general manager the following year, 'All Barbirolli had to conduct by way of an orchestra was a list of would-be players.'

This curious and surprising situation, when he had grasped it, rather appealed to John. It was a challenge—something to build on—and he knew all the ropes of training and control. Even the chilling fact that the optimists of the Hallé Concerts Society had gone on planning concerts and that the first was only a month ahead did not daunt him. It *looked* alarming, but he was fairly confident that, given players who were even potentially good, and with hard work, he could weld the orchestra into some shape in the time.

There were about thirty-six available players. All kinds of applications were received through the advertisements, scores of inquiries were made. He began to hold auditions daily, working as usual from morning till night in the black, blitz-scarred city, with its muddy bomb-damage—a city that nevertheless contained a population of dogged tenacity and tough Lancastrian spirit during those dark days.

The Hallé Orchestra, Britain's finest outside London, evolved indirectly from the Gentlemen's Concerts established in Manchester about 1770. The Gentlemen's Concerts (which ended in 1920) were inaugurated with twenty-four amateur flautists in a tavern and then a hall on the site of the Midland Hotel. A small orchestra developed and from 1803 Haydn, Mozart and Beethoven were being performed.

Charles Halle (or Hallé), the German musician who was appointed conductor and manager in 1849, was born at Hagen, in Westphalia, in 1819, the son of a Lutheran organist. He studied in Paris and became there a pianist of renown, but the 1848 Revolution brought him to London. At the first Gentlemen's Concert he attended in Manchester, Chopin was the pianist. Hallé was induced to settle there, conducting, teaching and playing in chamber concerts. Berlioz, a personal friend, described him as 'that model pianist, that musician sans peur et sans reproche'.

Hallé's ideas expanded when he was asked to provide a full orchestra for an art treasures exhibition at the new Free Trade Hall in 1857. Recruiting some players from the Gentlemen's concerts, some from London and some from the Continent, he made such a success of it and received so many plaudits that he started afterwards a weekly series of 'Hallé Concerts' in the hall on 30 January, 1858. Thus the Hallé Orchestra was born fortuitously as his own private venture. The first concert included Weber's *Der Freischütz* Overture, Beethoven's First Symphony, a selection from *Il Trovatore*, Berlioz's *Ballet des Sylphes* and piano solos by the conductor.

Hallé was a deeply serious man with a great capacity for work. In Manchester he found people who were equally serious and industrious and he instantly took to them and their environment as they took to him.

By 1865 the Orchestra was 80 strong and beginning its constant habit of travelling to other cities and towns. Much of the European classical repertoire was played, with one work new to Manchester audiences at each concert. Hallé, who was rewarded for his labours with a knighthood, played solo pieces at 370 of these concerts. He was the pianist in many concertos and at 63 first played Brahms' B flat Concerto. He gave the English première of Berlioz's 'Fantastic' Symphony in 1879. Bach's 'St Matthew' Passion was given in 1873 and Grieg conducted his Piano Concerto, with Hallé as soloist, in 1889.

Three years after Hallé's death in 1895, the Hungarian Hans Richter was appointed conductor and a non-profit-making society took over from the guarantors. An impression that the Hallé developed largely through the presence of German immigrant business and professional men and artists in Manchester has been questioned in recent years—its sponsors and supporters throughout were mainly of English blood.

Richter, a distinguished exponent of Beethoven and Brahms and an intimate of Wagner, was greatly admired and gave the Orchestra a glorious period, but he had conservative tastes, save for Strauss, Elgar and Sibelius. In 1903 he introduced Elgar's *Dream of Gerontius* (as well as Bruckner's Second Symphony) and in 1908 the first performance of Elgar's First Symphony. He was succeeded in 1912 by Michael Balling, German and a son-in-law of Wagner. An able and sensitive musician who had begun as a violinist, Balling performed Mahler* and Bruckner and introduced many composers new to Manchester. He was the first to suggest a municipal subsidy.

After the Great War, Sir Hamilton Harty conducted for 13 years. This romantic, fiery, masterful Irishman brought the Hallé again to great heights. He was a composer and pianist too, and as a conductor was famous in Brahms, Strauss and Dvorak, while his Berlioz may well have been, in its grandeur and poetry, the greatest that the Hallé has known.

It was a stirring event in the 1920s for a city to be visited by Harty's Hallé Orchestra, bringing Beethoven, Berlioz and a Dvorak symphony with a sonority such as only Manchester could produce for Dvorak and which enlivened the memory for weeks afterwards. The Orchestra then played an average of three concerts a week with one rehearsal. In summer some of

*Mahler was first performed in England by Sir Henry Wood, who gave the First Symphony in London in 1903 and later the first English performances of the Fourth and Seventh.

the players scattered to the seaside orchestras—Sam Geldard, the magnificent timpanist, for example, would be found playing less strenously the kettle-drums of the Ilfracombe Municipal Orchestra on the promenade.

Guest conductors followed Harty for ten years.

In that strange 1943 crisis of a wartime dearth of players, John Barbirolli worked away manfully. He auditioned for three weeks, listening to and testing out young people from music colleges, older people from theatres and various freelances. He didn't look for paper qualifications—he looked for ability to play with artistry and accurate sight-reading. Holding sway in a room of Forsyth's music shop in Deansgate, he discovered a girl horn player who was a teacher in a Keighley school and a girl trombonist who came straight out of a Salvation Army band. Another trombone was from the Palace Theatre, another from the Manchester Police. Livia Gollancz, the publisher's daughter, an LSO player, came as first horn. Some auditions could be quite amusing. One elderly double-bass candidate performed his part in the Scherzo of Beethoven's Fifth Symphony without moving his left hand at all on the instrument. Nearly half of those John eventually engaged had never played in a symphony orchestra before.

Harold Atkins saw him now and then at that time, travelling alone on a bus or a tram, looking very Italian, introspective and tense. He also looked grim. He must have been pretty anxious about the task he was engaged upon with so little time.

But gradually he got together nearly 70 players who passed muster—the average age of the Orchestra, it was said, was 26 and there were 24 women.

12 *Full Steam in Manchester*

Manchester is not so much a city—more a way of life. It has changed greatly since the war days; it is now brighter, whiter, cleaner; many of its buildings now gleam, where they were once black, with the reduction of belching chimneys, soot and smog in the massive streets. But at all times it is a city of impressive self-certainty and self-assertion.

During the war it was at is gloomiest, when Hitler's bombers had spread a fair amount of central devastation and jagged wreckage was visible all around; when you tramped to work or to the station or the theatre through depths of mud and pools of water amid ruins; and raincoats were black with the minute soot particles that descended along with the heavy rain, for it was a city of high rainfall and much industrial pollution.

But Manchester's people retained amid the devastation their stalwart, dour self-certainty, together with their throaty accent, homely humour, kind neighbourliness, practical commonsense—and sense of rivalry with London, a special Manchester characteristic that Londoners found inexplicable.

It is a myth, this rivalry, but it has a certain foundation and expresses worthy intentions—it comes from a wholesome feeling that the simple, direct virtues of the North, straightforwardness, honesty of thought, forthright speech and a no-nonsense approach to life, plus an abundance of energy, are worthy of ranking with the best that a dodgy, complicated and over-sophisticated London can produce. Added to that, Manchester people are essentially practical and feel they can do most things as well as or better than others can. And their unrivalled newspaper, the *Manchester Guardian*, that daily exponent of the best thinking and the best writing (derived largely from Oxford men) encouraged Manchester people to believe quite genuinely until fairly recent times that 'What Manchester thinks today, London thinks tomorrow'.

In the war days one felt at the centre of a very big dynamo indeed, mixing with the burly, purposeful, jostling crowds of the great cotton city all over the pavements (no walking on the left or right for these individualists) in Market Street, or talking and eating determinedly in underground restaurants, perspiring in a St Anne's Square teashop or fighting grimly to get on to a night bus.

In this aggressive, self-conscious, ugly and badly damaged conurbation, then, John Barbirolli, glad to be home in England, would climb rickety stairs to a rehearsal room. It was at the top of the old St Peter's school in Hewitt Street, set dismally in a back-street industrial milieu not far from the Oxford Road railway station. The building looked as if it had been a warehouse for years. There was a hoist that could be used to haul up the heaviest instruments and the players ascended several flights of stairs to the big room with its one coal fire.

Just before 9.30 am John entered, rather plump in those days, drawing on a cigarette that seemed to some of his players to be permanently attached to his lips, with that distinctive big black hat and walking-stick, already local 'landmarks'. He would get out the baton and plunge into rehearsal, putting his deep knowledge of the scores, his sensitive ear, his dramatic Italian temperament—and the monumental self-confidence he had gained abroad and at home—to the task of coaxing and galvanizing the various sections of this newly-constructed and soon-to-be-consolidated 'band' (many Mancunians had always called the Hallé 'Ally's Band' from the days of the founder) and inspiring them to play better than they thought they could.

He was an exacting taskmaster—at one rehearsal the rumble of a heavy railway train was faintly heard from a bridge close by. 'Tap-tap-tap' went the baton for the dead stop. 'What was that?' His expression was disapproving, and his voice betrayed a marked irritation. 'It's the free world outside,' came the plaintive response of a trumpet player.

A flautist recruited straight from music school at seventeen recalled that in the first week of rehearsals John told his players that he would not be annoyed with anyone who was trying, but that if anyone was careless or inattentive he could promise that he'd be very severe. He kept his word, too—but the effect was to imbue the players with a sense of confidence in their conductor's fairness. Some would find themselves responding in a short time to his compelling gaze, intense and ardent; his concentration and perseverance soon worked wonders. Rehearsals, held twice daily, developed into the familiar nine-hour Barbirolli pattern: three hours for the strings, three for the wind and brass, then three all together. Two rehearsals for each member of the Orchestra, but three for the conductor!

Evelyn was as constant an attender at the rehearsals as she had been at the auditions, listening intently to the orchestra taking shape.

She and John had spent their first days back in England in a hotel at Bowdon, nine miles out in Cheshire; then Laurance

Turner found them a small second-floor flat at Appleby Lodge, a large modern block between Rusholme and Fallowfield on the outskirts of the city. 'We had no furniture,' Evelyn remembered, 'so we borrowed some from an antique dealer friend who had gone to America and whose London flat had been bombed. I went along to the furniture depository, where a wide variety of furniture, old and new, mostly damaged and covered with soot, was stored. I collected what was usable for our very tiny flat. The only table to hand was a card-table so we ate off that! It was a case of necessity.'

Later, when securely entrenched, they moved to a larger flat in Appleby Lodge.

The first Hallé concert, fixed for 5 July 1943, Evelyn and John's fourth wedding anniversary, was not in Manchester but at the Prince's Theatre, Bradford—one of a series of seven in a festival week there. Five were to have had a piano concerto each—a popular concert-building item. Then John put his foot down. He refused to include more than one piano soloist. 'I haven't come from America to accompany guest artists', he declared. He would accept only one of the five, Clifford Curzon, playing Grieg. His aim was to build up the Hallé to draw audiences—not to rely on the ubiquitous popular piano concertos.

The reconstituted Orchestra's initial programme, in a hall only two-thirds full, was Wagner's *Meistersinger* Overture, Delius' *A Song of Summer*, Tchaikovsky's *Romeo and Juliet* Overture and Brahms' Second Symphony. Granville Hill of the *Guardian* felt constrained to mention the youth and inexperience of some of the players but prophesied a 'splendid unity and eloquence' in the future. The *Yorkshire Observer* said: 'The best Hallé traditions are safe.'

News of the Orchestra's prowess soon got round the town and there were crowded houses for the rest of the week. John declared to the Press that he was completely satisfied with the quality of the playing and that the financial results had been 'wonderful'. He took pleasure in mentioning that so enthusiastic were his musicians that when he arrived at the theatre one morning specially early for rehearsal entire sections were to be found already there, practising away in their dressing-rooms.

Six weeks of travelling to other cities followed—including a week each in Glasgow and Edinburgh—with more relentless rehearsals. The players were now being accustomed to hard concert conditions. Leeds, Wolverhamptom, Newcastle and Harrogate all received a taste of the renovated 'Alley's Band' with its dramatic new conductor.

Off the podium he was one of the band, always travelling along with the rest on tour, in trains or motor coaches, preferring—and Evelyn too—to have a seat with his players rather than using a first-class carriage or a special car. This became a lasting habit: fraternizing in pubs, drinking with the rest, exchanging jokes and anecdotes. Nobody took liberties because of this, they responded to his friendship, humanity and interest.

Was this tendency to 'travel rough', one wonders, part due to some intinerant strain which had caused his father and grandfather to wander in their younger days?

And then came the Manchester debut. On 15 August at the King's Hall, Belle Vue, six thousand people sat in ever-widening circles in an immense circus stadium, set in Manchester's big pleasure garden with its zoo. It was a hall used variously for conferences, exhibitions, fairs and boxing matches and it wasn't ideal for acoustics, but it somehow matched the widespread new audiences drawn to classical music as a relief from the war. John, an animal lover, was nevertheless a lover of circuses who had no objection to a circus hall, or even to using the room marked 'Ringmaster'.

Again the concert began with the *Meistersinger* Overture; then came Debussy's *Prélude à l'Après-Midi d'un Faune*, Elgar's 'Enigma' Variations and Tchaikovsky's Fifth Symphony. Granville Hill wrote: 'A crowd mighty in size and enthusiasm listened to splendid playing . . . a good deal of the orchestral playing was indeed finer than any we have heard in Manchester for many years . . . The strings are magnificent . . . Mr Barbirolli conducted superbly.'

This was a splendid Manchester beginning. The city was indeed satisfied. All was well; the 'new broom' had done it. Greatly cheered, the Orchestra embarked on a series of

ENSA* factory concerts for war workers in various Northern regions, gratefully received by another type of audience.

It also went to Sheffield, a city which showed enough continued interest in the Hallé to make an annual grant of £5,000 for regular concerts, an example followed by other cities. Manchester's initial contribution had been a mere £2,500, of which £1,000 was earmarked for children's concerts.

In September John wrote to Julian Herbage, of the BBC, 'Everything continues to go splendidly here and the orchestra is improving all the time . . . We have had packed houses everywhere.'

There was an interesting assessment of Barbirolli's conducting when in October he made a reappearance in London—his first since going to America. He was again directing a Royal Philharmonic Society concert, this time by the London Philharmonic Orchestra, at the Albert Hall and the *Times* critic said:

> Mr Barbirolli's general method is to treat the music he plays as a fluent plastic surface on which orchestral detail can be inscribed with great delicacy. He galvanizes an orchestra with animation and insists on nuance of tone. He is most successful with non-symphonic music, since the logical and structural aspects are for him secondary to the intensity of the passing moment. Sometimes it seems as though the basic, organic rhythm of a movement eludes him.

The emphasis on detail noted here might well have been due to a preoccupation at this time with rehearsing his own orchestra. His best symphonic conducting was yet to come, as the Hallé got into its full stride.

When it reached the Albert Hall, Nottingham, in December of that formative year during a tour of several cities, the *Nottingham Journal* critic was happy with 'a perfection of tone, a unity and a freshness', adding of the conductor: 'His musicianship, inbred and highly developed, has endeared him

*Entertainments National Service Association.

to his new orchestra . . . With the Symphony No. 2 by Brahms came some splendid playing and conducting.' And as the Orchestra became part of Manchester, appreciation was voiced of rich and polished playing and, in particular, fineness of detail attributed to strenuous rehearsing.

Mid-week subscription concerts were given at the Albert Hall in Peter Street, a Methodist mission that had escaped the bombs. The Sunday popular series was at Belle Vue, a standard weekly event.

News of Barbirolli's success in handling the Hallé soon travelled. In the spring of 1944 came the first of several tempting offers from elsewhere. The London Symphony Orchestra was looking for a conductor. But by this time John had become too fond of his work in the Northern city to accept. He had been impressed by his Orchestra's warm reception in many other parts of the region and he was emotionally involved with the big audiences at Belle Vue. He didn't want to leave. If he appeared to hesitate, it was to give warning to certain City Council elements, still philistine.

But he did want a better internal business management for the Hallé. In the event, he stayed—and in return for staying soon got it.

13 Front-Line Tour

He achieved something else. The Committee made an arrangement by which he would be released to conduct other orchestras, both at home and abroad.

This concession was substantial. It gave him freedom, but for a long time he did not use it, preferring to go on building up the Hallé in and near Manchester.

There had been a number of incidents such as some haggling and a threatened breach between the Hallé Concert Society and the BBC, who wanted Barbirolli to conduct for them on one or two occasions.

As for the business side, the Hallé was fortunate in securing Thomas Ernest Bean (later manager of the Festival Hall in London) as its secretary and general manager in 1944. He had been assistant circulation manager of the *Manchester Guardian* and his interest in music, noticed and stimulated by the percipient Neville Cardus, Granville Hill's predecessor, had led to his reviewing gramophone records for the paper. He was a clear-headed man with the ability to cope with unusual and difficult situations, a capacity much needed by an orchestra travelling about in war-time conditions.

Evelyn, too, had joined the administrative staff of the Orchestra; having taken a secretarial course in the United States at the time of John's concert visit to Britain, she was now a fully-fledged secretary. It was in this capacity that she acted for John, working partly at home and partly at the Hallé office.

When they first settled at Appleby Lodge they seriously discussed whether she should join the Orchestra as first oboe. 'But we decided that it was not a good idea.' She did, however, occasionally appear as a deputy in the early years when someone was ill or had to be away, if nobody suitable could be found.

It was during this early Manchester period also that they both developed their hobby of collecting rare Georgian glass. It happened that people were rather loth to buy fragile antiques like glass while the war was on, so the field was clear for some bargains and they liked hunting in the shops. They started their main collection before prices rose.

The Hallé's programme planning, according to Ernest Bean, was left entirely to John by the Committee. 'His choice was accepted as the finished product. We suggested things to him but the final pattern was his entirely. I don't remember any reaction coming from the Committee.' John who conducted over 190 of the Orchestra's 271 concerts in the first year, was also able to give the Society a good deal of experienced practical advice on ways of increasing the number of regular supporters. From 1944 it could rely on enough subscribers to fill the hall twice over for every concert in the Manchester seasons.

He paid an early tribute to his 'great predecessors' Hallé, Richter, Balling and Harty, adding of Harty, who died in 1941, 'During his period the Hallé reached heights that have certainly never been surpassed.'

Among memories of those early days, some veterans recalled

an informal 'hot-pot' supper that the whole Orchestra and their conductor enjoyed at the Denmark Hotel, near the Royal Manchester College of Music. One of John's cronies at such affairs was Tommy Cheetham, the Orchestra's librarian, best man at his marriage, and another whom both John and Evelyn liked very much was Wallace Jones, the tuba player and orchestral manager, a former Barnardo boy who had been in the Marines. It was he who declared that John was a 'sod' on the box but a 'toff' outside. A tribute which Evelyn overheard.

In September came one of the important engagements away from the Hallé—John flew to Italy to conduct the Rome Radio Orchestra, a very fine one, and also concerts for the troops at the San Carlo Opera House in Naples, as well as at Bari and Taranto.

But the big travelling event of the year was reserved for December, when the Orchestra went to the war zones in Holland, Belgium and Northern France—the first British orchestra to visit liberated Europe. It was the first time the Hallé had been abroad, too. Seventy-four players went on this 'ENSA' tour at the time of Hitler's Ardennes offensive in the last stages of the war, and seventeen concerts were given in fifteen days for troops of the British Army of Liberation, who showed great delight and enthusiasm.

The Orchestra went as near to the fighting line as Eindhoven and Nijmegen. They all set out one foggy night from Folkestone to Ostend, and then travelled by coach to Brussels. But John and Evelyn, who had slept in the open on deck, met with misfortune at the first concert there. In the dimly-lit hall both fell over the platform edge into the stalls and Evelyn fractured an arm. This made impossible their arrangement for her to be the soloist in an oboe concerto based on popular British tunes, written for her by Rosa's husband, Alfonso Gibilaro.

Seven concerts were given at Eindhoven alone, with thousands of troops on leave from the front arriving in Army vehicles. Other concerts were at Antwerp, Ostend, Amiens and Lille. When they played in Brussels an air battle was going on outside and at Nijmegen there was a machine-gun attack only fifty yards away. But no one seemed to mind and the uniformed audiences cheered and demanded many encores.

John was concerned with watching over the welfare of his

players and at one place where they were scattered in thirty different billets he walked round to each one to see that all were comfortable.

When transport was short, owing to the Runstedt offensive, the men in the Orchestra had sometimes to travel in Army trucks, though the women were more fortunate in buses. It was bitterly cold. John travelled in the trucks too, preferring to share all hardship with his players. Despite the freezing cold and bumpy roads spirits were high.

Some remarkable letters reached the Hallé from grateful Servicemen and women. One private wrote of a concert:

> It was wonderful. From start to finish I was held in speechless amazement that such music, which seemed more in keeping with the angels, was really being brought forth by man-made instruments.

A company quartermaster-sergeant wrote to his brother on New Year's Day:

> *Dear Willie,*
> I went to a concert last night and though we had a two-hour journey in a very cold truck it was well worth it. It was the Hallé Orchestra conducted by Barbirolli and though I did not expect to enjoy some of the items I found to my surprise that I enjoyed everything thoroughly.
>
> The concert opened with the 'Leonora' Overture No. 3, followed by a violin concerto by Mendelssohn played by a Belgian violinist. It was grand and I found that I knew part of it. Next came the 'Unfinished' Symphony and the programme concluded with a waltz by Sibelius and a short piece by Rimsky-Korsakov. But we brought the house down to the extent of four encores—'Londonderry Air', a march by Strauss, his *Tales from the Vienna Woods* and also a selection from *Die Fledermaus.* Barbirolli simply hung over the fiddles at times in the waltzes and drew the very best out.

A soldier wrote home:

> Into this indescribable dreariness of mind and spirit Barbirolli gave back to us something we believed we had lost—a sense of, and a belief in, beauty . . .

An RAMC corporal wrote:

> If anyone ever tells me that the Army does not appreciate symphony concerts I'll crown him. We all held our breath and let go in no uncertain manner. It was beautiful. Barbirolli was a stranger to me but to my mind he's a bloody good conductor.
>
> He told us he detested anybody who was highbrow and that as Sir Henry Wood ended the Proms with a sing-song he didn't see why we shouldn't end the series in the same way. So the Orchestra churned out a medley of Scottish tunes, and we didn't need a second invitation to join in!

Perhaps the most affecting letter was addressed to John on 8 January 1945, by a private signing himself 'A Yorkshire Lad'. He wrote:

> I was thrilled all night by the wonderful and charming music on January 5th at Ostend. There was hundreds of the lads who was left outside and as for myself I waited for 1½ hours and then only got standing room in the gallery, in an unhuman position but I would gladly do the same again.
>
> I asked my pal to come along and you could not have had a more severe critic as he had scoffed at me when I had tried to capture his interest in any of the classics, but I can tell you Sir with all true feeling that before your show was half way over he was actually cheering each item, and he has thanked me for asking him to go, and you know that is something from a dour Scot to admit. He has written his thanks to you as he was so amazed and overjoyed.
>
> As for myself Sir, I can only say thank you and as you played the 'Londonderry Air' at the close it seemed to tear the heartstrings out of oneself, and the scene at the finish as you played 'Auld Lang Syne' and each and everyone was singing it was surely the most lovely finish,

> and as the strains rolled on I am not ashamed to say that I was singing through my tears as it seemed to bring the Old Folks at Home ever so near to me and as it seemed to me then that you and your players were a Breath of that dear Homeland that we have left behind. I will close now and thanks again and God Bless and Guard you all.

After the end of the war there followed seasons of tours, extending all about the country, the Hallé competing with the great London orchestras, all trying to pull up their standards again with the return of players from the Services. Ernest Bean was hard at work with the detailed forward planning of tours for a full-time itinerary. And as time went on the repertoire of the Hallé often seemed wider and more flexible than those of the London orchestras, and they began to develop dovetailing policies of programme-building designed to avoid overlapping and duplicating among themselves.

The Hallé personnel changed a little. Some players left for the enticements of London—a recurrent loss always besetting the Orchestra—but others were demobilized and joined. One such was Charles Cracknell, the tall principal bassoonist, who was given an audition while still in battle-dress at Mémé's flat in Streatham. He had played in the Eastbourne Municipal Orchestra and joined the Hallé at £17.10s. a week.

He admired the conductor. 'Everyone who played for him' said Cracknell, 'felt almost instinctively devoted to him for his human qualities. It was a period of incandescence—doing every work afresh. J.B. put his whole self into the music. He was a wonderful mixture of Italian, French and Cockney—as much moved by a "Pomp and Circumstance" march as by Verdi—and he never seemed to tire.'

Another new arrival in 1946 was Audrey Napier-Smith, who joined the first violins from the WRNS. She had come in Wren uniform for an audition in 1944 in the Belle Vue Ringmaster's Office, and was 'demobbed' two years later. A contemporary of Evelyn at the Royal College, Audrey remembered her as very animated and full of life. In Manchester she considered her 'a very dear person and a big personality. There's so much to Evelyn that doesn't come out. There was one unforgettable walk, near Beachy Head—she loves the outside world of sea and country and dogs.'

Audrey, too, found the Barbirolli rehearsals exciting. 'He sometimes tore strips off us. There was nothing but Latin blood there—the Latins are very explosive and volatile people; they blow up at the slightest thing and then go down very quickly and it's all forgotten. He might blow sky-high and the next minute he'd be smiling all over his face.'

Charles Cracknell's view of such a situation was this: 'Devoted musicians themselves, the players recognized that if what the man wanted was right they'd go at it till doomsday for him'.

But the man could not please everybody, of course, and one Sunday morning after he had insisted on an extra rehearsal he overheard one player complain to another 'I missed my Mass through that bloody chap!'

J.B., as the players called him, resorted sometimes to Italian when a lapse of playing, or a piece of stupidity, provoked him beyond endurance. He did this, he said with tongue in cheek, so as to be reasonably careful when any English women players were about—they wouldn't understand what he was saying.

From 1947, when it first appeared at the Edinburgh Festival, the Hallé broadened out to link with a number of annual festivals, such as the Leeds, Harrogate and Buxton and of course the Cheltenham Festival of British contemporary music, at which much new music was played by Barbirolli during his eleven years' tenure. Many young composers were encouraged by his attention to their scores and kind suggestions. He once kept an orchestra waiting for rehearsal while he went over thoroughly on the piano, reading from the full orchestral score, a work by Stuart Scott, who was then a very young composer.

John conducted the Paris Conservatoire Orchestra (the third oldest in the world) and others abroad but it marked an international step forward in his career when in 1946 and 1947 he conducted the Vienna Philharmonic Orchestra, one of the most renowned in Europe, though somewhat battered by war-time vicissitudes. In April, 1947, he was in charge of *Aïda* at the Vienna Opera and Viennese critic described him as 'born to be an opera conductor'.

A rehearsal of Verdi's Requiem with the Vienna Philharmonic was marked by a curious incident. The cellos were playing extremely badly at an important point and of those available he had been provided with some of the least gifted. John said to the orchestral manager: 'I must have a better set of cellos.' The reply was a stubborn 'We have a rota—we can't alter it.'

John looked thoughtful and appeared to be resigned to the inevitable, but when the interval came he went down to the orchestral pit with a cello and played the passage himself. The effect was overwhelming. The orchestral manager, flustered but tamed, swiftly co-operated, saying: 'It's all right, we fully understand.' For the next rehearsal a much better set of cellists were provided.

Evelyn remembered especially one pilgrimage they made in Vienna. At the back of the Cathedral a short stone staircase led to two rooms where Mozart once lived and played in quartets with Haydn. 'It was wonderful to go up those worn stone steps that Mozart and Haydn must have used.'

Conducting the St Cecilia Orchestra in Rome at about this time, John took a day or two off to visit Rovigo, once his family's home, and to see his white-bearded old uncle and other relations. The other uncle from Rome described how the whole family (including himself, a Commendatore and a leading official on the railways) had taken to music. It was during this Italian visit, the second in his life, that John made some outspoken remarks about the hardships of Italian working people, especially the black-coated ones, and his concern over the wide differences between rich and poor.

The Hallé made its second tour abroad early in 1948—to Austria under the auspices of the British Council. Evelyn had the distinction in Salzburg of being the first soloist to play within living memory Mozart's Oboe Concerto, obtained from newly-discovered parts in the Mozarteum there. The following night in Vienna she had the humbler role of a rank-and-filer in the orchestra, taking the place of the second oboe, who had gone down with tonsillitis!

Performances in Vienna were praised with a natural restraint by the critics of that supra-musical capital. They recalled the

Orchestra's connection with Hans Richter and admired its verve, its intensity in handling the bow and the remarkable flexibility of the wind section.

The Hallé went on to play in Graz and Innsbruck too, and between these two towns a coach broke down and army lorries had to rescue half the players from an isolated mountain village. They spent several hours without food and John came to the rescue with cakes and coffee.

It was in Innsbruck that a quiet, shy woodwind player named Bert was billeted in a private house which happened to be plastered all over, inside and out, with religious slogans and texts. John, making his usual peregrination to ensure the billets were comfortable, was amazed to see Bert's habitat. He looked hard and long at the display, then turned a puzzled eye on the distraught Bert, who said, 'I'd 'ave you know, Mr Barbirolli, that I'm not quite so bloody sanctimonious as I look!'

While in Vienna the members of the Orchestra were invited to a dance. Audrey Napier-Smith found John more than difficult to dance with. He so much enjoyed listening to what the dance band was doing that he never minded what his feet were doing. 'They were doing all sorts of things,' said Audrey, 'but he didn't let them follow the orchestra.'

But, she said, he could dance on the rostrum. 'It was uncanny—he looked so graceful and his gestures were beautiful.'

14 At Home

If the Austrian trip had securely placed the Hallé in Continental esteem as an excellent orchestra, its second appearance at the Edinburgh Festival confirmed its standing at home. There was particular praise for some outstanding Sibelius—the *Times* critic said of the Fifth Symphony 'The finest performance it has been my good fortune to hear,' and the judgement was confirmed by Ernest Newman. Before 1948 was out a great compliment came to its conductor. Soon after the Orchestra had been appearing in London the BBC invited John to be chief conductor of the BBC Symphony Orchestra in succession to Sir Adrian Boult, who was approaching sixty, the BBC's retiring age.

John declined the offer. A number of considerations weighed with him, including the fact that the BBC Orchestra's programmes were chosen by a selection committee. To one who was the sole arbiter of his programmes this was an unacceptable shortcoming. But his main reason was deeper. He was well settled in Manchester and loved the Hallé Orchestra and its audiences as much as they loved him.

He let it be known in Manchester that the sacrifice he was making was a big one but that the Hallé also had been making big sacrifices. As a reward, he succeeded, through not going south, in securing for his players a rise in minimum salary from £10 to £13 a week, an annual tour abroad and the promise of increasing the Orchestra's strength to nearly a hundred (the size of Harty's) by the time that the new Free Trade Hall was built.

It was at about now, when the Hallé was fully ensconced with regular audiences of six thousand at Belle Vue, that Sir Thomas Beecham brought his new Royal Philharmonic Orchestra from London with his pianist wife Betty Humby Beecham to that immense auditorium. It was their first visit—and their last—and of the six thousand seats only two thousand were occupied on that unfortunate night. A Lancashire woman leaving the performance was heard to remark tersely, 'Well, he'd no more sense than to coom on washin' day!'

J.B. admired Beecham's powers, despite the personal antipathy between them, and told Audrey Napier-Smith 'He's a genius—an absolute genius. But an amateur, my dear.'* Beecham on his side had been attempting earlier to reassert his old position as President of the Hallé, but Barbirolli made it clear to the Committee that if Beecham came he would go. There was never any doubt of the result after that.

Barbirolli's stock of anecdotes included, of course, several Beecham ones from personal experience during his early days. A favourite, told with relish, was of going to Leeds to play the cello in opera under Sir Thomas. The orchestra, said John,

*Toscanini, less kindly, referred to him as 'le Pagliaccio' (the Clown).

came away without being paid and all he and his friends could afford at the railway station as they left was a meat pie and a glass of beer between them.

As time went on in Manchester Evelyn was continuing to develop her own independent career as a solo artist—a thing John had been encouraging her to do. When someone suggested that it might be better for her to stay at home he replied, 'Well! . . . what a waste of talent!' She accepted dates only for concerts or broadcasts that would fit to their joint convenience. As she explained, 'The conductor books his guest-conducting at least three—sometimes five—years ahead. Modest soloists like myself booked for much less time ahead—twelve months or a little over—so that when his diary was settled I'd fix my own concerts, and it was usually quite simple.'

She knew he was completely music-centred and her life revolved around his, but as individualists they demonstrated their mutual love of music in their own different ways. Their home life at Appleby Lodge was of the simplest—he cooked the dinner and they shared a bottle of wine and desultory listening to the wireless. There was a completely harmonious relationship between them; one reason was her sense of humour and warm-heartedness, another was the colour and emotion she put into her playing, which appealed to him and produced a close subconscious bond. She regarded him as 'a complete musician and a complete human being'.

To people who became concerned about John's neglect of relaxation Evelyn would reply: 'You might as well try to stop a bulldozer.' His idea of a break was work with no telephone ringing. He was relaxed when alone with Evelyn or playing his beloved cello and happiest of all when conducting. He liked quoting her as saying, when they were on tour abroad, 'One rehearsal a day at least—then he's bearable.' Depression sometimes produced contradictory moods. He was known to mutter on free days 'It disturbs me to go away . . . it depresses me sometimes to stay at home'. But of his day-to-day moods at home Evelyn said 'He was very undemanding and un-irritable. He wasn't temperamental at home; he said temperament should be kept for the place where it belonged—on the concert platform.'

John liked to wear old clothes at home—and even at

performances he had been known to say, speaking of one evening suit he sometimes wore for conducting; 'They don't make suits like this these days—do you know, I had this made in 1934.'

Fitting in her engagements with his could occasionally be something of a sacrifice for Evelyn. She wrote, for example, in October 1948, declining a tempting BBC offer to play the Vaughan Williams Oboe Concerto at one concert because she wanted to be with him on the opening night when he conducted the BBC Symphony Orchestra at another. She attended most of the Hallé concerts in Manchester, always finding John's presence stimulating. As time went on, beginning to see less of their home as she travelled with him, she developed the arts of the 'travelling' wife—quick and economical packing for both, working out such points as what 'un-iron' shirts to take, the exact weight of shoes for air luggage and the essentials for all types of travel. Robust and fond of good food, Evelyn enjoyed driving, having navigated a car since she was seventeen.

People noticed that at rehearsals she was often John's eyes and ears. She would move about strange halls testing the acoustics in different places—at the back, at the side, in the middle—while he rehearsed. He was often a bit on edge in a strange place, but Evelyn knew his needs and was able to help him.

Pauline Pickering, founder and chairman of the Barbirolli Society, said 'She understood him artistically more than anyone else in the world. She was so often out in the audience—and he could have nobody better.'

A nervous player, Evelyn was more nervous as a soloist with her husband conducting than with anyone else. 'I ought to have been less so, because he looked after me better than anyone else did. But I felt such a responsibility to play well with him—great musician as he was.'

One of John's few relaxations was cricket. He liked to umpire occasional matches between the scratch Hallé team and others and to send for the Test match scores at rehearsals. He was often at the Old Trafford ground and a visitor to Lord's and the Oval when in London. When staying in Sussex he and Evelyn would occasionally go to watch the cricket at Hove.

In the Members' Box at Old Trafford he sometimes ran into Neville Cardus, who had made so distinguished a seasonal 'double' of cricket and music for the *Manchester Guardian* for many years and now lived in London. Cardus, an admirer of Barbirolli's Hallé, suggested in 1952 that John and Mahler were 'made' for each other—a propitious idea that bore rich fruit later.

A comic fell-walking incident occurred one summer when John and three colleagues, T. E. Bean, Sidney Rothwell, his then secretary, and Kenneth Crickmore, afterwards the Hallé's manager, were staying in the Lake District for a spot of programme-planning at the home of Sir John Foster Clark (an amateur conductor) at Hassness. Early one evening, out for a drive and at the top of Honister Pass, John's three companions, keen fell walkers, decided to climb the steep footpath to the summit of Dale Head. To their surprise J.B. said he would come as well.

The notion that he, wearing light shoes and unaccustomed to it, should embark on a fairly taxing mountain tramp late in the day caused some misgivings in the others. But he came, and succeeded in keeping up with them to the summit, which they reached as the sun was setting.

The question then was the mode of descent. Rothwell was familiar with the terrain and said he knew a track ahead. Crickmore and John opted to press on with him while Bean went back, got the car and drove round to meet them at Grange-in-Borrowdale.

Reaching the village, he waited but there was no sign of them and after a long delay he set out to discover what had happened. Finally he ran them to earth, struggling sluggishly down after a rough and gruelling passage. Rothwell's supposed track had been ravaged by a hard winter and was a nightmare for an inexperienced walker. Part of the way they had to slide on their behinds, part of it the other two had to help John down the more precipitious sections of the eroded and barely discernible track. Looking exceedingly unkempt and rueful, the three reached their destination just before the last evening light disappeared, with J.B.'s crowning remark ringing in their ears: 'Now I understand what you were up to—you wanted to get rid of me so that you could put in Malcolm Sargent as conductor of the Hallé!'

During these informal planning sessions the capacities of distinguished solo artists were shrewdly assessed. 'We'd say of a soloist "He's asking £*x* these days, John." "Oh well," he'd reply, "he's not worth that much. We'll do without him." And he'd change the programme.'

The work was relieved by nightly walks by the quartet down to the pub at nearby Buttermere. Here, over pints, great conviviality obtained and John would regale his companions with salty stories from his past. This Lake District visit was a 'break' when work could be interpolated with refreshing periods of ease in that lovely countryside.

In June 1949, John received a knighthood. He was able to present this distinction to Mémé when he joined the family that summer at the house he now started to rent intermittently on the outskirts of Seaford, in Sussex. The British knighthood did not alter the strong Italian *tendenza* in that household, or trim the amplitude of the family parties and meals, either at Seaford or at Mémé's flat at Streatham, which was John's London centre. There would be his brother Peter, happily ensconced as a pillar of the Covent Garden Opera Orchestra playing the viola, a post he obtained after demobilization and still held in the 1980s, Peter's wife Pat, Rosa and Alfonso Gibilaro and three or four nephews and nieces, besides Evelyn and Mémé. The language would be English spiced with Venetian (of which Evelyn had a smattering). Sir John, donning an apron, would cook such delicacies as *boeuf à la Clémentine* and his various spaghetti sauces.

It was in London that he took the Hallé Orchestra to share in an Elgar festival. When it performed the 'Enigma' Variations at the Albert Hall, 'Dorabella' (Mrs Dora Powell, *née* Penny), the subject of one of the composer's most famous variations based on his friends, was in the audience.

Ernest Bean declared that both Elgar and Ralph Vaughan Williams (whose works John loved and fostered) had 'great enthusiasm' for the way he conducted their music and for the 'Englishness' of his interpretations. 'Elgar's Second Symphony under J.B. was absolutely shattering in its impact,' said Bean. 'But time and again in the Green Room he'd afterwards be overcome by floods of tears. The controlled force on the platform suggested the French side of his nature, the later mood the Italian one.' Elgar's Serenade for Strings was another work that affected him in this way.

Bean had an amusing story illustrating sensitive endeavour at a rehearsal which he had heard John tell against himself. It concerned an ardent young Dutchman who wanted to be a conductor and was allowed to be present. A word of direction on interpretation in the score being rehearsed was strange to John and the Dutchman said, 'Oh, it means this,' and taking his silk handkerchief out of his breast pocket he let it go shimmering to the floor.

Rehearsing the work somewhere else later, J.B. in turn tried to explain to the Orchestra the effect required. He took his own handkerchief out and let it go—but it wasn't silk and didn't shimmer but went plummeting down, to the general amusement.

Another of Bean's recollections was of the Orchestra's tour in Belgium that year, when John went round Knocke taking careful notes of the prices of tinned food—then on the last day laying in quantities of it to take back home in the large briefcase he always carried.

On other occasions when the others were dining in hotels, Bean recalled seeing him going quietly to his room carrying a picnic supper. Not relying on hotels or restaurants for his main meal of the day after concerts, John would take everything he needed for a cold supper—perhaps meatballs, cooked ham or fish, a bottle of wine and some bread, as well as the needed utensils. After a concert on tour he and Evelyn would sup together in their hotel room, unless obliged to attend a party.

Once in Berlin, on one of the rare occasions when they did have a late supper in a hotel restaurant, poor food was served; he got up half-way through and disappeared into the kitchen to supervise what the cook was doing. After that there was a great improvement.

In April 1950, six months after conducting the Berlin Philharmonic Orchestra for the first time, at the Edinburgh Festival, John conduced it in Berlin and began a lasting relationship of mutual admiration and affection. The initial

Berlin programme was Rossini's Overture to *La Gazza Ladra*, Delius' *Song of Summer*, Roussel's Suite *Bacchus and Ariadne* and Brahms' Fourth Symphony—something Italian, something English, something French and something German. This was the first of many concerts acclaimed by the Berliners and John considered their orchestra the best he ever conducted.

By this time the Hallé Orchestra had become by general consent one of the best in Britain, with its famous string tone. Perhaps the most vehement plaudits came in 1951, the year after John received at the hands of Vaughan Williams the Gold Medal of the Royal Philharmonic Society—its highest award—for outstanding services to music. When the Hallé first appeared at the new Festival Hall during the Festival of Britain the *Times* praised its performance of Vaughan Williams' Fourth Symphony and Verdi's Requiem while the *Manchester Guardian* summed up by saying that Barbirolli 'designed his programme in such a way as to show off all the virtues of his splendid orchestra in turn: its imposing mass of tone . . . its delicacy . . . the fire and precision of the strings . . . and the flawless articulation of his wind players'.

It was a hefty job arranging the Verdi event. To start it off, two hundred and fifty Manchester homes had to be thrown into early-morning action to get the Hallé Choir on to the 7.10 am special train from London Road station for Euston. At the end of the day the Choir, after dining at the Waterloo Station restaurant, had to sing by request the 'Hallelujah' Chorus for the benefit of the restaurant staff, after which they pursued their weary course to Euston to catch the 2.10 am train home.

At this time also there were fresh financial anxieties. Bean, pointing to two hundred and fifty concerts a year with still only seventy players compared with Harty's 100 and remuneration forty per cent less than elsewhere, called for a subsidy of £25,000 a year and a Treasury guarantee of the same amount. With Manchester's niggardly £9,000 and the Arts Council's matching sum the Hallé was barely breaking even.

Another source of anxiety was John's health. He returned with Evelyn from a nine-weeks conducting visit to Australia very run down after enteritis. An operation for appendicitis followed. His appetite was never the same again and he ultimately become very thin.

But the year had its grand peaks—Evelyn as soloist with the

London Symphony Orchestra in Strauss's Oboe Concerto, with John conducting, at the Festival Hall in September; John opening with *Turandot* (Eva Turner in the title role) the Covent Garden opera season as guest conductor in October and continuing with Callas in *Aïda* (Mémé seen sometimes in a box near the stage); John and the Hallé inaugurating the rebuilt Free Trade Hall in December and getting a great ovation for Berlioz's 'Fantastic' Symphony, with Mémé present and Kathleen Ferrier singing 'Land of Hope and Glory'; John's first performance of Handel's *Messiah* (he left it rather late, as he did Mahler) in December at Sheffield.

Here are a few of the Hallé players' comments:

'It was a different orchestra altogether when Barbirolli conducted it.'

'He imparted and inspired energy.'

'When he walked on to the platform it was like nobody else.'

'His concerts were events. There was always an atmosphere of nervous anticipation.'

15 *Women Friends*

Women were important in John Barbirolli's life—he had several deep friendships with them. He needed extra companionship with a woman, his friends knew, partly because he required a certain amount of hero-worship, partly because he often wanted to talk as he released the tension after concerts. He was attractive to women and they often felt they wanted to help him. One who knew him well said: 'He needed feminine company—he flowered in the company of women.'

Sometimes they were a nuisance. There was the American woman in the lift at the Festival Hall who, oblivious of everybody else, cried out, 'I've never been in a lift with you before.' Evelyn inquired, with a quiet laugh, 'Oh, would you like the rest of us to get out?' And there was the obsessive female who followed him into the dressing-room, whereupon he made a dexterous getaway and shut himself into a wardrobe until the coast was clear.

Apart from Evelyn, the greatest love of his life was Mémé, the dominating matriarch who had passed on to him French élan. He was inconsolable when she died in 1962 aged over ninety. With several other women his relationships became very close. He had an intimate feeling for Ginette Neveu, that great and intense French violinist who died in a plane crash in 1949. Later came an affectionate and confidential friendship with Audrey Napier-Smith, the Hallé violinist.

The friend with whom the relationship went beyond platonic affection was Norah Winstanley, sub-principal of the Hallé's second violins. Attractive and piquant, intelligent and always stylishly dressed, six years younger than John, she joined the Orchestra in 1941 and had shared in the battling years of the blitz period before the reorganization. Their close friendship at an early stage of his Manchester years caused concern. Evelyn treated it with tender understanding and recalled, 'There was certainly a relationship, though I don't think it went very deep. I think it was a fairly full one for a short time—he thought Norah very attractive and saw her a great deal.

'He went on being friendly with her over the years. I think their actual relationship was very short and fairly casual, but it certainly did exist. I don't deny that it wasn't the happiest time of my life but throughout the episode I didn't leave him. I was fairly busy playing at the time and away a good deal, which was probably a very good thing. It made it much easier to weather that particular period.'

Norah Winstanley, with the Orchestra for twenty-three years, left it during the 1964-65 season. She died in Cheshire in 1980.

Audrey Napier-Smith, as we have said, joined the Hallé Orchestra's first violins from the Wrens. She admired Evelyn as a former fellow-student and admired John as a fine conductor—and an explosive one. 'At rehearsals when he wasn't well or had been up all night for three nights running the atmosphere could be terrific, for he used to blow sky-high,' said Audrey.

She did not know him well till 1950, when the young Janet Craxton joined the Orchestra, becoming principal oboe. As she was only nineteen and he had known her from birth, John asked Audrey to keep an eye on her in Manchester. 'Janet used to go for sessions with Evelyn and I was often asked to dinner as Number Four. Then when they entertained soloists at their flat and we had dinner on the card-table I'd chat with the guests while J.B. and Evelyn cooked in the kitchen.'

So Audrey became a close friend and developed into a confidante of J.B. Extracts from some of his letters to her are given later. Sometimes calling her 'My dearest Wren' and signing himself 'Admiral Nelson' or 'Your devoted Admiral', he would recount to her his grumbles and candid views on people and institutions and would sometimes seek the relief of divulging to her the burden of his frequent deep depressions.

'He liked to write to me to tell me how the music was going; she said, 'particularly the music we were fond of, and comparing the orchestras. Then he'd suddenly break off to give me a cooking recipe or tell me about vibrato. And then of course he tried to teach me Italian. It fascinated me to listen to his family and his niece, Tina, talking. When she spoke to him or his mother they used an English-Italian jumble, going from one language to another in the middle of sentences. It made me laugh.'

Audrey had interesting comments to make on Barbirolli as a conductor. 'His hands and face had great expression,' she said, 'and you got more from these than from the beat itself. When he was doing music we knew very well he took liberties with the stick—it was always the correct beat but he got a bit wild sometimes, and he didn't always give you impeccably every lead.

'When he conducted anything modern or complicated he'd be very clear and economical with the stick. In romantic music the beat would become much more fluid and in moments of intense excitement the stick might even fly out of his hand.'

But the players knew he was a hundred per cent genuine, said Audrey, and if he became angry it was only that he wished to get the music sounding right. Sound was one of the most important things to him.

'Once I said to him "It's very hard for us to play *pizzicato* quietly together when you bring the stick down so gently that it's difficult to get the 'click'".* He replied "My dear, if I gave you a 'click' beat you'd make the wrong sound".'

*A dead-on down-beat executed with great precision for a pizzicato.

J.B., she added, had a wonderful horizontal conducting movement, resulting in a very fluid and flowing effect on the music. She thought he was perhaps the best accompanist of any of the leading conductors, possibly because of his opera training and deep sensitivity.

Audrey told of a pompous town councillor who walked into the conductor's room during a concert interval after some very beautiful Bizet had just been played. Insensitive to the point of crassness, he exclaimed, 'What on earth do you waste your time playing that stuff for?'

'J.B. merely looked at the intruder before turning his back on him, and said to me afterwards "I had my hand on the back of a chair and he didn't know how near he was . . . I nearly threw it at him!"'

John showed great kindness to Audrey's parents, who were both musicians. Her mother, a keen Wagnerian, was invited to his box at Covent Garden. He visited her when she had become bedridden and sent her flowers and postcards from many parts of the world. After her death he would come and dine with Audrey's father, then approaching ninety. 'He liked old men and treated them with respect. He had beautiful natural manners.'

Audrey was enthralled watching his cooking feats. 'He used to do pigs' kidneys with bacon, tying them up with cotton—a most delicate operation. Contrasted with that was his way of doing a lamb chop. He'd put it under the grill, right up under the flames, and the smoke!—you've never seen anything like it! It used to frighten the living daylights out of me! He was in a way abandoned with his cooking and his music. As with music, he could be meticulous—and at the same time so flamboyant!'

John first encountered Kathleen Ferrier, who had so enchantingly beautiful a contralto voice and so sparkling though tragically brief a career, at the Edinburgh Festival in 1947. He was there with the Hallé and she had been singing under Bruno Walter in Mahler's *Song of the Earth* with the Vienna Philharmonic Orchestra. Earlier that year she had sung the title role of Gluck's *Orfeo* at the Glyndebourne Opera. It was some of his Hallé players who induced John the following year to ask her to sing the Angel in his first essay at Elgar's

Dream of Gerontius. She was perfectly familiar with this, having had a round of it from 1944 onwards, notably with Malcolm Sargent at the Albert Hall.

Born in 1912 the daughter of a schoolmaster, the Lancashire lass who was to become a great contralto graduated the hard way—from a telephone exchange job and ardent practice with choirs and at the piano (initially she intended to be a pianist and gained the LRAM at seventeen and the ARCM at nineteen). She was twenty-seven before she gave her first vocal broadcast and appeared in war-time CEMA concerts. Malcolm Sargent heard her sing and encouraged her to go to London, where she was soon appearing at one of Myra Hess's National Gallery recitals in 1943, at a Westminster Abbey *Messiah* and with the Bach Choir. She asked Roy Henderson* to give her lessons and he developed her rich and noble voice and fine diction, taught her platform deportment and helped to launch her into leading engagements. She sang at a Royal Philharmonic Society concert (with Sargent) in 1944 and at a Promenade concert in 1945.

Her first operatic engagement was in the title role of Benjamin Britten's *The Rape of Lucretia* in 1946 at Glyndebourne and later at Covent Garden. Then the distinguished Bruno Walter took her in hand for Mahler's music and was eventually conducting her in Britain and the United States.

She made her Hallé debut with Sargent in *Messiah* at Belle Vue in December, 1945. Later a rehearsal with Barbirolli of Elgar's *Sea Pictures* at Sheffield did not ring a bell, for John lost his temper with a player and threw the score at him, narrowly missing Kathleen. Rendered over-anxious by the stormy atmosphere, she sang only distantly, giving him very little idea of her powers. However, later in *Gerontius* at Belle Vue in April 1948, there burst upon him for the first time the magic of Ferrier's voice, a mere five years before her death.

Instantly they became close friends, sharing a serious and meticulous attitude to music, a strong sense of homely humour and a preference for the simplicities of life.

He soon regarded her with deep affection and Evelyn, too,

*The famous baritone, born of Scottish parents in 1899, who was also one of Britain's foremost teachers.

came to love her, with a warm appreciation of her frank and direct nature and sense of vocation. Kathleen was full of gaiety and high spirits and liked to lapse into Lancashire dialect for fun, just as John did into a hoarse Cockney when he felt inclined. Tall and beautiful, she captivated everybody with her happy ways. But she had also a deeply serious and reflective side and after her 1935 marriage to Albert Wilson, a young bank official who was in the Forces from 1940 till 1946, was dissolved in 1947, she expressed the view that her nature was that of a 'loner'.

'We loved Kathleen very much,' said Evelyn, 'because she was a great person with a wonderful sense of humour.' She became their 'Katie' and almost immediately a regular visitor to Appleby Lodge. Soon she was invited to stay whenever she was in the vicinity of Manchester. John and Evelyn when visiting London would take a taxi to the loftily-sited flat at Hampstead, where Kathleen lived. Joyful hours were spent there in playing trios for oboe, cello and piano, for she was a facile pianist and sight-reader.

'She had a lovely voice and was a lovely person,' remembered Gladys Parr, and Charles Cracknell declared, 'She was totally devoted to her art and Barbirolli bathed in the wonderful artistry that shone out of her.'

Largely responsible for raising that artistry to its highest pitch had been Bruno Walter and Hans Oppenheim, her principal *lieder* teacher. John, fearing that she still might be in danger of becoming a heavy-voiced 'oratorio contralto', persuaded her to try French music, starting with Chausson, thus adding, he considered, to her range and interpretative ability.

He was constantly amazed at the natural warmth of her singing and the intuitive understanding she brought to music of classical dignity and deep spiritual meaning. He admired, too, her soft, low speaking voice, simple tastes and occasional off-duty comic songs, relishing her near-Rabelaisian shafts of humour. Besides golf, painting was her recreation and, when she visited the whole Barbirolli family in Sussex, she would paint country scenes. These visits were memorable for the drives to Sussex beauty-spots for them all to admire—and there were similar excursions from Manchester that took Kathleen deep into Cheshire.

The sublime period of her career was brief. In the next three years she was very busy and successful. Besides singing in Salzburg and Vienna and before Toscanini in Milan, she appeared throughout Britain at varied engagements large and small—never neglecting the small worthwhile amateur choral societies. She sang widely in Europe and toured America and Canada in triumph. One these strenuous rounds she enjoyed herself fully and her health seemed to hold up well—though in 1949 ominous signs of trouble appeared. She sought medical advice.

With John and the Hallé Kathleen sang radiantly in such works as Brahms' Alto Rhapsody, Chausson's *Poème de l'Amour et de la Mer* and music from *Orfeo* at Belle Vue, always spending a good deal of time with the Barbirollis, who were by now her closest friends. But in 1951 she was operated on for cancer and the disease pursued her remorselessly for her remaining two years.

There were further holidays at Seaford with John and his family. In December 1951, came the reopening of the new Free Trade Hall, Kathleen singing 'Land of Hope and Glory' with the Hallé—a moving performance that brought tears to the eyes of the conductor. A few more concerts followed in 1952 with the Hallé in Manchester and other cities, including Mahler's *Song of the Earth* and Handel's *Messiah*—John had conducted it for the first time the previous year. It was as busy a year as she could make it, with intermittent X-ray therapy in the morning and concerts at night, with periodical cancellations of engagements and a spell in University College Hospital, London. She would not admit to a serious disability and concealed the pain she suffered. Realizing her condition, John rapidly arranged a project both desired—for her to sing in an English *Orpheus*, this to be one of his 'guest-conductor' operas at Covent Garden. They jointly translated the libretto from Italian to suit her voice.

She was in Dublin in October for *Messiah* and *Gerontius* performances on consecutive nights. Here an amusing incident occurred to lighten her despondency. Between the performances she rested on Sunday morning in her room, feeling unwell and saying that she didn't know how she would get through *Gerontius* that night. John and Evelyn, to cheer her up, went out to try to buy her some flowers.

'The shops were shut but we thought there'd be a barrow somewhere,' said Evelyn. 'We asked a policeman where we could get flowers. He said (and as the Irish often are he could be terribly slow) "Whale now" (long pause), "and what kind of flowers would ye be wantin?" We said we didn't mind what kind. So he said again "Whale now" (and there was an even longer pause), "on a Sunday morning" (yet another, even longer pause), "on a *Sunday* morning" he said, relishing the Sabbath for all his might, "*ye'll not be getting any flowers at all, at all*".

'We took this tale back to Katie and she was cheered up no end—possibly more cheered up by the Oirishism than by the sight of any flowers, had we been able to buy any.'

Kathleen was the chief guest at the annual New Year's Party John gave for the family. She and John knew that her name was to appear next day in the Honours List and everybody raised a glass as he proposed a special toast to the new CBE.

It was now necessary to hurry on with the *Orpheus* arrangements at the Royal Opera House. When rehearsals began she was finding bodily movement troublesome and would arrive from the hospital walking painfully and with difficulty. John was one of the few who were aware of the extent of her struggle. He loved her deeply and she on her part felt his warmth and was lovingly grateful to him for the help he had given her in the past year.

Of the five scheduled Covent Garden performances she sang only in two. The first was on 3 February 1953, with Veronica Dunne as Eurydice, Frederick Ashton as producer and John as conductor. *The Times* said of Kathleen's Orpheus the following morning: 'She is ideally suited to it in vocal colour, dignified deportment and physical appearance,' adding, 'It gives her splendid voice space to unfold its beauties. Sir John Barbirolli in accompanying her with the closest rapport had ensured the success of the production by eschewing all romantic excess, yet making the classicism of the opera sufficiently ardent.'

But towards the end of the second performance a hip bone gave way and she had to lean on to her Eurydice as she bravely went on singing. After the final curtain John was to help her to the dressing-room. It was her last appearance.

No other singer was chosen to replace her and the remaining performances were cancelled, *The Times* stating only that she was suffering from arthritis.

For the next few months Kathleen was in hospital, receiving a few old friends with a determined and bright self-forgetfulness. To Gladys Parr, on one hospital visit, she shrugged off her illness with, 'Oh, never mind about me. Tell me about your early days with the Carl Rosa.' John visited at the hospital as much as he could. He planned her forty-first birthday party on 22 April, held in a ground-floor flat at 40, Hamilton Terrace, which she had by then rented for easy movement. Mémé cooked a special dinner.

In the next few months Kathleen's health worsened. She was much cheered and delighted by receiving in June the timely award of the Royal Philharmonic Society's Gold Medal. John, who had received the same award three years earlier, was a constant visitor in her last few days, when she sometimes sat up, looking at photographs and cuttings. On 8 October, 1953, she died.

16 'Kind and Generous'

The Hallé, delighted at moving to the newly-arisen Free Trade Hall, felt only a minor twinge of regret at leaving its vast war-time circus colosseum for regular subscription concerts (Belle Vue was still used for special ones).

The story was told of a man who wanted a particular seat at Belle Vue for the last concert under the old régime. 'But it's behind a pillar,' said the booking clerk. 'I've been behind every other damned pillar in the place,' said the man, 'and before they go I want to be behind this one.' That was true addiction.

The new Free Trade Hall was modern, handsome and spacious, the acoustics were about right and everybody hoped now for an orchestra the size of Harty's. John continued to throw himself into meticulous rehearsals, appearing at Hewitt Street in his broad-brimmed hats specially made for him by Borsalino of Rome, who had made them for Verdi. He was as concentrated as before, his eyes now deep-set and introspective; a stickler for preparation, fanatical about bowing and insistent on tone. The players said he worked with a 'player's mentality' and understood their problems.

He had proved a master of the large-scale Romantic repertoire. The chief criticism of his readings was that he sometimes over-emphasized expression and dramatic tension. 'He was never ashamed,' said Ernest Bean, 'of bringing out the emotional qualities in the music. Retrospectively you sometimes suspected that he brought them out too strongly—but at the time you didn't think so . . . From the first chord of a symphony the listener felt caught up by an irresistible magnetic force.'

This emotional intensity caught up artists as well as audience. David Franklin, the bass, was said to have been once so overcome while singing in *Gerontius*, at Belle Vue, that he had to remind himself that he was only doing a job. A leading soprano in *Messiah* felt she could hardly sing at one point because she was in tears.

Colin Mason, the music critic, described Barbirolli in the early 1950s as one of the great Brahms conductors of the day. 'His many Hallé performances during the past few years have been as fine as any to be heard in this country—perhaps any country, certainly not excluding Germany.'

Comparing Barbirolli's conducting with Beecham's, Ernest Bean said 'Beecham was rather aristocratic and *apart* from the audience but J.B., in all sorts of ways, made himself *part* of the music-making.' Some critics held that while Barbirolli was as assured as Beecham in Delius, Sir Thomas was perhaps the more fastidious while John was the more expansive and ruminative.

John maintained that it was impossible to teach conducting and he refused invitations to give lessons in the art.

He was decisive in handling practical affairs and generally made sure that things happened to his way of thinking. 'He liked to keep a little distance from the fray,' said one of his players, 'but nobody had any illusions about where the momentum was coming from.' He was no easier a taskmaster even in these more rewarding Hallé days and he drove rehearsals hard. At one that was flagging he called out, 'I'm the one that's meant to be half dead—not you!' On the other hand, he could be demonstratively grateful; after a London performance he was seen fervently shaking the hands of all members of the Hallé within reach as they filed off the platform.

Amongst cellists he was especially at home. One musician said, 'To see him walking among the cello section of an orchestra was like seeing a gardener among his prize roses.' He liked to use a cello to illustrate how a passage should be played. Once, rehearsing the BBC Symphony Orchestra, he jumped down, took a cello from a player and demonstrated a difficult passage. 'Of course,' he finally said, '*you've got to use your bloody elbow*!'

This was greeted by a round of applause from the players—and he bowed!

Preparing a concert with another orchestra, he remarked that in one work a certain small section should play extremely softly.

'But they won't be in for rehearsal that day,' someone said.

'Oh, good,' he replied, 'then we've a chance of getting it right!'

He was fond of the circus and enjoyed the clown Charlie Cairoli, recommending to some of his musicians that they could gain by going and watching how Cairoli played the clarinet.

Whatever John's occasional inner feelings of self-doubt and insecurity—generated partly by depressions, partly from the unreliable attitudes he had experienced in New York—which perhaps deflected him from accepting any of the tempting offers which came his way from London, he seemed certain enough of his position in his Manchester base. He told an audience at Bournemouth, where there had been a council decision to disband the municipal orchestra, 'They daren't take the Orchestra away from me in Manchester. There would be a revolution if they did!'

Evelyn was completing her handbook *Oboe Technique** for the Oxford University Press. She asked her friend Natalie James to run an eye over it so as to make sure it was clear for beginners. Later translated into other languages, this short useful book described control of tongue and finger muscles,

*The revised third edition was republished in 1982, following her larger three-volume manual, 'The Oboist's Companion' (Oxford, 1978).

breath control, embouchure and tone quality. Evelyn also discussed problems of nervousness, the care of the instrument and the technique of its boon-companion, the cor anglais.

Ernest Bean by now had gone to be general manager of the new Festival Hall in London. Besides managing the Hallé Orchestra he had run for many years the excellent *Hallé Magazine* and now he introduced into the Festival Hall programmes those quaintly juxtaposed extracts from contradictory criticisms of the same concert that so greatly amused the London public and so incensed the music critics, such as:

> '. . . two well-differentiated tones, the father's sweeter and more silvery, the son's weightier and more penetrating . . .' *Guardian*

> '. . . Mr. Oistrakh, senior, had the more penetrating, his son the more silvery, tone . . .' *Times*

Bean was succeeded by Kenneth Crickmore, an appointment urged by John that he later had reason to regret, and Clive F. Smart came in as secretary, later becoming general manager in his turn.

A continual problem for the Hallé was the large turnover of players. Smart estimated that in John's time it was about ten per cent a year. London, of course, was the giant magnet; Audrey Napier-Smith said that ten or fifteen years after John came to Manchester there were forty-eight principals in London who came from the Hallé. John grumbled that he found and trained musicians and then London took them—but he kept on finding more. He was not amused when told that he had become recognized as one of the best trainers of young orchestral players in the country.

So the Hallé went on touring cities and towns in common with the (also busily travelling) London orchestras, returning to its northern bastion for rehearsal and replenishment. One of its lighter moments at the Free Trade Hall was the near-Christmas concert in 1952 when J.B. played a tiny plastic trumpet in Haydn's 'Toy' Symphony. George Weldon, his deputy conductor, provided cuckoo effects and the baton was wielded by Alderman W. Collingson, enjoying a night off from being Deputy Lord Mayor of Manchester.

John caused a minor stir at Covent Garden that winter when, conducting *La Bohème*, he turned at the beginning of Act III and requested the audience not to start clapping at the end of acts until the last notes had been played. It was particularly irritating in this opera to have bursts of applause at highly emotional moments.* Beecham had more brusquely shouted 'Shut up!' on similar occasions.

Bohème, Turandot and *Madam Butterfly* accounted for a good number of Barbirolli's guest appearances during three Covent Garden seasons, after an absence of fourteen years, pointing the fact that though he had conducted Verdi a good deal (his father had told him a lot about the tempi Verdi liked) he was as much associated with Puccini. Just as Lorenzo remembered Verdi and his ways, so John remembered Puccini. At twenty he had played the cello in that same building in the first London performance of *Il Tabarro*. He would tell stories of Puccini's courtesy to the orchestra at rehearsals, his dash, his dandyish dress and his liking for colourful English ties which he bought at a special West End shop and thought were discoveries, without realizing (or being told) that they were the ties of famous English regiments and schools.

Early in 1953 John conducted *Tristan und Isolde* for the first time at Covent Garden for three performances, described by a critic as 'lyrically intense and convincing'. Sylvia Fisher, the house's leading dramatic soprano, was making a debut as Isolde, with Ludwig Suthaus as Tristan. Some people had hoped after this that John might succeed Karl Rankl as Covent Garden's director of music. David Webster, the general administrator, offered him the post but he said he was not interested—he would not leave the Hallé at that time. Erich Kleiber became a powerful candidate but his demands proved too onerous and ultimately the post went to Rafael Kubelik.

After the 1953-54 season John did not appear again at Covent Garden. He intended to undertake more opera but the travelling demands of the Hallé and other orchestral commitments were too exacting for him to find time. Yet he shone brilliantly in opera, maintaining that this was the field in which the Italians had made their unique contribution. Of his strong sense of 'theatre' Charles Cracknell said, 'He had an intuition for character in opera and brought the best out of his

*Such requests and warnings to audiences were to become a feature of quite a number of J.B.'s concerts, abroad as well as in this country.

soloists.' In later years he conducted concert performances of operas and made some fine recordings and in the late 1960s conducted a new production of *Aïda* in Rome.

One important aspect of Barbirolli's work during the early Fifties continued to be his performances of contemporary music. Bartók, Berg (played from early years), Hindemith, Shostakovich, Walton, Schoenberg and Stravinsky were in his programmes. At the Cheltenham Festival there were works by Rubbra, Rawsthorne, Finzi, Hoddinott, Gardner and Fricker among others and many first performances were given.

It was a knock at his door at the end of one of his London concerts that brought John a big surprise: his former wife, Marjorie Parry, who had come round to tell him how moved she had been by it.

At about this time, too, Michael Davis, many years later leader of the London Symphony Orchestra and the son of Eric Davis, a Hallé violinist for thirty-two years, first demonstrated his youthful prowess with the violin to John. Michael was then about eight and recalled, 'He wrote me a marvellous note congratulating me on getting through my grade.'

John kept him in mind after that, encouraged and advised him on teachers as the years passed, till the time came in 1967 when he invited him to join the Hallé as assistant leader. He ended as co-leader, his father leading the second violins.

'Extremely kind and generous,' was Davis's summing-up, 'though a bit of a slave-driver.' When his father had a growth on his finger that might, according to the doctors, have necessitated amputation and caused the end of his violin career, John arranged for him to see a noted surgeon, who successfully removed the lump.

'He spoke affectionately of the Orchestra as "my children",' said Davis. 'It might have seemed a little out-of-date but they could really count on him a hundred per cent.'

Evelyn shared in his solicitude for his players. Natalie James said, 'If there were people in the Hallé who were unhappy about anything both would help, and Evelyn would be so kind to them.'

'If he heard that a back-desk cellist's wife was ill,' said Clive Smart 'or that his son had fallen off his bicycle he'd want to know all about it.'

What always surprised Smart was that after being sometimes

at his lowest ebb at the end of afternoon rehearsals, John would walk through the curtains at a concert 'as if somebody had super-charged his batteries'. After the concert he might again appear 'burnt up'.

Among personal Barbirolli traits was a great admiration for Winston Churchill, whose speeches he stored next to his Elgar records. He admired both the medical and the legal professions and held that he would have cheerfully been a doctor or a barrister if his lot had fallen differently. He perused medical books and made occasional visits with a surgeon friend to watch operations at a Manchester hospital.

John enjoyed telling stories of his early days, particularly in London, which retained his constant affection. In public houses for the occasional sandwich and beer he could hold forth on cricket and Suvi Raj Grubb, the gramophone record producer, remembered when, using a tankard as a wicket, he described the 'exquisite poetry' of a cover drive by Frank Woolley, adding, 'They don't make 'em like that any more.'

For his friends he could be a devastating mimic, using the Lancashire, Yorkshire, Cockney and American dialects, or imitating Welsh and Irish intonations, but unable to get the hang of Scottish despite his sojourn in Glasgow. He was a keen judge of dialect. When he took part in a radio show with Harry Corbett (whom he greatly admired in television's 'Steptoe and Son') he asked Corbett 'Are you a real Cockney or a false one?' Corbett admitted that he was not a real one.

When one of the authors was walking down a country lane in 1981 carrying a book bearing Barbirolli's name a car drew up at his side. The driver leaned out and said, 'So you're reading about Barbirolli. I remember him. His Elgar and Vaughan Williams were wonderful and he was one of the few conductors well liked by the players. Goodbye.'

And with a wave of his hand he drove on out of sight.

This percipient but unknown personage had epitomized the conductor in ten seconds. John's insight into Elgar's music was superb and he understood Vaughan Williams as few did. Both composers recognized it, and he was a friend of both.

John had admired Elgar from his youth, had played under him at nineteen, had broken into conducting with the Second

Symphony. With Adrian Boult and Malcolm Sargent he was a faithful advocate of the composer over the years. 'I know it's sometimes been wondered at,' he would say, 'that I, a Cockney of Latin blood, should have such an affinity with one whom some call a purely English composer . . . My affinity with Elgar perhaps has its origins in the fact that I was brought up in Edwardian London in a period which Elgar evokes so ardently.'

They were both Romantics, both had had uphill battles in early life. John's insight into Elgar's emotional intensity stemmed from youthful acquaintance with the poignant Cello Concerto and his admiration for the Violin Concerto. The symphonies, with their prolific invention and inner drama, moved him greatly. Elgar, who had marvellously said, 'Music is in the air; you simply take as much as you require,' was grateful for his interpretations.

A fair amount of Elgar's music had been received in Britain with reserve and indifference. John knew of this barrier in receptivity and wanted to help overcome it. He had come to know Elgar in the early Thirties, shortly before his death. He would tell of meeting him at his home, of how the reserved composer showed him the wonderful view from his bedroom window overlooking his beloved Worcester, saying, 'I wake up and see this,' of his sense of humour when playing a record of *Falstaff*, often the subject of criticism, when he remarked at a drum-roll, 'Well, that's a good bit, anyway!' Elgar, said John, embraced and thanked him for appreciating his music so much.

He resolved after the composer's death to enlarge as much as possible public appreciation of his music, both at home and abroad. He became a master of its essence. 'Elgar', he said, 'wrote noble tunes, with wonderful contours . . . little rhythmic figures built up into lovely melodies. He is one of the greatest craftsmen.'

One of John's earliest records had been of Vaughan Williams—a Fantasy Quintet for Strings. In his conducting career he performed faithfully in London, Scotland, the United States and with the Hallé throughout Britain the works of the great composer who had based so much of his music on English folk-song and madrigals and who helped

English music to throw off the yoke of the Continent. The Fifth and Sixth Symphonies were John's special favourites. In 1952, when Vaughan Williams was approaching eighty, John included in his season all six of the symphonies then written. They had become close friends and Vaughan Williams made certain revisions for the occasions, seeking his advice. While rehearsing, they would try different balances in certain parts and the composer adopted some of the conductor's ideas and suggestions.

During this season Vaughan Williams himself took the baton with the Hallé in his 'Sea' Symphony in Manchester and Sheffield. The Sheffield performance was notable for John's unexpected appearance among the cellists. Their principal was ill and, with the conductor's amused permission, John took the sub-principal's desk, receiving a special round of spontaneous applause from the audience when he was recognized.

In January, 1953, he conducted in Manchester the première of the composer's Seventh Symphony, the 'Antartica', developed from themes for a score for 'Scott of the Antarctic' four years before. It was bleak music, with its wind-machine, and portrayed heroism versus implacable nature. John's performance met the composer's intentions and Vaughan Williams was delighted. Later V.W. composed especially for John his Eighth Symphony and after its first performance he wrote on the title-page 'For Glorious John'—a name which stuck and which gave John endless pride and pleasure. (The MS score is now in the British Museum. A facsimile of the title-page may be seen in the Barbirolli Room at the Royal Academy of Music, together with that of V.W.'s 'Fanfare for Glorious John'.)

The Hallé Orchestra for the first time appeared at the Promenade concerts in the Albert Hall, London, that August. Its initial concert included the 'Fantastic' Symphony, Ravel's 'Mother Goose' Suite and De Falla's *Nights in the Gardens of Spain* with Iris Loveridge as pianist—and the opening drum-roll of *La Gazza Ladra* brought some loyal citizens to their feet as usual. Then, on 27 August Vaughan Williams attended to hear Barbirolli's 'stunning eloquence', as *The Times* called it, in his Fourth Symphony—the violent work thought by some to be a presage of war, though the composer denied this—as well as the 'Tallis' Fantasia and others of his works.

There was a story that V.W., at the first performance of the Fourth Symphony, muttered to himself, 'Well, if this is modern music, I don't like it.'

After the composer's death John declared that the only other British composer in the past sixty years to stand beside Elgar had been Vaughan Williams.

17 *'Ally's Band'*

Often the person who achieves great things is not the one who had the original idea. And so it was in 1943, when Philip Godlee had the idea of inviting John Barbirolli to return to England and reconstruct the Hallé Orchestra. Godlee, Manchester business man and patron of the arts, as well as influential chairman of the Hallé Society, was himself a talented violinist; he delighted in running amateur string quartets and chamber music groups (his daughter would later play in the Orchestra under Barbirolli). The conductor rightly received the praise for the resuscitating of the Orchestra—starting almost from scratch, when he had expected to take over at least a hundred musicians—but the idea of reconstruction had been Godlee's, and so makes him a man who cannot be forgotten in any account of Evelyn and John and the Orchestra which so influenced their lives. He was a bit of an intellectual farceur at times; most serious when he was appearing to be amusing, placing to the last fibre of his being his service to his 'child', the Orchestra. It was an idea flashing through Philip Godlee's mind that dictated what could have been a disaster had the recipient of his cable from Manchester to New York been of a different calibre. But as it was, the 'long-shot' produced the ultimate result: Barbirolli, with talent and imagination as well as a superhuman energy, promoted the Hallé as *his* child, now. And Godlee, in the words of one observer of the northern musical scene, went on to encourage him 'with rare dash, wit and resource'. John never let down the city of his musical adoption, but endeared himself to all—orchestra and audiences being made into a total whole—and Philip was his friend's strongest ally. The over 6ft 3in Godlee with the 5ft 4in

Barbirolli made a notable sight upon those occasions when they were together, and not infrequently photographed, justifying the amused comment that 'here come the long and the short of it.' Both men were musicians to their fingertips; Godlee was highly professional in outlook, albeit an amateur in musical practice, and, like John, he subscribed to the belief proposed by Molière's Music Master in *Le Bourgeois Gentilhomme*:

> who demonstrated irrefutably that wars and other ills of the body politic arose simply because not enough people took the trouble to learn music, a sure means towards harmonious brotherhood and universal peace.*

It was this patron of the arts, Philip Godlee, who apparently first put to the Manchester City Council the idea of opening a bigger and better Free Trade Hall.

With Barbirolli, who was working himself in to become a Lancashire idol, Godlee compelled the dullards and the ant-J.B. factions to agree with him. When he was stuck for any advanced music point he would, theatrically, utter a sotto-voce stage whisper audible to everybody in any council chamber, however large: 'I do not know everything—but I know who knows'—and then his glance would fall meaningfully upon J.B. And Barbirolli's ability to carry on from Godlee's groundwork was attributable to his flair for gathering around him the right people to work for the right money. Or, at any rate, such money (sometimes only tiny sums) as the budget would allow.

'To *share* music is very important. To be able to help and almost disappear at times, when necessary, is sometimes even more important.' J.B. thought this in principle, though his personality was often too vivid to disappear. Despite his wide popularity and a general consensus of opinion that he had put the Hallé back on the map (creating an entirely new sound for an orchestra at its peak in the process), it cannot be denied that there was a resentful faction in the city—the civic bureaucrats congregating in council chambers, committee rooms, the Lord Mayor's parlour and public libraries—who disliked the 'international' aspect of their conductor. Manchester having

**John Barbirolli:* A biography by Charles Reid (Hamish Hamilton, 1971)

become Barbirolli country, and the Hallé John's base, it was perhaps natural that those elements opposing any public expenditure on the arts should intrigue and occasionally stand up publicly in the council chambers to make denouncements, reported freely in the Lancashire Press, to the effect that 'tha 'Ally wasn't as popular as it was cracked up to be'. Philip Godlee was one of those people who would give of himself to further the 'cause' as he put it, quite selflessly and with a unique attack, humour and energy. He, in company with the critics Michael Kennedy, Ernest Bradbury and C. B. Rees, believed that 'an orchestra's affairs cannot be judged in the same way as those of an ironmongery store'. The majority of Mancunians agreed with them, but it took Godlee's dark hints that Barbirolli might be driven to shake the dust of Manchester off his feet to promote the solid resistance to Town Hall 'politics' that became an issue in the Fifties. Accusations flew, there were newspaper and magazine articles, and the battle waged between those who wanted increased help in the way of subsidies for the Orchestra, and those who were busily accusing Barbirolli of Beecham's extravagance; of having returned from abroad with big ideas that made him too big for his boots. 'Manchester is not America' said one councillor, adding, 'Manchester hasn't as much brass.'

In a reply that would seem to have been directed as much to Manchester's Town Hall as to an inert Arts Council of Great Britain (waiting at the sidelines to see the result of the battle rather than acting as a pathfinder to lead an artistic way), the conductor spoke out with spirit:

> On the question of having big ideas for Manchester, I would like to know how one can establish an orchestra worthy of the city we serve on little ideas . . . If Manchester wants a little orchestra, run by little men with little ideas, I agree that I and my colleagues of the Hallé Society are not the men for the job.

But it took several more years of bickering, allocating blame here and there, the local establishment doing its best (or worst) to upset any hope of smooth-running by infusing a philistinism that was anathema to artists; before the City Council climbed down. In his biography, Charles Reid wrote:

> Meantime the Hallé Committee, wondering where the money was to come from, put up the players' 'basic' wage by three pounds per week and promised Barbirolli a playing strength of ninety-six as soon as they had a platform big enough to seat that number. On the strength of these concessions he announced that he was turning down a BBC offer. It is doubtful whether he had ever intended to accept. Two more years of dickering followed. The orchestra had asked for a direct grant in place of guarantees against deficits. This the [Arts] Council conceded, promising nine thousand pounds a year for three years: ludicrously less than comparable orchestral subsidies at home and abroad, but mollifying for the moment.

Local politics and the niggardly grants extended to the Hallé Orchestra by the Arts Council continued to harass the Hallé members and their conductor for the rest of the decade. On 21 May 1960, the *Guardian* delivered a stern leader:

> Sir John Barbirolli's threat to resign from the Hallé unless there is an inquiry into the whole question of subsidizing orchestras in Britain has brought a long-standing grievance to a head. For all its fame and the immense value of its work the Hallé is not treated generously either by the Arts Council or by Manchester Corporation. It has to work harder than any other orchestra of standing to keep going—last year the Hallé gave 238 performances, compared with the Royal Liverpool Philharmonic's 190, the Scottish National's 151, Birmingham's 201, and Bournemouth's 210. The Halle's musicians—with reason—feel this to be a hardship, and there have been an uncomfortable number of resignations from the orchestra recently. Moreover, the Arts Council's allocation of its grants is puzzling: why should the Hallé last year have been given £12,000, and Liverpool, with a much bigger local authority grant than the Hallé, £20,000? The Arts Council must have reasons for this apparent discrimination, but they may not be good reasons, and Sir John Barbirolli is justified in asking for an inquiry into the system of allocating grants. Manchester

> is niggardly to its orchestra compared with Liverpool and Birmingham—the Hallé's grant from local authorities last year was £17,181, compared with Liverpool's £29,131 and Birmingham's £30,000. Moreoever Manchester takes back a large part of what it gives by charging the Hallé some £7,000 a year for the rent of the Free Trade Hall. The notion that music can be provided on the cheap must be dropped if the Hallé players are to be free from constant anxiety.

However, if many thought the Arts Council niggardly towards the Hallé and less than gracious in many of its dealings with Barbirolli, he himself never permitted the cumbersome structure of that Council (in a state of bumbledom in the 1950s, with high and low officials, countless committees and often choosing to make complicated 'arrangements' with artistic bodies) to obscure the idea of subsidy of the worthwhile by the State. All too much could be traced to an unimaginative and parsimonious Treasury, but since the Council's formation in 1946 a small but invaluable part of its work had been the administration of a number of private trust funds.

One such fund, known as the Suggia Gift, was established in 1956 to fulfil a wish expressed by the eminent cellist, Guilhermina Suggia. In November 1950, shortly after her death, Barbirolli had taken the Hallé to Portugal on a visit that ended with the conductor playing the cello in a Haydn string quartet during a Mass in memory of Suggia. The two had recorded together in the past, when, under contract to HMV, Suggia (along with such instrumentalists as Heifetz and Rubinstein) had made a disc under Barbirolli's baton.

The 'wish' that was to become widely known in musical circles as the Suggia Gift was formed to respond to approaches from exceptionally talented cello students of any nationality under the age of twenty-one, who could be judged to possess the potential qualities of first-class performers. An illustrious panel was formed under the chairmanship of Barbirolli. Who better than one so distinguished, whose favourite instrument the cello had always been?

Barbirolli was a generous man, rarely—if ever—refusing a deserving cause. Until the year of his death he would lavish his experience on the problems and aspirations of the numerous youthful musicians paraded in front of him. And those who came forward to catch his eye and ear with the cello were, on the whole, especially likely to attract the most detailed comment. His status as a conductor of international renown was freely placed at the disposal of the Arts Council, he probably feeling about it what he felt about the BBC: that while they were no better than they ought to be, and while much of their work was misguided and unadventurous, in the long run they *were* on the side of the angels. Something of what he felt was made clear:

> They [the Arts Council] do it as if it were a Welfare State-means-test. If you go down the drain and can't get engagements you get a lot of money. If you earn 81 per cent of your income, as we [the Hallé] do, you get penalized for it.

Since the inception of the Suggia Gift a number of prominent members of the Council's music department, including Eric Thompson, have placed on record their department's indebtedness to both Evelyn and John for the immeasurable value of their work, jointly and individually, down the years. But in John's lifetime it was generally conceded by many to be an administrator's nightmare. Very carefully timed audition schedules had to be devised in order that the throng of applicants (and accompanists, parents and teachers) that milled around backstage throughout each session could be smoothly dealt with.

Theoretically, each applicant would complete an approximately twelve-minute audition, leaving the stage before the next one emerged from the Green Room. In fact, timetables were often shattered by impromptu guidance shouted from the back of the hall, which could often develop into brief, long-distance cello lessons mimed by John. Holding a bit of furniture for an instrument, he would hum a tune, sometimes even bounding forward with upright chair or stool under one arm. Then he would stomp along and, reaching a startled child's cello, wrench it away as he commenced a practical lesson illustrating the right sort of technique that he expected from a pupil playing this or that particular piece. Chaos seemed to reign, but it was all made smooth in double-quick time after the Master had shown the students, explaining with as much detail and illustration as he would had he been talking to a seasoned member of his own splendid Hallé.

The very first Suggia Gift audition took place at the Royal Academy of Music on 25 July, 1956.

Evelyn was not present upon that first occasion, although much later she was to be on Arts Council music panels. John had four fellow-panellists, including Lionel Tertis and Ivor Newton. Five young instrumentalists were to be heard, including the quiet and winsome Jacqueline du Pré, then aged eleven. Her audition was successful and the advisory panel recommended an Award to enable her to have additional private lessons, on condition that she could devote at least four hours a day to practice while still continuing her general education. With the consent of the Headmistress of Croydon High School for Girls this proviso was made possible and a sum of £175 was offered by the Arts Council.

At the audition, Jacqueline played movements and pieces by Vivaldi, Saint-Saëns and Boccherini. John's written notes were brief but perceptive:

> *Vivaldi*: Certainly talented. Nice tone. Good intonation. *Swan*: Very immature musically. Not very imaginative. *Boccherini*: More advanced technically than musically. Feel that she should now really get down to her cello.

With John's helpful observations and the panel's endorsement of these, the Council continued to invest in Jacqueline, whose progress was both marked and rapid. In 1958 he was writing about the young prodigy:

> Certainly fulfilling her promise and would definitely recommend continuation of financial assistance. But on what lines? Needs developing in terms of real beauty of sound, poetry and imagination and warmth. Vitality, she has plenty.

In another few years, on 12 July, 1962, he once again expressed the advisers' view that she should be helped to go to Paris and wrote: 'Had a little talk with her and was delighted to find how unspoilt she has remained.'

Standards, application and overall dedication were qualities he looked for in all the candidates, whatever their age, and he was ruthless in his insistence that they be observed minutely. His busy schedule prevented his attendance at the 1966 meeting of the advisers, but he was back in the following year for the Arts Council audition in the Great Drawing Room at 4 St James's Square. On that occasion, twelve cellists between the ages of nine and eighteen were being heard by John, who had alongside him Amaryllis Fleming, Ambrose Gauntlett, Bernard Shore and Lionel Tertis. Seven of the applicants were seeking renewals of awards that he been made in previous years, and five were submitting requests for the first time.

A crescendo of dissatisfaction through a long morning welled up into a vehement outburst by John after the last player had been heard. Rounding on his fellow-panellists and without mincing his words, he reminded them of the terms of reference all were supposed to be subscribing to: 'exceptional talent', 'potential qualities of a first class solo performer', and so on, and so forth. He believed that the high standard of performance required had been allowed to decline, that it was now necessary to enforce a stricter observance of the terms set out in the Trust Deed. He quoted from his audition pencillings the most favourable observations he could make of all the cellists he had heard that morning:

> 'I think there is promise here.' 'Has a nice bow—and a nicely positioned left hand.'
>
> 'About the best intonation we have had yet . . . I suggest this grant, of forty pounds, is made, and he play to us again next year.'

The nine-year old Marius May was the only beneficiary in 1967.

That John Barbirolli was able to give so much time and effort to help the Arts Council administer the Suggia Gift, when he was often at odds with the Council over the subsidy it would grant the Hallé Orchestra, is a tribute to the way in which he was able to rise above the particular to the general when the good of musicians was at stake. He gave valuable time and encouragement to youthful cellists, even though he could have been excused for thinking that there were too many amateurs (he was a professional to his fingertips) in positions of power deciding grants and the size of the handouts they would recommend should be made. His devotion to the cause of his Orchestra did not blind him to other considerations, but the Orchestra did come first. C. B. Rees observed in 1958 that what had brought it from its beginnings into the present was not only the vitality inherent in its being but also the integrity of its musicianship; not only its invincible will to endure but also its deep, assured awareness of its mission. The citizenry of Manchester—and other places where it travelled—were able to 'praise it with devoted pride, and cherish it with rightly jealous zeal'.

For many years 'Ally's Band' had brought credit and renown to the city, as well as to the whole world of music. As Rees wrote in *100 Years of the Hallé*:

> Do not let us forget that the Hallé, though a hundred years old, is a young orchestra, as one glance at it will reveal. Its conductor is a young man, and a young man who looks a young man. It is not easy to realize that Sir Charles Hallé had been dead for four years when John Barbirolli was born; and that Barbirolli was only two years old when Richter was appointed conductor of the Hallé Orchestra. Both for its pulsating youth and its honourable age, Britain's orchestral centenarian deserves and commands our fullest loyalties and our most generous practical support for its future.

But these plaudits were not merely the product of centenary enthusiasm. Five years, earlier in January 1953, Neville Cardus had written in the *Radio Times*:

> Under different conductors, naturally, any orchestra cultivates different traits of style. Under Sir John Barbirolli I think the Hallé players have acquired an almost Latin cleanness and brightness; Sir John, in a way, had Mediterraneanized Manchester music—to use the

> expressive language of Nietzsche. He has, for our epoch and for the present generation, made the Hallé Orchestra his own, as much his own as it was ever Richter's.

It might have been known as 'Ally's Band', but it was entering into legend as Barbirolli's.

> *There was a young lady from Calais*
> *Who wanted to visit the Hallé;*
> *So she swam o'er the Channel*
> *Wrapt up in red flannel,*
> *Crying 'Oui, oui! Fol-de-rol! Barbirolli!'*

18 *Conductor On The Box*

John loved the feeling of *live* music. He rarely listened to records—his own or other musicians'—and only appeared on television in the first place because he felt that by such exposure to a nation-wide audience the Hallé would be seen as well as heard, its standing enhanced, and that this might lead to bigger subsidies for the orchestra with which he had become chiefly identified.

His first television engagement was with the BBC in 1952. The *Manchester Guardian* reported on 22 November:

> Last night the viewing public saw and heard fifteen minutes of the Hallé Orchestra, under Sir John Barbirolli, in the second programme of the series 'The Conductor Speaks'. For most of the afternoon and early evening the submerged nine-tenths had filled the Manchester Free Trade Hall with toil and striving.
>
> The muzzles of the television cameras threatened from several directions—upwards from the floor of the house, where rows of seats had been removed to allow them free passage; downwards from the balcony; slanting across from a point on the stage. All over the place young men listened raptly to what came through their headphones, or signalled urgently but silently to each other . . . 'Does

it start with me talking?' asked Sir John of the nearest young man. 'Sir, it begins with you speaking,' said the young man's formal voice, followed by Sir John's comfortable tones, familiar, yet beautifully avoiding the buttonholing mode: 'My friends, I suppose I am meeting you this evening more intimately than ever before . . .'

He went on to introduce the overture to *The Barber of Seville* . . . The brilliant ripple and chuckle of Rossini began; the muzzles of the cameras swung and stilled; Sir John's hands moved in a fluid pattern while he uttered to the orchestra those inarticulate, affectionate, exasperated noises which one makes to a beloved but refractory horse.

After that the Preludes to Acts I and III of *La Traviata*, which, said Sir John, his grandfather used to say were written not by Verdi but by God, and which he had chosen because their melodies should dispel any prejudices viewers might have against classical music, 'whatever that may mean.' Then Mozart's *Eine Kleine Nachtmusik*, and finally Berlioz's *Carnaval Romain* overture.

Nobody ever heard the opera that came after the overture, said Sir John, but there was a tune one of the ladies sang, 'like this . . .' For a second or two all present listened spellbound while there was uplifted that highly individual instrument, a conductor's voice. 'In the overture the cor anglais has it.' It came, cool and hollow and plangent, from the woodwind desks . . .

A solo drum roll, to show how that was done, then Berlioz's orchestration blazed out, blindingly magnificent in the empty hall. Sir John, rejecting any attempt at verbal flamboyance, hoped only that the unseen audience had enjoyed his orchestra, which he thought worth looking at as well as worth listening to. He looked surprised when the players, as he finished, applauded him.

Barbirolli went on conducting intermittently and selectively on 'the box' over the next six years. A BBC poll found him to be the most popular conductor on television at that time.

But there were no 'noises to a refractory horse' in 1958 when, to celebrate the Hallé centenary, and after John had signed the first contract (as Head of Classical Music for Associated

Rediffusion) for classical music to be transmitted on the still new Independent Television, two important music programmes were lined up for one transmission by Association Rediffusion from the Free Trade Hall, Manchester under his complete musical control.

The first part consisted of 'The Rehearsal—Before', and was precisely that. The second part was 'After—Rachmaninov's Rhapsody on a Theme of Paganini'. The soloist was Peter Katin and the date was 1 September 1958.

The conductor actually went with Peter Cotes, who directed and produced the programmes, all the way to 'headquarters' to ask that no 'commercials' be inserted between the two parts of the programme, so that the flow and continuity would not be impaired by the abrupt advertising of some product entirely unassociated with the great rhapsody of sound. John had his director's full support, and the request was acceded to, one of the very few times when an artist's plea—directly contrary to a commercial television contractor's policy—was granted by the powers-that-be.

However, the success of this first programme was of even greater importance to Associated Rediffusion than to the Hallé. The goodwill of Barbirolli on this occasion, so early in the television company's life, represented at least as much clout as did the advertising agencies who—in those comparatively early years of the 'commercial'—were jockeying for position. Those at the top had wanted J.B. for prestigious purposes, and had offered him greater artistic freedom and a more acceptable contract than he had had with the BBC, where he was a valued asset. But, as always, Barbirolli of the kind heart and generous temperament was nobody's fool where musical integrity was concerned. He showed his abiding loyalty by demanding decent amenities for his orchestra.

Throughout his ITV contract he chose his own director/producer, as well as his times for rehearsals and the slots to be scheduled for the transmissions.

So, with commercials to precede and follow, but not to interrupt the programme, preparations went ahead in line with the concept worked out between conductor and director. Peter Cotes recalls that, in his talks with the conductor prior to rehearsals, John was chiefly interested in presenting an abstract sound visually, which, although most interesting in itself, is an extremely difficult feat to accomplish.

Clearly, Barbirolli's aim was for the television cameras to catch the instruments themselves; concentrating on the sounds and the look of each instrument rather than watching music-stands and gilt chairs or passing up and down and across rows of instrumentalists.

He made pictures in music, too—also lines and tones, colour and composition. Business and art. Mostly art. But he could be 'big-business' when the occasion arose. His integrity was his guide, as well as his artistry, and he liked to think of the instruments in relation to the cameras, as having personalities of their own. He once quoted the words of Heifetz, who had whispered to John that 'the violin is the carpenter of sound, sawing away contentedly', to which he'd made the reflective reply that every instrument in the orchestra was vibrant with life if properly played, 'even the bass drum: prophetic, stubborn, slightly rude!' Cotes recollects:

> John felt that most of the instruments had lovely shapes and varied, interesting textures. To him, the cello, with a sheen rich as a conker, or the sparkle of the brass section, glistening with their shower of notes, was absorbing to watch. He wanted, he told me, to see the fingering of a clarinet in profile, close up. This would, in his view, be better than seeing a man puffing away from afar.
>
> John's idea was that, as each section of the orchestra came into dominance, there should be a fade-in of one beautifully photographed instrument from it, so that the sound would seem to be drawn from the wood, the metal, the drum-skin, or whatever, and not from a labouring musician. This has since become a generally accepted principle. When the orchestra is in concert or crescendoes together, then the conductor is all; and how lucky I was to have such an exceptionally photogenic conductor, whose hands, with their eloquent back-bending thumbs, seemed to mould the music out of the air.

One idea that Peter Cotes discussed at great length with Barbirolli, one that television audiences are now familiar with, was that when a solo instrument was predominant (in a concerto, for instance) the solo line of music should slowly cross the screen *as it was played.* The idea was adopted with that enthusiasm so characteristic of J.B. It was found fairly simple to have the notes on a winding device, like that used for credit titles, only wound across horizontally instead of vertically.

'If you feel that there are not enough people in the audience with sufficient musical knowledge to follow the line of score,' suggested Cotes, 'why shouldn't we have it on the bottom half of the screen with you, John, in, say, a medium shot, conducting above the music?'

In fact J.B. never doubted that many more people than one imagines have sufficient elementary knowledge to follow one line of music. But Cotes, working for commercial television in its infancy, was more cautious than Barbirolli himself, who made the point that most people have, at some time in their lives, possessed a recorder, a ukelele, a Jew's-harp or even a penny whistle. Some tinkle in treble on the piano by vamping ad-lib a sentimental tune. And even for those who couldn't read a note of music the shapes of crochets and semi-quavers might be pleasant to look at.

The well-constructed shots of instruments, as well as of instrumentalists, helped to secure a general admission that these were the best classical music productions on television in which Barbirolli had ever figured. The orchestra and pianist were shown in the final stages of rehearsal of the Rhapsody. Through this pioneering programme many people were enlightened as to just how a concerto is rehearsed. Some think that the great virtuoso arrives, informs the conductor of *his* tempi and interpretation, and then throughout the actual rehearsal continues in the grand manner—most often perhaps associated with the proverbial prima donna style and attitude—treating both orchestra and conductor as 'accompanists'.

The script expounded first this point of view, and then the diametrically opposite one, with a soloist shrinking on and sidling on to the piano stool as though it were a trapdoor that might open and swallow him up while the conductor told him exactly how he wished the concerto to be performed.

Finally the viewers were shown Barbirolli's way, in which conductor and soloist collaborated to do the fullest justice to the music. What had always been regarded as an extremely difficult piece in the pianist's repertoire (and in the orchestra's) was transmitted first in rehearsal, then in performance. The national Press's response the next day indicated that this was television's classical music programme of the year.

'London sees Barbirolli rehearse first', wrote Philip Purser in the *News Chronicle*, and went on to say:

> Every ITV station carried last night's performance by Sir John Barbirolli and the Hallé Orchestra. But only in London and the North were viewers also let in on fifteen minutes of rehearsal beforehand. The others undoubtedly missed half the fun. Although it was a rehearsal, it revealed enough glimpses of practical orchestral mechanics to enhance the finished performance that followed. You recognized with pleasure the moment when Sir John had asked the brass to be more aggressive—and, by Jove, now they were! The best treatment of the Hallé I have seen and the producer was Peter Cotes.

Colin Frame of the *Star* applauded Barbirolli's return to television.

> ITV's treat—like watching a beauty make up her face. Sir John at rehearsal, wearing a muffler and pah-pah-pahing what to emphasize was such fiery fun that it was thoroughly worth while.

And Peter Black, the doyen of television critics at that time, wrote in the *Daily Mail*:

> Associated Rediffusion really pulled one out of the bag last night with the Hallé at work. From the Free Trade Hall, Manchester, we had first a telerecorded rehearsal, then a live performance of a Rachmaninov rhapsody by Sir John Barbirolli and the Hallé Orchestra. The substance of the programme is not new to radio listeners, who for some time have been able to hear similar dissections of music. *But it was the first time that television had offered such a thing.* It was remarkably effective. The orchestra was seen rehearsing in shirt sleeves and

sweaters, with Barbirolli in a suit and choker scarf and soloist Peter Katin in pullover. The sound rolled round the hall, stopped as decisively as a slammed door, moved on, stopped again while Barbirolli, generating enough vital force to light a small town, encouraged, suggested, exclaimed. He stepped down to tell the pianist, 'I rather lost track of you there.' Katin repeated the passage. The two heads nodded agreement. The music moved on, with Barbirolli shouting 'That's it!' No doubt it had been planned, rehearsed and repeated. No matter. I congratulate Sir John who advised, and Peter Cotes who devised and directed, on presenting something that really extended television's range. It was new, exciting, worth doing, splendidly done.

(It *was* in fact 'planned, rehearsed and repeated', proving what a marvellous actor John would have made.)

Telegrams, letters, phone calls and personal messages followed John's début on commercial television. Both Associated Rediffusion and Granada TV, who had respectively arranged the transmission and provided the amenities and floor space, quickly got to work on the second programme John's contract promised them. Peter Cotes was reappointed to steer *Master of Music*, which John insisted the same team should produce and direct. It was more of a condensed tribute than a life history, for it also commemorated John's fiftieth year as a professional musician, and was to be transmitted in November 1958.

Evelyn appeared in person to recall memories of her husband's early life and musical career from a family scrapbook. At first she resisted the suggestion. Self-effacing as always, she felt it was John's evening, and that that was what most people would expect—to see John and the Hallé at work again. However, she was drawn in when she learned that Mémé was to appear in the programme. Now aged eighty-eight, Mémé could be a difficult—even turbulent character, but Evelyn promptly undertook the role of daughter (rather than that of John's wife). By looking at Mémé and soothing her nerves, she enabled John to concentrate on the job in hand with no need to worry about his mother. And, largely thanks to Evelyn's tact, Mémé seemed as proud and happy to be on the studio floor amongst the lights and bustle, the cameras and the actors and musicians, as she had been in her many kitchens down the years, when she had been chef and matriarch in charge of combined operations.

John appeared as himself with the Hallé, being impersonated as a youngster by a boy actor who managed to span the years from childhood onwards, while a real-life father and son, Victor and Robert Rietti, played John's grandfather and father respectively. The musical part—the main feature—had the Hallé rendering a selection of popular orchestral pieces such as Elgar's *Cockaigne* Overture. Vaughan Williams' *Fanfare for Glorious John*, specially composed for the Hallé centenary, rounded off the dramatized biography and musical proceedings.

The whole entertainment represented a further success, though to some—both the musical 'purists' who wanted John and the Hallé undiluted and, paradoxically, sections of the popular Press not overfond of classical music—the second programme was a big let-down after the first. It may be seen now, however, as a pioneering programme of its type, increasing the viewing figures for serious music, and making Independent Television increasingly aware in the years ahead of the arts programme as a worthwhile contributor to the schedules.

Looking back today, the 'Manchester TV musical experiment', as it was to become known, represents at the very least a *succès d'estime.* Not only were the general public made increasingly aware of 'Ally's Band', but the national and provincial Press found in favour of more programmes of a similar nature.

Evelyn, diffident but impressively to the point, charming and intelligent, had made a distinct impression. One critic suggested that, should she have wanted to, she could have given up the oboe the next day, for a career as a chat-show hostess or news-caster well above the average!

But perhaps best of all from the point of view of the production team, and all those who had sweated behind the scenes to put across these two pioneering experiments, was John's appreciation of all their hard work, and his refusal to alter his view that the programme was a good one just because the critics disliked it. 'I have never taken any notice of critics,' he wrote to Peter Cotes at the same time as he presented him with a copy of C. B. Rees's *100 Years of the Hallé* in a luxury presentation binding. This volume, one of a limited edition of just a hundred copies, was inscribed:

> For dear Peter, whose sensitive collaboration has given me hopes for Music in Television.
> In affectionate admiration and with warm thanks
> 11-11-58 John

This stands as his personal attitude to critics and reviewers. In writing as he did, he was allying himself to the entire project; it is an insight into an artist's loyalty, an impressive illustration of what J.B. was known to be by all who worked with him—a real trouper.

Barbirolli's conducting style was as fascinating to watch as his 'sound' was to listen to: it combined hands, wrists, elbows, knees and facial expressions. First he pulled and then he pushed, straining for the exact effect he wanted to create. His left hand, with its widely extended thumb, constantly executed a rapidly waving 'come-on' gesture, and his thick black hair flew wildly in spirited passages. In quieter moments, his wrists and arms moved in fluid waves, every motion one of grace on the television screen.

The camera's job was to catch, pin down in close-up and then show the strength of his hold over his audience through his orchestra. That flexible and sensitive left hand, every quivering finger expressing a special something, supplemented the baton; the swaying figure, the expressive feet, all combined to lift and inspire the players and his orchestra too.

A bigger British audience had been caught, at one viewing, by the little box, than had ever seen it before at any of the performances given in the concert halls and great stadiums throughout the world, or even at the vast open-air Hollywood Bowl. It is difficult to recreate the sense of excitement and involvement that J.B. produced: these fragments from the 'rehearsal', transmitted from the Free Trade Hall Centenary performance, go some way to enabling us to relive those moments.

J.B. asked for warm, felt, sounds (referring to string bowings):
'Let me say several things—take the last four bars—three before 7 and then come forward and back.'

Pause–much clucking and baton-tapping before:
'Timpani—that's a solo; a theme. We need you . . . Now that's a tricky one . . . (pause) . . . that's much better—remember to *point* it up—the ones behind didn't hear you'.

Wagging finger admonishingly:
'Now the trumpets: let me hear the bar before—no, before that—not enough underneath you. That's better, much better . . .'

He whispers coaxingly, rather than demandingly:
'Please let me have a sound from all of you, because I must hear all of you individually. No, no, *no*. That's too loud; with this crescendo open . . .' (*pause and further baton tapping mixed with much coughing in silence, before renewing*) . . . 'Now, from the start, remember, one and two are simple—that's terrific.'
(*Music plays for some 20 seconds without interruption*)

J.B.'s eyes are closed and he sways, a rapt expression on his face:
'All together now. All right—let's go again (*tapping to stop*). So good I wish I could convince you. The air should be electrifying now—let it happen *by itself*. Keep it as pure and noble as you can—stop it. *Now . . .*' (*Pause, and then*) 'Fantastic. I'm proud of you. I'm not absolutely satisfied of course.' (*Laughter from members of the orchestra*) 'But it'll be all right. Meanwhile, it's as near as dammit right.'

And then the piece is played almost to the end before the tapping restarts and J.B.'s voice:
'It's heaven. I'm serious. Now do it with the tuba. You can do more—so now let's hear *more*. That last run-through was much more staccato. But it should be more traceable to its roots. Its origins . . .'

He dances up and down in order to make his points and his hair is dancing up and down in the swift and sudden breezes of his own exuberance. He taps his baton for silence, preparatory to rehearsal-transmission-picture coming up on the director's monitor, after so much noise having been registered on a 'wild-track' . . .

19 *V.W. at Cheltenham*

The Fifties were an important decade for Barbirolli and the Hallé for many reasons, not least of which was the part they played in the festivals at Cheltenham. That spa had become a showcase for British composers and Ireland, Elgar, Delius, Walton, Britten and Vaughan Williams—especially V.W., who was 'our greatest living composer' pronounced John—had their airings here. The Hallé played under John's baton never fewer than four orchestral concerts. Whenever he was asked the state of British music the reply came in John's best 'taken for granted' tones that the state of *our* music had never been better. He regretted that the music of Arnold Bax had been, on the whole, passed over and put that fact down to the possibility of its intricacies and overlong passages. But Cheltenham with all its ups and downs had some signal compensations, not the least of which was the deep pleasure enjoyed by both Evelyn and John in seeing so much of many dear friends, including the Vaughan Williams, Ursula and Ralph.

As Ursula Vaughan Williams has since reminded us:

> I was at the concert at the Albert Hall at which Ralph gave John the Royal Philharmonic Society's gold medal: this was in December 1950, and at the party afterwards I saw both John and Evelyn, though I did not meet them. Evelyn was tall, elegant and beautiful, a remarkable figure in a not so well-dressed collection of concert-goers.
>
> Later we met frequently, for Ralph's 'Sinfonia Antartica' had its first performance in Manchester, conducted by John, and we were up there for rehearsals as well as for the first performance. There were always dinner parties after concerts, and John was an enchanting host. He arranged the menu with extreme care and chose the wines. If anyone upset a glass he would rush to the place, dip his fingers in the flood and touch each person's forehead with a drop. I never discovered if it was a

Venetian custom, a spell against the Evil Eye or a ritual of his own devising.

Hallé rehearsals were long and frequent, so a new work, such as 'Antartica' and Ralph's Eighth Symphony, was thoroughly known and understood before the first performance, which made those occasions less alarming for the composer. Ralph showed John the score of No. 8 when the Barbirollis dined with us in London in 1955, just before they went to Australia. John was obviously interested, and when we were in Manchester for another concert during the following winter he arranged an evening session for us with the Hallé pianist, Rayson Whalley, who bravely played through the symphony from Ralph's manuscript—not an easily decipherable matter, but he did it. John then took us all out for a meal to some nearby café; to my surprised amusement all three men were delighted to find tripe on the menu, and so strengthened returned to another play-through of the score and further discussion.

When John took the sick cellist's place in the 'Sea Symphony' at Sheffield, Ralph, who conducted, was, of course, touched and delighted. The rehearsal was much enlivened by the leader of the Hallé, Laurance Turner, sending messages across to say that there was 'too much noise coming from the first desk!'

During these years Evelyn and I became friends, and there was little I enjoyed as much as the evenings we spent together, sometimes with Michael and Eslyn Kennedy as well. The Cheltenham festivals were enormous fun: all the extras—you might call them the fringe benefits of Festivals—the parties, the meetings for drinking and conversation after the concert was over, sitting with each other at the official garden parties, and the many other friends, Herbert Howells, Gerald and Joy Finzi, Anthony and Ruth Scott, John and Alice Sumsion . . . The combinations and permutations were endless, and great fun.

I had the pleasure of staying with Evelyn and John, after one of the concerts at the Free Trade Hall. We came out of the Artists' Entrance, John splendid in opera hat and full regalia, but when the door of their flat closed on the world he changed into grey flannels and produced a delicious supper for us; cooking was, he said, a good unwinding process after conducting.

Evelyn and he had collected a number of beautiful things, furniture, glass and pictures. One of Evelyn's finds was made on a West Country tour, a picture for which she paid £2 in a junk shop. When she returned to London she had it valued and was told it was worth £100. She naturally, felt that she had made a profit of £98 for further spending and of course she kept the picture. This form of arithmetic puzzled and outraged John, but I told him that it was a perfectly correct way of thinking. He shook his head over this, but he was too nice, or too bemused, to use the word innumerate which he obviously thought both Evelyn and I must be.

The last time we went to Cheltenham, in 1958, John gave a dinner party at their hotel on Cleeve Hill. The Kennedys were there, and driving up in the late twilight we stopped to get out of the car and see the gigantic splendour of the sunset, a strange vastness of crimson sky and ultramarine clouds, a solemnity that dissolved in the lively company of friends, but left with each of us an echo of foreboding, perhaps an intimation of 'look thy last on all things lovely'.

When Ralph died John was one of the very few people who saw him, as still as an effigy, and who came to the cremation service, where William McKie, organist of Westminster Abbey, played for us.

I went to Berlin once, for a week when John was conducting Ralph's No. 5 with the Berlin Philharmonic Orchestra. By this time John was eating as little as a dragonfly, as far as I could tell, and seemed to live on his nerves and draw nourishment only from music. One particularly endearing episode was when we came back to the hotel after the second of these concerts. It had been broadcast, and the hotel staff who had been listening surged round John with cries of admiration, touching him, thanking him, and obviously happy that he was once again staying in their hotel.

It was a firm friendship they all enjoyed and no Cheltenham

Festival was complete without the familiar personality of 'Uncle Ralph', as he had come to be generally called by musicians and those members of the musical public who admired the man and his work, and bathed in his kindly presence. He, in turn, loved his 'Glorious John'—his nickname for J.B.—and early in the morning at the start of each rehearsal, he would turn up to be one of the watchers who drank in the intoxicating sound of the Hallé. According to Ralph, there was no other 'sound' like that of J.B.'s Hallé and they, the V.W.s, spent never less than four days at the Festival. In 1958—which was his last visit—'Uncle Ralph' seemed to be at his best, his most alert, that massive frame and genial smile winning friends, as much in his mid-eighties as at any time in his long and splendid life that, like his friend's, had been devoted to music. With no more than a few more weeks to live, he was able to close his eyes and listen to his 'London' Symphony.

It was known to be regarded as the composer's favourite of all his nine symphonies; he confided to John that he thought it the best of the lot. But John was admiring of everything his friend wrote, and each enjoying the company of the other, their warm and cordial correspondence discloses a respect that cannot be exaggerated. Ursula has kept the letters received from their friends and a selection makes striking references to the Symphonies—music that both John and Evelyn found very special indeed:

> *My dear Ursula,* 4 October 1954
> . . . I was thrilled at the contents of Top Secret, though I fear that if Edinburgh have earmarked it for themselves they will want a first performance. However, whether it be Cheltenham or Edinburgh, you know what an honour and privilege I shall ever deem it to produce a work of V.W.'s.
>
> By the way, you might tell him that he has been much in our thoughts during this last tour as we have given several performances of No. 5. What a heavenly work it is. Sometimes I think perhaps one of the loveliest of them all.
>
> The performance in Salisbury Cathedral was an experience I don't think I shall ever forget, and I think he

would have been touched had he been there to see how deeply moved the players themselves were by it. In fact, at the end of the slow movement, I saw quite a few of them perilously near to tears.

Delighted to hear that Ralph is so fit and that you are keeping him to sea air and novels for the time being.

Evelyn joins me in best love to you both,

Ever, JOHN

My dear Ursula, 22 April 1955

A real thank-you is much harder to say than an ordinary conventional one. I do wish I could tell you more articulately how we loved being with you and V.W. last night. Please believe that we shall treasure that evening and hold it warmly and gratefully in our memories.

John is deeply touched to be entrusted with the Score. He couldn't resist having a look in the small hours of today! and says his first impressions are that he loves it. He wants to spend more time with it, though, and also he has a concert nearly every day before we leave for Australia on May 1st, but he will send it back then and write to V.W. soon after. I don't think that you and V.W. can have any real idea of how happy he is to have it now.

It was wonderful for me to be able to ask V.W. about oboe concerto bits and I can only hope Australia will prove conducive to fruitful practising for the recording.*

Thank you Ursula for showing me the house which is lovely—John and I are both covetting hard (or is it 'coveting'?)—and for such good food and drink. For a Mary to be such a good Martha is indeed wonderful. Bless you.

We send much love to you both and thank you again so very much.

EVELYN

PS: My apologies for our 'journeying' military paper.

*Vaughan Williams wrote to Evelyn Barbirolli about the recording of the oboe concerto saying: 'We listened to your record the other night and it is lovely. I cannot imagine anything better in the way of a performance. Thank you again . . .' (Dated July 1956).

My dear Ursula, 30 April 1955

. . . . I have had a good look at the Symphony and can quite *honestly* say (I realize V.W.'s insistence on this) that I am greatly intrigued by it; although absolutely authentic V.W. it has touches of most charming originality, both in harmony and orchestral texture, as well as some very lovely music.

The four movements are excellently contrasted, in the rather etherealized opening and closing of the first movement, the most attractive march for wind and brass, and a really beautiful slow movement, whilst the finale should prove extremely effective in performance

I can only hope and pray now that he won't decide to tear it up when he looks at it again.

I know Evelyn has already written to you about our evening together. I can only add that it will remain for ever a treasured memory.

My best love to you both,

Yours ever, JOHN

My dear Ralph, 20 June 1956

We leave for Italy again on Thursday, as I shan't work again (*hoorah!*) until Palermo on the 25th. But this is really to say 'thank you' for your sweet thought in sending me the printed F.S. of my beloved No. 8 with its inscription. Another prized possession.

Much love to you both, in which Evelyn joins.

Ever, JOHN

My dear Ralph, Friday, 2 November 1956

I have been wanting to write ever since we spent that wonderful day with No. 8, but we have had a continuous run of concerts and travelling since then, which I have unfortunately had to face with a severe bronchial chill, and, to cap it all, '*lumbago*' for the last three days. So every spare moment I have had to try and rest a little . . . Last Tuesday was rather a 'black day', when lo, your adorable, inimitable letter arrived, and I was enabled to set forth again in renewed strength. Ralph, I feel rather shy in the face of all the honour you have done me, and my lack of words must measure the depth of my gratitude for the Symphony, the MS and your faith and confidence. We have had quite a V.W. week since the 7th. Two performances (Bradford and Wolverhampton) of 'Wenlock Edge' (Richard Lewis) and 'Tallis' last night (Leicester). 'Wenlock' sounded magical, I think, with orchestra (the texture is more lovely and appropriate and never too thick if properly played). Richard sang most beautifully and it had the greatest success. Parts were full of wrong notes, but all is correct now. We do it again in Manchester in April, and would like to record it if you consent. No. 8 is, I am sure, going to be a great success, and we are all waiting for May 2 and 3. Hanley, Newcastle and London follow immediately.

Best love to you both,

Ever, JOHN

PS: Must congratulate Roy (O.U.P.) on the extraordinary accuracy of the parts of No. 8.

And a short time later, at the end of November, John was writing to Ursula one of his 'fun' letters, this time enclosing a photograph of 'Uncle Ralph' rather ornately attired in satin robes and wearing a skull-cap, looking not unlike a picture of the recent peasant Pope, 'John the Good', as he was called—that had been clipped from a copy of an English illustrated periodical:

My dear Ursula, 21 November 1956

Why have you kept it from us, that Ralph had been created a Prince of the Church!!?

Much love, JOHN

Early in the New Year, also from Manchester, John was writing again:

My dear Ralph, 11 February 1957

After our Festival Hall Concert tomorrow I am off (with Evelyn) to Scandinavia, and give No. 8 in Gothenburg on the 21st. Also I am giving it its first Zürich performance on May 17th. We played it last night at the Free Trade Hall to an enormous audience and the greatest enthusiasm. I wonder how many symphonies have become so immediately loved?

Do hope you both keep well.

Am fine now and happy and grateful to be back at work.

Much love to you both

Ever, JOHN

PS: Cheltenham Panel have chosen a symphony by one of my boys, Arthur Butterworth (2nd trumpet) *without* any prompting from me; probably would have had the obverse effect. Feel rather pleased.

John was constantly being encouraged by audience reactions to write and let his old friend share the experience of emotional gatherings in crowded and unusual places:

My dear Ralph, 5 October 1957 (here till Oct 12)
I feel I must write and tell you what an incredibly moving experience it has been to play your Tallis Fantasia in the Cathedrals of Winchester, Exeter and Truro these last few days. I don't want to sound fulsome (for how you would hate it) but your genius never seems to flower so exquisitely as it does in such surroundings. The orchestra join me in humble and grateful thanks.

I have been studying the 'London' for your birthday concert and what a lovely work it is. As a genuine 'Cockney' I am in a position to know!! Tried the 'Flourish' through the other day and it sounds *grand*.

My love and blessings to you both, and I am happy to gather you are now fully recovered.

Ever, JOHN

In the following month he was renewing V.W.'s birthday celebrations by evoking his 'Uncle Ralph's' presence on the day itself:

My dear Ralph, 4 November 1957
Thank you for your lovely note.

I don't think I need tell you what a joy it was to have you and Ursula with us for your Birthday Concert, an occasion we shall all remember with affectionate gratitude, in that we were privileged to honour in our Centenary *the greatest of living composers.*

What wonderful news about No. 9. Let us know as soon as it becomes available (after its initial performances) and eager hands will be clutching for the score.

Best love to you both in which Evelyn joins.

Yours ever, JOHN

There were many letters couched in a similar vein, as well as scores of postcards and telegrams that passed between the two friends. In 1957 a card from Zürich announced that:

> The Tonhalle Orchestra here gave magnificent perf. of *our* No. 8 last night. Press and public and orchestra most enthusiastic. Evelyn joins in much love to you both.
>
> Ever, JOHN

and a sample of the type of postcards that came through the post was one from Innsbruck in 1958:

> Your and *my* 8th! had a great reception in Prague, Warsaw and Lodz (where next day I hear the local orchestra rehearsing the Antartica). Am now on my way to Lisbon, where it has to have its first performance. You know, Ralph, I love it more and more. Looking forward to No. 9. Much love both,
>
> JOHN

It was the spirit of looking forward towards the few years remaining for Ralph, also, that prompted John to send a cable from Swansea to the composer on his eighty-fifth birthday:

> GREETINGS TEL: DR RALPH VAUGHAN WILLIAMS O.M. 10 HANOVER TERRACE, NW1 ALL THE MEMBERS OF YOUR DEVOTED HALLÉ ORCHESTRA JOIN ME AND EVELYN IN SENDING YOU OUR AFFECTIONATE GREETINGS AND WISHES ON THIS GREAT OCCASION OF YOUR 85TH BIRTHDAY
>
> JOHN

Vaughan Williams was very soon to die in the arms of Ursula.

She, realizing how deep the Barbirolli friendship was, immediately picked up the first thing that came to hand and wrote a pencilled note so that they should hear the news before all others.

26th August 1958

John dear, I want to tell you, before everyone knows, that Ralph died early this morning—he didn't suffer and the doctor who was there says it was coronory thrombosis—he had no realization that he was ill, just restlessness and he had a most normal day yesterday. We had just had a lovely week with Joy Finzi, who took us to Stonehenge, and into Dorset, which he loved—the country looked so rich and ample and golden—and over the Berkshire downs. All this time he has worked, and been with friends, and we have had no illness, or lowering of mental capacity to face—it has been absolutely lovely and I was with him all the time, and he died at home, in his own room, just before the dawn.

Will you tell the orchestra and give them my love? He was always so happy being with you and them.

My dear love to you and Evelyn.

URSULA

20 *Disappointment and Success*

'However long he stayed away and however far he travelled, his heart remained in Manchester,' wrote Charles Reid, the music critic. The 1950s and 1960s were a period in which John and Evelyn were often away from their adopted home as his fame spread, and in which the Hallé undertook more and more successful concerts.

It was also a period in which John and Evelyn found that what they had thought was a friendship was betrayed. Following Ernest Bean's move to the Royal Festival Hall in 1948, Kenneth Crickmore had taken over his position with the

Hallé. Crickmore had been invalided out of the Services, and then became Secretary of the Sheffield Philharmonic Society, from where he was able to become familiar with both the Hallé set-up and with J.B. While he was a shrewd and far-sighted business manager at a time when business imagination was needed upon both Barbirolli's and the Hallé's behalf, he was unscrupulous in using his position of trust for his own benefit.

Sidney Rothwell, who was for a time John's personal assistant and is still a trusted friend of Evelyn's, was well-placed to see just what was happening. (Despite the shared surname, he is not related to Evelyn.)

> I was in at the beginning of what one should, I suppose, describe as the Crickmore Saga. Crickmore came into the Hallé/J.B. ambit after his service career in the RAF, and a brief period as a cinema manager. He came via the Sheffield Subscription Concerts which were, and still are, an integral part of the Hallé scene. It was soon obvious to those behind the scenes that Crickmore was only there to feather his own nest. Obvious, that is, to all except J.B., who—once he had made a friend—went on trusting until it was manifestly clear that the friend was in fact an enemy. In 1948 Crickmore was appointed to be J.B.'s personal manager—a post that had not existed before. To my knowledge, the closest J.B. had come to having someone—other than Evelyn—as his 'representative'. (she was his secretary, chauffeuse and many other things as well), was with John Woolford, his wonderful secretary in New York who became (and remained till his death) a dear and trusted friend. Crickmore was different: he carved out for himself, unquestionably, a controlling influence, almost Svengali-like, I should say, where J.B. was concerned. The irony of those early days—1945 to 1948—was that Crickmore was even then known in the trade as a 'musical spiv'. That was the expression applied to him.
>
> The litigation that followed J.B.'s discovery that Crickmore had been 'cooking the books', was a traumatic episode in the lives of Evelyn and John. It was also a horrifying experience to have to fight in the American courts, with all the expense involved. Rosalind Booth,

who had been J.B.'s secretary, had now become Mrs. Crickmore—they had married in the United States—and her subsequent action in fighting the Barbirollis, as his widow, contained her claims: a) that they had defrauded Crickmore of his rightful earnings; b) accelerated his death by their wrongful and thoughtless treatment of him; c) deprived them, the Crickmores, of all their liquid capital. It is generally known that J.B. died, leaving virtually no capital—no estate. The measure and the flavour of this episode is best summed up by Evelyn herself, when she told me that grievous though the loss of what was virtually a fortune had been, it was nothing compared with the pain of experiencing a betrayal of a valued friendship.

It was on their tours in the United Kingdom and abroad that John took risks at the box office that few other conductors were prepared to take. Many gambles paid handsome dividends. He was to voice his feelings about Vaughan Williams, Elgar, Sibelius and their like of the day-before-yesterday, as well as the William Waltons and the Humphrey Searles of that time, when he spoke on 'Musical Taste' in the Sixties:

> All in all, I think we in Britain are the most catholic-minded musical public in the world today. But publicity ventures of the Musica Viva type are a waste of public money, for they lead nowhere and have already died what I would call a timely death.

And when, at about the same time, Colin Mason was celebrating Barbirolli's reign at the Hallé in the *Guardian* under the heading 'Barbirolli and the Hallé' (1 July, 1963) then, one felt, it was time to put out more flags:

> The orchestra has much to be grateful for to Barbirolli. During his first ten years it was consistently the equal of any orchestra in Britain, and perhaps the most consistently excellent of them all. Since then it has had its

ups and downs, the last great 'up' being the centenary season in 1957–8 . . .

John had left EMI (HMV) to record for Pye—a company which offered him and the Hallé a very wide choice of repertory. Evelyn and John now renewed contracts with EMI, and three major works were recorded during twelve months. The Sunday series in Manchester showed an even bigger jump in popularity and increased income. The public Orchestral Rehearsal series continued and in the mid-week series also the Society presented many works which John had introduced, now firm favourites with the public after his score of years as conductor-in-chief. At the first Sunday Concert on 29 September 1963, John was presented with the Hallé's Gold Medal in recognition of his twenty years with the Orchestra. There was a special twenty-first anniversary concert to follow and in this season 189 public concerts were performed including school concerts, broadcasts, recording and television sessions.

Recordings with HMV included *Gerontius*, *Butterfly*, *Otello*, the Brahms Symphonies, Verdi's Requiem, Mahler's Fifth, Sixth and Ninth Symphonies, as well as Purcell's *Dido and Aeneas*. The company, greatly elated by the result of the new contract, now intended to use the Hallé as much as possible for future recordings.

During this time, the early and mid-sixties, John was busily working on a performing edition of Bach's 'St Matthew' Passion. In all it had occupied him for over five years and he finally gave the first performance of it at the Free Trade Hall, Manchester on 26 March 1961 with Janet Baker. (In 1967 they did Verdi's Requiem together.)

He was serious, almost solemn, when he prepared himself for such occasions, but his ebullience was constantly recurring despite the gravity of the theme. Michael Davis recalled meeting J.B. one evening after he had played Mahler's Symphony No. 2 ('Resurrection') at the Festival Hall:

'I passed Barbirolli in the corridor and he said "we showed 'em tonight, didn't we?"'

Indeed, the London Symphony Orchestra still talks about him not only with great respect, but with a touching affection.

Much of 1967 was spent in Israel—in 1965, at a Toscanini memorial concert given in Manchester by the Jewish National Fund, John had been presented with a piece of land in Netua, Upper Galilee. It was to be called Barbirolli in recognition of his service to the Israeli Philharmonic Orchestra. 'He always longed to see his land,' said Evelyn, 'but, sadly, when he visited Israel for the last time, just after the successful Six-Day War, that part of the country was still being shelled intermittently and no civilian was allowed to go there.'

Evelyn went with him on this trip to Israel. (Her reports sent back to England at this time make arresting reading; if she had not adopted the oboe, might she have made a good foreign correspondent? Her graphic and sympathetic accounts of a country recovering from war lead one to suspect that she might have done.) She was also with him on another major foreign adventure . . .

In 1960 John had been appointed conductor-in-chief of the Houston Symphony Orchestra, the beginning of a friendship with that Texan city crowned with instantaneous success, and less than ten years later he was made conductor emeritus for life.

Both Evelyn and John quickly became famous as locals, were taken by the generous people of Texas to their hearts and were recognized wherever they went as two accomplished artists.

Tom M. Johnson, for many years manager of the orchestra, recalled their friendship with him and his wife, Kathleen. J.B., shortly after his arrival, paid him a compliment reserved for those to whom he felt attached:

> The 'me boy' bit came about early in our association. Sir John was sixty and I was forty-seven. He began to call me 'me boy', but I transferred the appellation to him, whereupon he referred to me as 'Dad'. While this was amusing to many it also proved to be confusing on occasions. Early one morning at a small town airport, Sir John was 'putting' about the lobby with his cane while Evelyn and I were fixing the tickets. Overhearing my reference to 'me boy', the man at the counter handed me the tickets for 'yourself, the lady, and your son'.

At restaurants he was known as an expert chef himself, who would enjoy good food and who knew earnestly what he wanted and was prepared to go to pains to get it—even to the extent of a specific item that the dining room, or diner, might not happen to have.

He once described with much affection how his mother cooked ham. Curiously enough it sounded much like an old recipe that my wife's mother had used. So when he came to dinner, the dish was put in front of them both: Evelyn was overjoyed, and John was unbelieving. When 'Me boy' and his Missus left us later that night, the remains of the ham were tucked under his arm like a fiddle case!

But it had not been easy to get J.B. signed up. He was Conductor Laureate of the Hallé still, and his loyalties were equally owed to London and Manchester; to his birthplace and to his showplace for so many years past. The British Press had a field-day speculating whether or not they would ever see J.B again as a permanent fixture at the Hallé, and coming only two years after the Hallé Centenary celebrations his Texas appointment had made front-page headlines. *The Times* proclaimed 'Sir John Barbirolli For Texas' and the *Daily Telegraph* 'Sir John To Conduct U.S. Orchestra', while the *Guardian* had 'Sir John's New Post' and the *Daily Mail* treated the story as if it belonged to the financial pages: 'Take-Over Bid for Barbirolli: Texas orchestra wants Sir John full-time!'

But John and Evelyn never had any desire to settle permanently anywhere else in the world but England, though the new conductor's debut was treated as one of the most significant events in the Houston orchestra's history. Special red white and blue bills announced:

The Grand Alliance!
SIR JOHN BARBIROLLI
conducts the
HOUSTON SYMPHONY ORCHESTRA
Season 1961–62

The bills went on to cite other attractions: guest conductors of the calibre of Kostelanetz and Rachlin would be assisting

Barbirolli during the season with its thirty-two 'great concerts'. Among the soloists to appear would be Evelyn Rothwell, oboist.

The outcome of that first limited contract was another longer one that would engage, intermittently, the services of J.B. throughout the frantically busy decade of the Sixties. There were short periods when Evelyn and John had time off from Manchester, New York, Germany and Texas, and one of their regular activities was to take part in the King's Lynn Festival, founded and organized by their friend Ruth Fermoy (herself an accomplished pianist). John would conduct orchestral concerts, and take part as a cellist in a chamber concert with Ruth and Evelyn and others.

It was in Texas, while he was rehearsing the Houston Symphony Orchestra during the day, that news was brought to John and Evelyn of the assassination of President John F. Kennedy.

The orchestra's principal viola player (Wayne Crouse, a close friend) wrote:

> Sir John said many comforting things to us about the terrible tragedy that had struck us that day. He was a student of our Abraham Lincoln and knew many of his quotations, some of which he uttered in praise of Lincoln at the memorial concert we gave a few days later.
>
> One last thing: Sir John was in Houston on his seventieth birthday—there were many celebrations when he returned to England, but he was here in Texas on his birthday—and it coincided with a series of Berlioz Centenary concerts, and I was fortunate in being the soloist in *Harold in Italy*. The entire audience stood and sang 'Happy Birthday' when he came on stage and it was obvious to all that he was very touched. That night we gave him a birthday meal of fresh salmon and hollandaise sauce.

Of that time, also, Fredell Lack Eichhorn who was a well-known violinist herself and a teacher at several American universities, recalled:

> Although I was soloist—a great privilege for any musician—playing with the Hallé under Sir John, I knew Evelyn especially well because she played chamber music with us so often. I was so in awe of him that I often couldn't talk intelligently in his presence. And yet he was not an awesome person. No more simple, natural, unaffected being ever lived; the one conductor I've known (among many) who was not consumed with vanity, ego and a power complex.
>
> In any other one of the performing arts he could have been a great comedian, for he had that wonderful mobile 'rubber' face that could easily assume any expression from moment to moment. He could use crude expressions without being ever crude. I felt personally, and this seemed to be the general consensus of opinion out in Texas when he paid us visits which were so rewarding because he brought his darling and talented Evelyn with him, that he could make the most elegant and sophisticated and heartrendingly sensitive music and with all that talent and charm on the one side there was the precision and emotional temperament on the other. What a combination! Texas still talks about him today, in 1982.
>
> It was our good fortune to have known them both as people who became the city's friends as well as—during their times here—its most important musicians.

During the Sixties, John was less and less with his favourite of all orchestras, through his foreign commitments, recordings and work in London. It was during this period that he received the award of Companion of Honour from the Queen, when he discussed with her the finer points of the cello, an instrument that Prince Charles had learned to play.

John kept going at a great pace; he slept little, and in his waking hours he had a fund of energy he insisted on calling upon—however tired he might have been inside. For ever on the alert, he displayed a ferocious galvanizing drive when working, never letting anyone think that he might be tired. This vitality forbade any of those with whom he came in contact to droop or show signs of listlessness. His very last recording session was at the Kingsway Hall in London, less than a fortnight before his death, where he was working on an old favourite, Delius' *Appalachia.*

21 *J.B. And His Friends*

To Barbirolli the word friendship meant something special. He expected loyalty from those who were his friends and once he had given of his own he was a friend for life. (It was this aspect which had laid him open to exploitation by Crickmore.) Perhaps his rather exaggerated view of friendship was because the old melodrama was in his blood—in his love of the live stage, his hero-worship of such giants, in his view, as Winston Churchill, Pablo Casals (whom he considered the cello's greatest exponent), Henry Irving, Lord Nelson.

He had many friends: 'Billy' Douglas the surgeon, Herbert Walenn his old cello teacher, Ralph Vaughan Williams, Kathleen Ferrier, Sam Oddy the Cockney greengrocer (he was J.B's 'mate' during the last years of his life, and, with his wife, continued the friendship with Evelyn), Sidney Rothwell, Philip Godlee, Tom Johnson, Beatrice Hancock, Michael Kennedy, Valda Aveling, Audrey Napier-Smith, Ernest Bean, Clive Smart, Laurance Turner, Janet Craxton, C. B. Rees, Natalie James, Ronald Kinloch Anderson, Geraint Evans, Janet Baker, Margaret and Hubert Furtwängler, and many score of others who must figure in any assessment of his life.

Nothing was more rewarding for him to feel than that he could count upon his friends. When let down by any of those he trusted, he was greatly wounded for months on end. As he was never disloyal to his friends, he argued, why should they be disloyal to him? A few of them remained white in his eyes long after they should have appeared a darker hue.

The last letter ever written by the actress, Yvonne Arnaud, concerned John's friendship. Sent off to her husband, Hugh McClellan, from the Midland Hotel, Manchester, where she was on tour with a play being tried out before coming into the West End, it was dated 4 May 1958.

On 24 August 1959 Martinu's Concerto for Oboe and Orchestra received its first public performance in England when John conducted the Hallé in an Albert Hall promenade concert, and Evelyn played the solo part. (Below) A chamber music concert for charity at Bramham Park, Yorkshire, in July 1962, with (l. to r.) J.B., Ruth, Lady Fermoy, Evelyn (turning over), Martin Milner, Sydney Errington, Joseph Segal. This concert was soon to be repeated at the King's Lynn Festival.

also Page 101 to number 22 + Page 117 number 33

3rd movt (I almost forgot this!)

Page 58 Fig (14). I have tried the following at rehearsal and found it a more satisfactory sound, but would not like to adopt it without your approval.

8va lower

loco

the tuba same as the contra + seems to blend better, but you may not like this.

J.B. and Vaughan Williams worked together closely. Here are John's notes on part of the composer's Eighth Symphony, and (below) the two men pore over the *Sinfonia Antartica* during a Festival Hall rehearsal.

BBC Hulton Picture L

Her mannerisms in the 1st movt. of Franck

very distracting, + frankly rather unpleasant.

The 2nd movt however had many v. good

qualities, especially in one so young.

Debussy Sonata

In this performance there is no gainsaying

her great talent musically + instrumentally

but she needs really first rate ~~musically~~

musical guidance in the next two years

say, years which are vital for her.

7 July 1961 signed [signature]

JB's audition notes on 7th July 1961

J.B. was one of the first to spot the talent of the youthful Jacqueline du Pré, as his audition notes made in 1961 show. (Below) His friend Ronald Kinloch Anderson, head producer at EMI, masterminded many of J.B.'s recordings. Here the two men confer with an older Jacqueline du Pré.

David Farrell

Hermann Ran

Encouraging, admonishing, controlling – J.B. taking a rehearsal of the Houston Symphony Orchestra.

Hermann Randolph

Hermann Ran

An evocative picture of J.B. taken in the 1960s. He loved this photograph, and used to say that it couldn't be of anyone else's back.

Perpetuating a famous name still, Evelyn Barbirolli – as she is now known – is seen here accepting a boxed set of J.B.'s recordings; and at the presentation of a conducting triptych to the Town Hall, Manchester, with the sculptor Byron Howard – who also did the excellent bust in the Royal Festival Hall.

Evelyn as teacher (above), after a master class, and as performer with Iris Loveridge (The Barbirolli Duo).

Evelyn with Sir Charles Groves, Sir Lennox Berkeley and Sir Geraint Evans in 1980 in the effort to keep music 'live'.

Lady Barbirolli, then President of the Incorporated Society of Musicians, picketed for the Musicians Union in the fight to retain BBC orchestras. Deeply involved with music and musicians at all levels, she is determined to speak out for what she knows to be right.

My darling, Sunday 10 pm

I'll continue this in the morning, but how I wish you could have been here, as you would have enjoyed the music *so* much. I told John and he wrote that little message in the programme. He treated me as if I had been the Queen of Sheba! As generous and kind as ever.

I go to bed now, full of the most divinely *played* music. It did me good to refresh my mind with something so beautiful. It was a grand evening.

Good night, my darling.

Yv.

Yvonne Arnaud was an accomplished pianist, who frequently achieved the insertion into straight plays in which she appeared of a sequence where she was able to play sometimes to accompany her singing of songs. As a child prodigy she had won first prize for piano-playing at the Paris Conservatoire in 1905. Knowing of her admiration for the conductor, her widower sent on this last letter to John three years after his wife's death. It now lies inside a book about Yvonne—a short memoir—on Evelyn's bookshelf.

Friendship was much prized also by Evelyn. She, too, when she made a friend made one for life. To both friendship came naturally, but not lightly; they took time in that most difficult of tasks, knowing another human being. Acquaintances (those who merely admired, camp followers and the like) were never confused with friends. But the two were always prepared to take people as they found them; they would rarely sit in judgement, and then only when principle was at stake.

Family was important as another source of friendship. John never liked being away from his family for long, and would make every effort, wherever he was and whatever he was doing, to be with them. There were long walks in the spiky cold air of the Sussex he loved, which his niece Cecilie Jaggard later recalled with nostalgia. (Cecilie, daughter of Peter Barbirolli and his wife Pat, married sound recordist Timothy Jaggard. Their son Jonathan is a horn player, the only musician in the family's younger generation.)

Pat Barbirolli can reminisce indefinitely about their beloved J.B.'s culinary propensities, and about a thousand and one things that were said and done in Mémé's warm, lovable and friendly household. 'Like many, but not all, great men he was simple at heart and enjoyed it all because of his great love of the family,' she said. John certainly enjoyed being at Mémé's home, or at his brother Peter's flat in London; he also enjoyed haunting second-hand bookshops or browsing with Evelyn, frequenting antique shops and looking for that glassware they both loved to collect. Reading biography, attending the law courts, caught up by a fascination with medicine—these were other aspects of his life.

He preferred, like Evelyn, being away from consciously arty musical people wearing their culture like a badge; from the beginning he never cared much about 'reputation'. He had a horror of being cornered at some 'posh' reception and asked to define his music. He preferred talking to his own chums, his boys in the band.

His music and the composers he revered were in part responsible for that process of self-awareness and exploration of others' character, rather than mere theorizing and pontificating. Philosophies are sometimes ascribed to conductors, as to composers, but John never climbed on to a podium, delivered a speech or wrote about a piece of music with the idea that he might be expounding a theory or a philosophy. Though he was an exponent of so much great music, and showman enough not to discard the pomp and the circumstance (arriving at a Lord Mayor's banquet to a blare of trumpets, for instance), the memories of him that linger longest are of the small things.

To his niece Cecilie, going to his hired-for-the-summer-house in East Sussex was always fun. 'Uncle Johnny slouched around in his oldest clothes and bedroom slippers when indoors. There were his simple Italian dishes, too, and rough Italian wine or equally simple English fare.'

His admiration for those he knew personally among statesmen, such as Churchill and Roosevelt, vied with that for Disraeli and Gladstone, with whom he was acquainted only through reading biographies. Sidney Rothwell, his private secretary at the time of Roosevelt's death, recalled:

> On the day that Roosevelt died, the Orchestra was playing in Chester Cathedral, and I had an urgent telephone call from Wally Jones to bring the music of

'The Star-Spangled Banner' so that the Orchestra could play this in tribute to Roosevelt. I grabbed the music and took the train to Chester. In the event, John did not use the music but chose instead to dedicate to Roosevelt the performance of the slow movement of the 'Eroica', which was in the programme.

Rothwell, who talked about his old chief in tones of awe and admiration, also remembered his great love of Corot and said he was remarkably well informed about which art galleries had the best collections of his paintings. 'There may well be an affinity here with his capacity for interpreting Delius.' He also recounted a characteristic example of John's spontaneous generosity.

Shortly after the first Edinburgh Festival in 1947, when the Hallé was the star orchestra, a letter arrived from Hertha Balling, saying how pleased she was to have read that the orchestra of which her husband had been the conductor from 1912 to 1914 was still flourishing. (I should mention here that there was a marked disparity in their ages, Hertha being only nineteen when they were married, Balling himself approaching fifty; he died of pneumonia shortly afterwards through fulfilling an engagement at Bayreuth when he ought to have been in bed.)

She said that she had treasured the mementos of his Hallé period—including all the programmes of his concerts—but they had been lost in the air raid that destroyed by fire the major part of Darmstadt.

John immediately wrote to the *Manchester Guardian* asking if anyone having copies of the programmes of the period would let him have them to send on to Hertha Balling; and Edward Isaacs, who had the complete set, said he was very willing to give them to her. The problem then arose of getting them to Germany, because at that time communications were extremely difficult. Here, again John was resourceful and arranged with the British Council to have them sent to Darmstadt in the diplomatic bag.

Beatrice (Lady Hancock) remembered John from before his Scottish engagement, when he was a friend and colleague of her first husband, André Mangeot, in whose chamber orchestra Beatrice Mangeot had herself been a talented violinist at one time. She recalled for us in a tape-recorded interview what he had been like nearly fifty earlier.

> He used to talk a lot in those days, and I heard him tell André that I had my bow on the string, and I thought "What does he mean?" And then I saw what he meant. This is what he got from his string players: instead of the way string players go crash if it's a big chord—crash, scratch, double-stopping—which is horrible, he got them to curve into a big chord. You don't go bang, you come in on course, and when you're nicely there, you let the strings and the bows have it.
>
> But you can't *just* attack—you would almost stop the sound as so many fiddlers do, even the best. Anyway, that's what he taught all his string players.

According to Beatrice, it was the *bowing* which really produced the 'Barbirolli Sound', so well-known to musicians.

> His contemporaries. I suppose, are all dying off, but it must have come down in musical circles. The Barbirolli orchestras were known for their wonderful strings. He married Evelyn because she was jolly nice and pretty and all those things, but I'm sure he also married 'the sound'—because *her* oboe has got the Barbirolli *sound* . . . Although I met him regualrly at André's, I didn't, for the many years before Evelyn appeared on the scene, really get to know John. Here was I, on the corner, in this house of music, and he was just one of the people who came in. And I thought, 'You're a darling little Italian, I'm afraid of you because you play the cello like an angel and you're important and who am I?' I was just emerging from the student 'scene'. I was also an Australian; unsophisticated to an extraordinary degree, so that I really wished to creep away.

But she didn't creep away, and the young violinist, who had

had her profession forced on her by an over-zealous father, began her real education in musical discrimination.

J.B.'s friendship with André Mangeot seems to have been of the kind that thrives on frequent heated arguments:

> My husband had a quartet, and John played in it for a while, but by the time I met him he was not playing in the quartet. He was, of course, still a friend of André's. And he used to come to Cresswell Place, where we lived, to have jolly musical evenings. They'd snatch up their instruments, and there was always a quartet. Everybody played something in those days.

Percy Grainger, the composer of so much that was melodious, was an admirer of Barbirolli, and after writing to the conductor a letter of praise for his interpretation of Delius' *Dance Rhapsody*, 'Such satisfying speeds, such faithfulness of moods—one might wait long to hear such a faithful, sympathetic and inspiring rendition as yours', he was asked how he compared Beecham and Barbirolli, to which he replied, 'I wouldn't work with Tommy—his eyes are too "brown"—but Johnnie—ah, there's another cup of tea!'

J.B. played Grainger, and Lehár's popular waltz *Gold and Silver*, and, best of the lot, the lovely lilting Strauss dance tunes of another era, long past, when he played solos at the annual Hallé Ball. At its centenary festival ball in 1958, few soloists could have received the thunderous applause that he did after his own version of the old McCormack song, played on the cello, *I Hear You Calling Me.*

Among his close personal friends and professional colleagues, no singer was ever quite to win his admiration and affection to the same extent as his adored Kathleen Ferrier. 'My beloved Katie', he would call her. But his respect and high regard for Janet Baker led him upon more than one occasion to dub her the greater singer. According to Michael Kennedy, 'His professional honesty forbade him to say otherwise.' It was the same Janet who, on 27 September 1970 when *The Dream of Gerontius* was performed in his memory, broke down and wept.

Those who admired the man and felt protective of his talent were forever fretting about his moods, his sleeplessness, the manner in which he drove himself. 'Don't overdo it,' they would urge, and invite him to share their relaxations. This message gave him great pleasure:

> The three of us are celebrating a superb concert and wish to conclude the evening by including the raison d'être—our maestro.

It was a note in pencil handed to J.B. by the doorman at the Free Trade Hall from three of the Orchestra in the pub opposite the hall, hopefully awaiting his arrival at the bar to join his pals—Pat Ryan and Len Regan (first and second clarinets) and Charles Cracknell (first bassoon). But John always liked to go home after a concert, to have his one meal of the day; or if he was away, he liked to return to his hotel room for a picnic supper.

The way in which he put so much into his work aroused the protective instincts of Ernest Bean (among others), as this letter he sent, together with some antiquarian lyrics he thought John would enjoy, for his birthday in 1946 showed:

> *My dear John,* Merionethshire 2 Dec 1946
> Yours must seem at times an ephemeral act—intensive preparation for a Concert. Then the performance! Tumultuous applause and what is left but that vague depression of spirit which so often follows in the wake of violent disturbance—a depression only to be overcome by starting the cycle all over again? In black moods you may sometimes wonder if anything remains which can compare with the tangible fruits left by one's creature artists—sculptures, paintings, poetry, quartets. You know, of course, there is something left just as abiding though less tangible and communicable: an awakening of the spirit in perhaps half a dozen hearts. The beginning of an unending Iliad in the life of some youngster hearing the 5th for the first time. But just because the fruits of your work are so unpredictable and unseen I sometimes fear that you can't go on giving out your energy and recovering so little in (tangible) return without suffering from what the agriculturalists call 'exhaustion of soil'.
>
> Basking in acclamations of applause is not a substitute

for quiet refreshment of spirit which you need. It merely continues the process of 'giving out'. That is when I am often so dumb and ineffectual in my spoken appreciation after a concert. I have a wish to clear the room of all those who have gathered to praise Caesar—the sincere and insincere alike. And to whisk you away to some bower of quietness, where all your agitated molecules can be ironed out; where JB, the crowds, the personal aspects of your triumph can be shed completely and you can enjoy that refreshment of mind you need—unless you are to justify Dickens's belief in the possibility of a man going up in spontaneous combustion! That—in a few words—is what I wanted to find, a birthday gift which would take you a million miles—in space and time—from the arc lights of Belle Vue. I haven't found what I wanted, but a few of these ancient lyrics may give you pleasure, so here they are with my love and all good wishes for you 45th birthday, as ever,

ERNEST

PS: You'll find no farts set to music. But there is the same earthiness to rejoice the spirit, in one or two.

Brenda Bracewell was John Barbirolli's secretary from 1961 to 1970:

To work for the Barbirollis was to work *with* them. They were friends, and I was regarded as a friend of them both for the last nine years of his life. John became a sort of surrogate father. I think, looking back, that I worshipped him really, and talking about him even now makes me very distressed.

I remember staying with them in their apartment in Houston; I felt very much part of the family. Lady B. cooked a scrumptious dinner on our first Sunday, helped a little by J.B. and me; we went shopping for those lovely avocados which J.B. delightedly said were only tuppence as against about three shillings in Manchester! I also fondly recollect two evenings when I went out with some young people from the Houston Symphony offices—when I was collected from the apartment and both J.B. and Lady B. welcomed them inside and chatted to them

> before seeing me off for the evening.
>
> He would deny himself essential things, for he often used to say to me that one of his main aims in life was to provide for Lady B. and his family; this really did become an obsession with him, after the Crickmore affair and the financial insecurity it brought in its wake.
>
> He had a great love for traditional things. He hated so many of the hideous modern buildings that had been substituted for those which were beautiful to look at. He was a true Cockney and had a possessive pride in London and its places and traditions, its landmarks and its smells, shapes and colours—and he seemed to yearn for the past. He would rail angrily at the changes 'because everywhere I now go I notice a change'. It was true that the concrete jungles had taken over, London was desecrated and the spoliation of the big city had been copied by the smaller cities and country towns, where once there had been a rustic grace and well-mannered discipline.
>
> He would have me write to the city fathers in various places warning them that he would never return to play good music if this was how they intended to go on ruining *his* England. Why should festival organizers expect those with artistic feelings to play for them in settings which were no longer lovely—and which in time would become more hideous still?

It is interesting to speculate what John's feeling would have been had he lived long enough to contemplate the Barbirolli Street and Hallé Square, prominent features of the ultra-modern Arndale Centre in today's Manchester. He would doubtless have felt honoured by his adopted city's choice of name, but would almost certainly have wished for a different style of architecture.

He loved London, especially his own area in WC1 (where once one heard nearly as much Italian spoken as Cockney) that spread around Southampton Row, Theobalds Road, Lambs Conduit Street, Russell Square and Queen Square. Even after the Second World War, when it had been knocked about so much, it still retained some of its former charm and personality. J.B.'s love for London is touched upon by yet another friend:

> I well remember during the winter of 1947 I made my first visit to London and John met me somewhere near Fleet Street and took me on a personally conducted tour, arm in arm, round the area of the Law Courts and Lincoln's Inn Fields in particular. The night was dark and the ground covered with snow—just like an evening out of Dickens. The climax of the tour was in Gough Square when, with the air of entering Aladdin's cave, he revealed with a magnificently theatrical gesture his *pièce de résistance*—the house of Dr Johnson! As you can imagine, this was quite an experience and what was particularly touching was John's proprietorial sense of identification with everything—as though he had built it all himself!

He also recalled that as they left Gough Square and were traversing a plank across a trench which some workmen were digging there was some spirited repartee between John and the navvies.

And here are two ancedotes of Casals and J.B. by a friend of both, one amusing and one rather touching:

> During Casals' first visit to England after the War in 1945 he played at Belle Vue and was taking the midnight train to London. John saw him off on a dreary, wintry night at London Road Station, where a couple of drunks, observing him carrying his cello, said, 'Give us a tune, guv'nor!' Casals, in a good-natured aside to John said, 'Zey will not be so merry in ze morning!'
>
> Travelling down from London in the summer of 1969 I met John on the train and noticed that one of the lenses of his glasses was broken. He told me that he had just come from the Puerto Rico Festival, where he had been conducting with Casals. At the end of one particularly outstanding performance Casals had hugged him with such ferocity that he had broken his lens, but John had kept it in this state as a token of his affection for the great cellist.

The two men had enjoyed a lengthy friendship, and Casals had a great admiration for the younger man. On 12 January 1962 Casals wrote to John:

My dear and admired Friend:

Your kind words and wishes for my birthday have honored and moved me. I wish so much to see you again . . . I do hope that it may be soon.

I am deeply grateful for your friendship, which has enriched my life.

With all good wishes and admiration,

PABLO CASALS

Much has been written about John Barbirolli's wide circle of friends. Sam Oddy, the Cockney ex-greengrocer, referred to in previous books on John, was prepared to recall his 'mate' in a tape-recorded interview when we saw him in May 1982. Sam, a jocular man in his late fifties was then working as a security officer for Marks and Spencers.

First time that I run into Sir John was when I was down in Huntsworth Mews, off Baker Street. A little gentleman with a great big black hat come up over to me and he asked for some fruit and vegetables, and I said, 'Who might you be, sir?', and he answered, 'I'm Sir John Barbirolli, but you needn't worry about that, mate.' So anyway I got to know him very well and he treated me just like a son.

There were times when I was down the Mews and he come over to me and said, 'You must come in and have drink,' and I said, 'Well, you've got your friends, and I can't invade your place.' 'Rubbish,' he said, 'You can come in now.' Anyhow, he dragged me over to his house, and there were some very high-class people there, well beyond my reach, so I said: 'No, some other time,' and he got hold of me and just pulled me in and said, 'You just sit your arse down here . . ., you're going to have a drink with me.'

He said, 'You look a bit embarrassed,' and I said, 'Well, so would you be, in the same position as me,' he said, 'Drink up and have another drink,' Well, the wine was everywhere, and we'd had quite a few Scotches as well, and I was beginning to talk and mix with those people in there, who all enjoyed the Cockney speech. Yes, that first time was 1967 to be precise. But he was such a nice man. Well, he went away, and I didn't see him for some time.

My daughter who worked in the florist's nearby came home on Thursday, and she said: 'Your mate's very ill,' so I said, 'And who might that be?' She said, 'You know, Sir John Barbirolli, he's had a heart attack.' Well, I was choked.

She said 'I've had hundreds of flowers ordered from our customers, to go to his home at the Mews. Would you like me to send anything from you?' I said, 'No, I know just what he likes.'

So I went over to my own warehouse and picked up a nice bunch of freesias, and went around. I told Evelyn to put them by his bed. And he didn't know that it was from me, and apparently he looked around the room and said, as sick as he was, 'Nice flowers, we've got in this room. And these freesias are the best we got.' And Evelyn said, 'Well, they're from your old mate, Sam.'

Evelyn's a darling. She's been so good to me, in fact too good at times. There were times, after I'd packed up my work, we'd chat. This particular year, we were going to Australia and we were saving our pennies, because we started work at the Marks and Spencer down the road, too. I really had to push to find a way of saving, and I got a bit short. Evelyn said to me, 'Are you financially embarrassed or anything?' And I answered, 'Well, I'm about £200 short.' So she said, 'Well, I'll give you a cheque for £200.' She was as generous as that. Money was money you know; in those days £200 meant something.

A moment of pause, whilst Sam's mind rested on John's last hours.

It'd been snowing and I was round there. Evelyn offered me a cup of coffee, and asked me to go up and see John. So I went up . . . and I've never seen anything like it in my life. There he was sitting up in bed, because he'd been studying music, and he'd just fallen asleep into the book, right there. That was the last time that I saw him, asleep like that. He looked so peaceful there, when I saw him that last time.

They took him off to hospital, but he was dead on arrival . . . He was so good to me, I'll never forget it. And

> Evelyn still keeps the friendship going. To me she's one of the family. If ever I wanted to take anyone out, she'd be the one I chose sooner than anyone. She's down-to-earth, and a good mixer. It doesn't matter who she's with, or what you're talking about, she can hold a good conversation, and she's a good listener.

Ernest Bradbury, an old friend of both Evelyn and John, is fond of recounting to friends at the Savage Club bar musical stories that feature John; fewer tales include Evelyn—perhaps because, unlike J.B. she was not a member of the Savage, which Bradbury, music critic of the *Yorkshire Post*, has been since the mid-Forties. At that time, when John was also a much-revered member himself, according to Ernest, he was joint guest of honour with Evelyn at a civic banquet held in Bradford. But when he rose to speak in answer to 'Our Most Distinguished Guests' he found, to his consternation, that he'd left his reading spectacles at home. Concealing his anxiety and deciding not to let a specially prepared speech go by the board, he turned to Evelyn sitting next to the Lord Mayor, and suggested to her that perhaps she could let him borrow those she kept in her bag.

Evelyn, not lost for the quick quip whenever she needed to help J.B. make a point, said she hoped that, although their eyesights were different, her lenses might suit him in the pressing circumstances 'and that, in any case, something might prove better than nothing!' Quick as a flash back came the stage-whispered rejoinder, at the same time that J.B. was trying the glasses on for a searching look that took all of a second's pause: 'Blimey, that's the first time we've seen eye to eye since we met!' The incongruous Cockney that J.B. loved to affect (especially upon such an occasion in the heart of Yorkshire) brought the house down.

It was Ernest Bradbury who was to write one of the most poignant of all the many obituaries that would follow his friend's death. He was on holiday when the news came, and his Editor sent him a telegram. He received the wire just as he was starting off for a journey with his family, and composed his tribute at the wheel of his car.

I pulled into a car park, wrote it there and then without a pause from the mental notes I'd made on the half-journey since I'd heard the news.

I made no corrections before phoning it through to my Editor at the first post office I came to, and I was glad to note when I re-read it the next day that it had gone in actually as telephoned.

Rachel Godlee, the viola player (Philip Godlee's daughter), was born into a musical home, her parents and her brothers and sisters all being musicians, and playing chamber music was one of the favourite pastimes of every member of the household until Rachel herself joined the Hallé in 1952, staying with the Orchestra under Sir John Barbirolli for the following eight years. She now plays with the Philharmonia as well as free-lancing. She can recall aspects of Barbirolli not known to everyone.

He was held in awe by all of us. In spite of being a small man he had an incredible personality which would dominate any gathering at which he was present, certainly in any ordinary sized room. That's how I felt when I was small. We as a family—the four of us and my father—all played string instruments so it was natural that we all played chamber music together, and we did so very occasionally *with* Barbirolli. I know that in the absence of any of us my father would say 'Come on John, old boy, let's play some Beethoven duets. We'll have three duets for one large Scotch.' And I can only suspect—without actually knowing for certain—which they enjoyed most! You see, in spite of being a businessman all his life, my father was a genuine music lover. He loved it very much indeed and I suspect he went into his textile office every day thinking about music rather than about textiles. In fact he did spend more time 'chairing' Hallé meetings, organizing chamber concerts and the famous Tuesday Midday Concerts, than anything else. He was a true musician. He could sit at the piano, pick out tunes and harmonize. But he mainly played the viola.

When John came to Manchester and found virtually no orchestra there, he did nothing but audition for a number of weeks. He found solace, I think, in coming to meet congenial spirits, with whom he could drop the conductor's baton and posture and just play the cello.

I remember an occasion at Belle Vue when I was still a child and we were taken to see him as a treat. R. J. Forbes and his family used to give us, after the performance, tea and bread and butter; and when he'd come to J.B., Forbes would be heard to say, 'Here, John, here's your Russian tea,' and it would be produced in a tall plain glass. But everybody knew without a word being spoken at the time—that the 'Russian tea' was really diluted Scotch whisky. He got up to so many little tricks that he fondly imagined were not seen through. In that way he was without guile, thinking that he was doing something that nobody might know about, and it was all very endearing and childlike.

Like so many performers I suspect he didn't really know how good he was. A fascinating man. Always uncertain what sort of figure he was cutting in the eye of the beholder. More afraid of public opinion and the social scene than he pretended to be. Full of contradictions; he took us to Bulawayo and acted as umpire in a cricket match and used to joke that he couldn't count the number of balls in an over! Then, later, he acted as chef for us all that night at a barbecue. He cooked the steaks and the chops and the sausages—forgetting *himself* . . .

In my knowledge J.B. was the only conductor who has demanded *total* silence as he walked on—and that applied not only for each concert to a crowded audience, who had to be quiet before he started, but also to a rehearsal. And I do remember once (because the violas sat on the side of the platform where he walked on, and he had to pass us all to get to the rostrum), I was still tuning-up and he furiously snapped his fingers to get silence—walked out and then, after a pause for complete silence, started walking in again. I don't know of *any* other conductor who would have done such a thing. Most of them just arrive and you get silence once they're there, ready to start work. With J.B. this had to be *before* he arrived.

Tribute of rather a different kind could be discerned in the two memorial services held in John's memory—in Westminster Cathedral and in Manchester Cathedral. While the Westminster Cathedral service was impressive in its own right, it was during the Manchester tribute that one was especially conscious of the sense of deep personal loss, sustained alike by members of his Orchestra, civic dignitaries and the people who had formed his devoted audiences.

Audrey Napier-Smith had once ventured to question J.B. about his religion. As a Protestant, she wondered what he really thought about such customs as the kissing of St Peter's toe.

> He said: 'Oh, my dear . . . I don't know. If you're born into a Catholic family . . .'—and would have left it like that.
>
> I asked: 'Well, you do believe in God, don't you?' and after surveying me in silence for a few moments he said, 'You have to.' He pointed out of the window, waving his arm at the trees and the sky.
>
> And then: 'Well, *I* leave it to the priests. If anybody wants to know about a Mahler score they come to me. If anybody wants to know about religion, they go to the priest.'

Leaving J.B.'s Memorial Service Evelyn remarked to the same friend, 'Dear John, he was such a good Christian and such a bad Catholic.'

22 *Beyond These Shores*

The Barbirollis' travel abroad had begun early; when John returned to the Hallé from New York in 1943 the Government was in the process of deciding to ask the Orchestra to play to the troops in Belgium and Holland (see pages 93—96). This tour was a great success, and a war correspondent for *The Times* wrote back despatches from the Ardennes offensive saying how well things were going not only with the Allies' resistance, but with 'Ally's Band'. Travel conditions for the

Orchestra were not always easy, and during a particularly gruesome journey by truck one trumpet player grumbled, 'It's all very well for t'*Times* man to talk about our wonderful doings. 'E should see us now, hangin' up 'ere like bloody bats!'

After the war travel was easier, and John began to make plans. Evelyn remembers a discussion on the bus going to the first International Eisteddfod in Llangollen in 1947 on the opportunities for taking the Orchestra abroad presented by the development of long-distance air travel. A rather different recollection of that same Eisteddfod was that of the concert given by the Hallé to mark the end of the festival. The orchestra and about four thousand people in the enormous marquee played and sang with heart-rending fervour the Welsh national hymn, 'Land Of My Fathers'.

John shared his artistry and his joy in music with almost all the peoples of the world. To begin with Great Britain's nearest neighbour, John and Evelyn used to love their frequent visits to Ireland, and had a special affection for Dublin and for the choir of Our Lady, formed from the best members of choirs in the various Roman Catholic churches elsewhere in the city. It is a choir with a beautiful and very warm sound. (The manager, Father Andrew Griffith, became a very close friend.) John enjoyed conducting it regularly, every time he made the journey to that troubled but exciting land.

One of the first tours undertaken by the re-formed Hallé was as already mentioned to the recently liberated Austria in 1948. Conditions throughout that unfortunate land were exceedingly bad. The bomb damage had neither been repaired nor even partially cleared. There was little fuel, even less food and no meat of any kind. When the Barbirollis were there it was bitterly cold.

The Hallé played five concerts at Salzburg, Vienna, Graz and Innsbruck and included in the repertoire the *Enigma Variations,* Mozart's Symphony No. 34, Beethoven's Seventh and Dvorak's Fourth as well as Vaughan Williams' *Fantasia on a Theme of Thomas Tallis* and Barbirolli's Purcell Suite. In Vienna one of the concerts was held on a Sunday morning, coinciding with one of the brief periods in which the Viennese had the gas and electricity turned on.

All the same, much to John's surprise, the concert was packed to capacity and afterwards a number of the audience came round to see the Barbirollis, including a young woman with three small children. John loved children, always liked talking to them, and he said to the mother: 'I'm rather surprised that you're here; I should have thought that you would be using this fuel time to cook your little children a nice hot meal.'

Smiling shyly, the woman pointed out that if she had cooked a Sunday dinner the children wouldn't remember it—'but now they will remember this concert for the rest of their lives.' It was a moment that moved both John and Evelyn intensely, for they knew how much music means to the Viennese.

About their last visit to Innsbruck, Evelyn recalls:

> We had two excellent baggage men, a father and son called Wilson. When an orchestra travels the baggage van goes ahead. The baggage men get to the theatre or concert hall in time to set up the stands, bring on the double-basses and the harps and the other heavy instruments. They also put out the music so that when the conductor and the orchestra get there the stage is ready for action—rehearsal or concert.
>
> The Wilsons were both very reliable and conscientious, and had never been known not to be there when they should be. They got to Innsbruck on this occasion well ahead of rehearsal time, and were preparing to unload. As they were walking on to the stage they became aware that round the back of it were about twenty men dressed in a very exotic manner with helmets and elaborate coloured uniforms, breastplates and things, and they were all standing, silently watching. The Wilsons, understandably enough, concluded that this must be the chorus of an opera and some mistake must have been made. They therefore tried to explain in broad Lancashire, which was all they spoke, that they must continue their work and the uniformed ones must go away. The watchers replied in German, which was all *they* spoke, that they were not going, and continued to stand and stare.
>
> The Wilsons went off to the hotel to see John, who was conversing rather deeply with the administration. We took some bilingual colleagues to the theatre, and found

> the explanation. The Wilsons always had cigarettes in their mouths. Smoking is not allowed in most opera houses, especially European ones, and the characters ranged around the back of the stage were the local firemen.

The Hallé visited Czechoslovakia in 1958, the first post-war visit of a noted Western orchestra to that unhappy country, for the famous festival known as the Prague Spring. They had a tremendous welcome, for the Czechs are a very musical people, and they wanted to show how much a visit meant to them at that moment.

At the end of the concert the audience did a most heart-warming thing—quite usual on the Continent but rare in England. When people have been particularly stirred by a concert, they rise all together and move in a body towards the stage, where they continue clapping and looking up at the artists, as though to get as near as possible to those who have given them so much pleasure. Evelyn recalled:

> We weren't used to such behaviour and had not had it for some while past. What made it unique was that in the springtime lilies-of-the-valley grow in great profusion in the woods around Prague.
>
> When the audience surged up to the platform, many little bunches of these wild lilies-of-the-valley were thrown on to the platform. John and the orchestra were standing in a sea of lilies-of-the-valley. When John went out, there were more people on the pavement throwing them down, so that one couldn't help walking on them. I can never smell that flower now without recalling that very wonderful occasion.

Shortly after the war there was an exchange visit between the Hallé and the great Dutch orchestra of The Hague. That orchestra came to Britain and performed the regular subscription concerts in Manchester, Sheffield and Bradford, while the Hallé played at The Hague and other leading cities of Holland. Dutch musicians were taken around the Lake

District and their English counterparts escorted to the bulb fields.

With a shuttle service of planes laid on for this visit, there were lunches of welcome on both sides. John and Evelyn, upon arrival, had semi-official gastronomic greetings made to them over the various gins and liqueurs for which the country is justly famed. Evelyn sat next to the Chairman of The Hague Orchestra, who spoke excellent English. The main topic everywhere then was the Black Market, how far butter would go, and above all rationing. Food queues would stretch for miles in the lands that had been so long under the jackboot. The Chairman told Evelyn: 'It was worse for us than it was for you. We were occupied, you never were. We were desperately short of food because the Germans took it all from us—and you know, for six weeks we lived on nothing but boiled bollops.'

Evelyn misunderstood the word, thinking it had a rather rude connotation, so queried the meaning; and then hearing the word pronounced again in exactly the same way, she felt a kick under the table from John, who had been silently overhearing the conversation. He whispered, 'Bulbs, you fool!' (The Dutch tend to pronounce the word 'bollops'!)

It was in 1950 that John made his first appearance in Berlin, the first concert in what became a long-standing relationship with that city. His visits to Germany, particularly Berlin, during the last ten years of his life were among the highlights of his career. The West German Press called those years 'a love affair'. John and the Berlin Philharmonic Orchestra did indeed love each other, whilst Evelyn, as both woman and artist, shared in that love.

There was something very special about those concerts. They were always sold out well in advance. The audiences were enthusiastic, but there was something even more—a strong personal rapport. The contact developed into such an intense affection that a dozen years after his death John's memory is still fresh, kept alive by the visits that Evelyn makes to see their old friends there.

No account of the Berlin and Munich engagements that filled those last eventful German years would be complete without personal discussions with a number of those who had contributed to that German rapprochement. Evelyn had kindly suggested a number of those who would be willing to advise us, and journeys between London and (both) Berlin and Munich were undertaken in the spring of 1982, where a good deal of the atmosphere of the Sixties in musical Germany was very generously evoked, with the use of tape-recordings.

In evaluating John's high status in Germany, it is interesting that while it is contended in one quarter that in some ways he was the peer of Toscanini, it is also held by two of the people we interviewed that his humanity gave him the edge over Beecham. (And, curiously enough, two of the four made an unprompted comparison with Charlie Chaplin.)

Dr Franz Roehn. A musicologist and music teacher, now in his eighties, he was brought up in a musical household—his mother was a fine pianist and his father was also a musicologist. Today he works on behalf of the Hugo Wolf Society in Munich.

> I consider that the great Toscanini did not play Beethoven as well as Barbirolli. Although many people admire him, very few put him or any conductor in the same class as Toscanini. I always preferred Barbirolli conducting Beethoven but in the case of Verdi, Puccini—any Italian music—or Wagner, then of course Toscanini was one of the greatest conductors in the world. Only not with Beethoven.
>
> While Toscanini was, in a strange way, very hard (as if he didn't know what rhythm was—only to attack it and he was convinced that was the way Beethoven wrote it, but he took it too literally), Barbirolli's Beethoven was one of the most wonderful experiences of my life—and I had heard this music all my life, played by Furtwängler, Bruno Walter. And now, after the sad experience of Toscanini, I was so relieved because Barbirolli was a 'loving' conductor. He gave his whole soul and body, everything, to Beethoven, as if Barbirolli had disappeared and Beethoven was there, breathing. He had the soul of a dancer. He was a born dancer—I think he had a great likeness to Charlie Chaplin. He had that diminutive, balletic, fastidious delicate thing. There was a great humanity to Barbirolli.

He was opposed to musical snobbery, he didn't like people who take scores to the opera to read instead of looking at the stage and listening to the music. He was very simple, he didn't like pretentiousness.

Friedrike von Wedelstaedt. She has occupied a unique position in Europe, and in Berlin especially, for more than half a century, having been for much of that time Music Officer for the British Council in the city. Now in her eighties, she has been awarded an OBE by the British government for her services to music, having worked to build a bridge between Germany and Great Britain.

I knew them since 1950, the year J.B. had his first concert in Berlin after the war. It was from the very beginning such a success . . . it was as if you had known him all your life, with this wonderful mixture—French, British and Italian—married to this very English wife. I found the greatest charm of both Barbirollis was that they knew what friendship was and they could be friends in a way that only a few very gifted people can. Most people like to give something, but they don't like to accept from other people; and that is just the great art, and it was something both the Barbirollis were wonderful at doing. They were the best friends I have ever had. I have never found people with such delightful ways.

They were more like Siamese twins than husband and wife in one way. Although they went in different directions—she with her career and he with his—they were so complementary to each other. He took the floor and she always knew when to stop him. You need never fear they wouldn't be reliable. You just did what you wanted to do and it was right by them. The greater the test, the greater the friendship which could survive it. It is a wonderful feeling when you know anything can happen and nothing will disturb the friendship.

The Berlin Philharmonic is still one of the top orchestras of the world . . . Sir John was quite different from any other guest conductor. When he entered the concert hall and went on the rostrum the whole hall was like one family. The audience was with the orchestra as one personality . . . You could see the difference between him and many other guest-conductors, most of whom were very good indeed. But Sir John had the great gift to be loved. He had a great humanity and great compassion as a man.

Wolfgang Stresemann. Son of the renowned German Liberal statesman, Gustav Stresemann, he is a well-known musician and was the distinguished Intendant of the Berlin Philharmonic Orchestra. He was at one time a conductor, and had known John (with Evelyn) during the New York period. He lives in the Dahlem area of Berlin, with his American wife Jean.

The wonderful thing about Evelyn is that she is playing better today, in her seventies, than ever before. Evelyn is at the top of her form and has never played better. I would place her in the front rank of oboists. Her books on this instrument are masterpieces of technical excellence and respected by musicians throughout the world. John had—and Evelyn still has—a wonderful sense of humour; a quality that seems unusual in most musicians, especially conductors.

Evelyn is selfless—both as woman and as artist, with a way of her own when handling people. I have seen people who were indifferent to others won over completely by her charm. She loves her friends, and if she cannot say nice things about those who are not her friends—then she'd rather shut up. Except for Beecham! Her loyalty to her beloved John is paramount there.

John had real charm, and although Beecham was a fine musician, John had that incomparable something over Beecham—humanity. That was lacking in Beecham. Admittedly they had one thing in common: both would stand up and hold the floor—Barbirolli was of course able to improvise at the drop of a hat. But he enjoyed a personal popularity that Beecham never had.

John was childlike in some ways, and when the time came for Evelyn, with firm kindness, to tell him to 'stop it', she did; then she'd let him know in no uncertain terms who was the boss!

> John was—apart from Herbert von Karajan—to my certain knowledge the most popular and beloved conductor we've ever had. All who played with and under him knew that he was the 'head man', that they could not relax for a moment, that he'd demand their complete co-operation and concentration—that nothing less than perfection would satisfy him.

Stresemann enlarged upon the team spirit that John encouraged. Although he was a volatile character, and such a marked individualist, it was his wish to be one of the players:

> He liked to be one of the band, not a man apart in the manner that so many conductors are, with their reserved places on trains and planes and buses, special VIP treatment in hotels and the red carpet down at functions. He was 'one of the boys'—part of the team, yet such was his power and natural authority, the respect and love in which he was held, that his position was never in danger of being usurped by those who mistake kindness for weakness, even by implication. He never demanded leadership. He just was the head—and woe betide those who ignored that fact. His chief concern was music. That had to be first wherever he was, whatever he did.
>
> I never heard him comment much on fellow conductors, although I know he was greatly honoured to be guest conductor on Bruno Walter's ninetieth birthday. He admired Toscanini of course, and it was a dreadfully perilous undertaking for John, as a young conductor, to step into the older Italian maestro's shoes.
>
> It could not always have been any too easy for Evelyn living with such a temperament, such a 'life-force', but they emerged triumphantly together and her personal success, both as woman and as artist, persists to this very day.

Margaret Furtwängler. The beautiful concert pianist and exponent of Schumann, who had been soloist under Barbirolli at the Hallé some years earlier, is now semi-retired. A painter and water-colourist of note, she lives in Munich.

John Barbirolli was of that warm family of musicians, the same family as Furtwängler*. Therefore we had immediately to love him and feel at home with him. We didn't much care for other guest conductors—Beecham, for instance, because he was like a bandmaster. He was a very good conductor for small pieces, but for big works he lacked the real greatness which is necessary. Even Toscanini seemed very dry, and I could never think Toscanini could be called greater than Barbirolli.

In J.B. you had a man who was vital, emotional and volatile. He had all the lovable things of the Italian—the charm and a childlike ingenuousness, and also the panache of a conjurer's assistant.

I remember the only concert I gave with him, I was very ill and very depressed and he said, 'Oh, if you have a fever, you don't feel any nerves!' The disappointment was almost too great when I found the piano was inadequate for that huge place. Also, I was weak. I was playing the Schumann Concerto. But it was quite incredibly easy to play with Barbirolli. In the last movement, when many have failed and stopped in the middle—Cortot and Gieseking and God know's who—because it is so difficult that many conductors just get entangled, Barbirolli had a way of doing it with a different kind of beat and it went like nothing you can imagine—just fantastic. At the end, because he knew how ill I'd been feeling, he applauded me, which was very sweet.

I would say he was a bit too sensitive for those huge works such as Mahler, although he had a tempestuous temperament.

I've never met two married people who appeared so outwardly unsuited to each other and were so lovable as a pair. Unsuited, not in their souls, but physically—this big, lovely Evelyn, full of life and wonderfully lively. But that is a façade. She is very delicate inside. She seems always to be laughing at life and to possess a lot of strength. And I think this is what he needed—because he had something about him—not feminine but a

*Wilhelm Furtwängler, the conductor, to whom Margaret Furtwängler is related through marriage.

fastidiousness. He needed somebody to put wings around him. He had a unique delicacy, like Charlie Chaplin impersonating Hitler when he was doing the dance with the balloons. But he was human—the laughs we had together!

He liked to eat in an Italian restaurant, just a simple pasta with a good red wine. But he ate very little and then always non-gourmet fare; and he was a great one for going down to the market and doing a bit of bargaining. He took after his mother.

When I was in Venice I wanted to paint his portrait, and I had to know what the Teatro la Fenice was like inside. We had no tickets for the performance, so I offered the doorman a tip. He wouldn't let me inside until I said, 'I'm an old friend of the Barbirollis',' and showed him the sketch I had made of John. He immediately opened the door! He said he remembered J.B. with such love. You see all kinds of Barbirolli types in Venice: outwardly very much like him, but without that magic spark.

Evelyn stands up to life with a valiant spirit. We were with her on the night that John had his first big heart attack [in Munich, where he had conducted two concerts]—Evelyn rang us from the clinic where John had been taken. I shall never forget; there was a telephone call from the Press to the ward where we were all assembled, and we could all hear a harsh voice calling out, 'Ist Barbirolli todt?' ('Is Barbirolli dead?') John was already sitting up in a chair, and his eyes began to sparkle in a humorous way. 'Tell them I am not *todt*, but very much alive,' he said.

In what was to be his final season in his home, Manchester, in 1969–70, Mahler's 'Resurrection' Symphony and works by Elgar, Vaughan Williams, Holst and Delius were featured in John's programmes, and the Hallé's 112th season, 1970–71, was brought to a close with another performance of the Verdi Requiem, whilst in his very last appearance in Manchester on Sunday, 3 May, Sibelius's Sixth Symphony preceded Stravinsky's 'Firebird' Suite.

In this month, too, John undertook the final recordings of all the Sibelius Symphonies before journeying with Evelyn to conduct the Orchestra at the King's Lynn Festival. It was not without point, perhaps, that his beloved Elgar's *Sea Pictures* preceded a grand and rousing performance of Beethoven's Seventh Symphony. His last conducting of all, alas, was only to be seen and heard at rehearsal. Of what happened at another rehearsal near the end we have an account by Rachel Godlee:

> I was in on one of the last rehearsals he did. I had seen him arrive in Manchester when I was still a little girl; and I played in the Hallé with him later. Then when I was playing with the Philharmonic Orchestra he was rehearsing it to go to Japan for Expo 70.
>
> There had been a rehearsal break at the Bishopsgate Institute, and he came out of his private room; we heard him emerging to descend the three or four steps to the main hall area.
>
> I saw him start to come down to floor level—and he just crumbled. There was no weight in him—he just crumbled down the steps and collapsed. The rehearsal was finished. Word came through—the announcement: 'Barbirolli's collapsed', and the ambulance from Bart's came and they took him away on a stretcher, covered by a red blanket.
>
> He was released from hospital and, with that indomitable will and galvanizing nervous energy, he started work again. J.B. always said he wanted to die on the rostrum: 'I want to snuff it with my boots on and a baton in my hand.' Well, he almost did: as good as . . . going out on the stretcher, he looked dead then.
>
> It was all very tragic but it was amazing to go on like that—in harness.

'In harness' they both were in the short while that followed the collapse and the end. Evelyn, taking command and sole responsiblity as was her wont throughout their married life when any emergency occurred, was encouraged by John's recuperative powers. 'After his last rehearsal (before the Japanese tour) he was in good form and came back to Huntsworth Mews very happy after a long, hard day.' Her written instructions during this last period, dictated to Brenda Bracewell, indicated her sense of the occasion:

> Memo: *Huntsworth Mews*
> *Dear Brenda*,
> 1. Sometime this morning I have to ring the Philharmonia about our flying to Japan on the 2nd instead of the 1st because of flying with Dr Heighway. Also must ask about routes there as Dr H and Dr Linnett feel that a very long hop should be avoided. I'll do this in your office as there may be notes to be made.
> 2. I promised Mary that J.B. would sign a photograph for 'Len and Dot'. Could you produce one for him?
> 3. These records are—sometime at your leisure—to go to Solc (in Brno, Czechoslovakia).
> 4. Note from J.B. to you and/or Sidney Rothwell: Kindly see if Watson library have a min. score of 'Lieder eines Fahrenden Gesellen' of Mahler and have this sent up here as soon as possible. Also, if possible, a vocal score of Elgar's 'Caractacus'.
> ***
> I had hopes that we might have had a productive session on the schedule (to cut it down) today. Unfortunately J.B. had a bad night and so may be very tired. We'll have to see how we go, but it MUST be done today or tomorrow!
> As we won't be here for some while, what are we doing about records? The Rome Embassy ones are the urgent ones. J.B. suggests writing a note to the Hancocks telling them that records are being sent direct and that he will write on them when we are back in Rome in January. Perhaps we could have a word about this.
> Love, E.B.

Later it happened. He had returned to work after his short spell in Bart's. On the last day of his life, 28 July 1970, he rehearsed all day, even giving an interview to the Press between sessions. It was to the *Manchester Evening News*, who subsequently headed the piece 'Last Hours with Sir John'. And, in the early hours of the following day, Evelyn phoned Brenda Bracewell to say, 'He's gone.' Brenda remembers the simple way the two words were uttered. He had been warned. They had been loyal to each other. At that moment in eternity there was little else to say . . .

23 *Music His Passion*

He was, up until the last decade, a youthful personality, hair black and thick, enthusiasm infectious, discipline sharp as a razor. And what order he commanded! 'No, no, *no*,' came the instructions from the podium, 'don't play like stuffed shirts—or like members of Fred Karno's Army! If his band didn't like hard work—well then, they could go. On the rostrum he never stood for any nonsense. After the rehearsal he'd stand the lads a drink—only after a session, though; nothing in between—and he'd cap their yarns with better ones, always within reach of his memory, or sparked off by a tale just told.

His passion, music, to which he applied a sizzling concentration that had to be seen to be believed, was life itself—the left hand vibrating, the powerfully communicating eyebrows. The rapt expression would occasionally appear and, as quickly, vanish when a wrong sound was detected. A frown before the storm.

The many-sided J.B. came into one of his other 'selves' each year when he pretty well controlled the annual Hallé Ball. Standing on the bandstand, with dancers all around him, and friends and supporters of his Orchestra amongst the guests who mingled with the Hallé Society members and staff, he enjoyed the revels, looking down at the general gaiety like a jovial father at an old-time Christmas party. He was with friends and the man who relished friendship so much was at his happiest.

Zenovia Goonan, who held various offices in the Hallé club and now runs the box office, was always present at these events and recalled something of the atmosphere that J.B. engendered from his elevated position among all present:

> On one occasion John introduced a surprise item; a can-

can from a Divertissement by Ibert. He dictated a dance rhythm and cajoled the dancers into dancing to the tune. (He also introduced the versatile Rayson Whalley, his percussionist, who had just acquired a goatee beard, crying out to all who could hear, 'My Mephistophelian friend.') This was a 'one-off', for on other occasions his tactics varied and he would conduct a popular dance tune in anything but strict dance tempo; offering to kiss the first female who could make head or tail of what he was playing and could guess the title correctly!

It was left to Evelyn to confess that he loved romantic 'Smoke Gets In Your Eyes' and the haunting refrain became a regular feature of the Hallé Ball each year. Each time his 'lovely orchestra' got the nod, the opening bars would be started by the leaderless orchestra and J.B., having abandoned his baton, would take up the cello. In this way the orchestra would stop playing, leaving the 'romantic' John as solo cellist. Dancers stopped dancing and crowded round to listen and to watch J.B. who, with eyes closed, a rapt expression on his remarkable face, would be far away from the hustle and bustle of that festive occasion.

But generally, he expected respect as well as admiration from his audience. An example of this other aspect was given when he conducted the BBC Symphony Orchestra in Moscow in January 1967. Latecomers were groping for their seats in the vast Tchaikovsky Hall and ignoring requests for silence. J.B. entered and bore patiently with the confusion until something snapped. He had rapped the podium for silence; now, with noise unabated, he walked off. Then about a hundred further latecomers, apparently students, came up near the front, and he entered again after an absence from the platform of over five minutes. The students led the applause for his entrance, and J.B. rapped again for complete silence before starting on a concert of Rimsky-Korsakov, Bliss and Beethoven. The reception he was given at the end is still talked about in Russian musical circles. Barbirolli's orchestra retain vivid impressions of his personality. His impatience with the slovenly and even semi-competent was short: he was nevertheless lavishly generous in appreciating those who tried.

His tastes varied. His masters were not always the classics;

he went to pains to explain that the 'masters' could be modern, if good enough, as well as ancient. Forever willing to help the unsung, when they were good enough, he was the friend of talent wherever it was to be found, helping new workers of promise; in America as well as at home composers, instrumentalists, and fellow conductors had much reason to be grateful for his advocacy. In the early Forties in New York he gave the first performances of Britten's *Sinfonia da Requiem* and Violin Concerto at a time when Britten was not well-known.

His treatment of singers like Ferrier and Baker has often been remarked upon. They considered it important to have someone like J.B. when they were essaying demanding roles. John, of course, took them with him—working with, and not against; being aware that there must never be competition between soloist and conductor. He had plenty of ideas and imagination and he made his singers feel that everything was wonderful. They responded to J.B.'s magnetism as whole-heartedly as instrumentalists did.

J.B.'s players were devoted to him, both because of his magnetism and his unfailing concern for their welfare, and would have had no reservations about calling him a great conductor. None of them entertained any doubt of his genius as an orchestral trainer and his ability to conduct by the strength of his emotive output. After one performance of a concerto, a double-bass player received the ultimate in compliments from the allegedly egotistical John, who said, 'If I could play the double-bass, that's just the way I would have played it myself!'

Martin Milner, who succeeded Laurance Turner as leader of the Hallé, wrote:

> J.B. was completely loyal to those who had taken the authority he'd given them. As leader he'd always stand behind me, giving his support if things—as they sometimes did—went wrong. If there was an aftermath following an instruction he'd given that could seem to reflect upon one of his subordinates having 'muffed' the assignment, then he'd step in to accept full responsibility. Never once can I remember J.B. passing the buck under any circumstances. He may have been illogical and

unwittingly unfair because of that fact upon occasion, but never once did I know him to lack courage—moral or physical. Indeed, his loyalty to his musicians—who were all his friends when faced with trouble—was proverbial. J.B. had this ability to trust people, and sometimes that trust proved to be misplaced. It was odd, really, because he had a wonderful sense of assessing character for much of the time—but his judgment could let him down. He wanted so badly to believe, and couldn't properly understand why, when he was 'let down', people were not behaving as well as he would have done in similar circumstances.

Audrey Napier-Smith was another who benefited from his loyalty: she frankly admits that she was 'never much of a fiddler.' On one occasion Laurance Turner, then leader of the Orchestra, said to J.B. 'Audrey hasn't got much technique.' His reply was: 'No, but look what she does with it.'

I used to argue with him and fight with him. We had one furious row. I thought he ought to encourage the fiddles more and not be so angry with them. He got very angry then with me and said, 'You expect me to go cap-in-hand to all these little creatures?' Then he stopped and said, 'I'm sorry I shouted.' The next minute he was shouting again, and that made me laugh, and so of course it was all over, because he laughed, too.

I remember at one rehearsal four of us coming in a few minutes late together. John was very angry, and asked what was the reason. We said we had overslept.

'What, *all* together?' he asked.

He once said to her, 'What I like about you is the way you respond to me, and you don't do that to please me. That is the way the music works for you.'

Elizabeth Godlee, one of his protégées, wrote that her four years in the Hallé (1950–54) under J.B. were:

the most inspiring years of my career—and I have been playing for a living ever since—the memory of which will

> always remain with me; and I shall always feel the benefit of playing under his baton. He just drew the music out of you. I used to enjoy his rehearsals because they were so fiery and concentrated. Music oozed out of him, and he usually achieved results by actions rather than words, though he used to shout at us, and could be rude, which personally I used to enjoy.

Anything like 'upmanship' in performance was anathema to him; never did he subscribe to the belief that the conductor was there to upstage the visiting artist, famous or otherwise. He upheld the idea that without collaboration in music, between all concerned, no single member of an orchestra could artistically come out on top.

It was an example of John's rare intuition in sensing talent that youngsters like Rachel and Elizabeth Godlee in their teens were invited to play in the Hallé. He knew latent or partially developed talents for what they were worth at the time and would gauge their potential, never choosing a second-rate player.

J.B. would not tolerate the word 'accompany'. His contention was that the visiting soloist and the conductor were in a sense equal partners. There were few soloists who played with him who did not pay tribute for what he did to make them perform better than they might have done with another conductor. He desired complete co-operation, the ability to make of the music the most that he could, though rehearsals were not always as long as he would have wished to achieve his standard. (Apparently, upon at least one occasion he admitted that he had allowed a certain soloist to dictate the tempo of a particular concerto; but it was someone for whom he had a great deal of respect. Nevertheless, it goes some way to counter the notion that he had a 'thing' against all soloists.)

His liking for the lighter composers was only equalled by his hatred for musical snobs. Why compose, why conduct, why play at all, he would ask if the only audiences who attend are to be those who are more interested in themselves than they are in the music itself? Musical snobs masquerading as music lovers and musicologists at the same time wished to bend every composition to their narrow, restrictive and sometimes inhibited natures and blinkered points of view. Music, asserted

John, demanded commitment and an effort from the listener, and how much more infinitely rewarding it could be for those who gave it a fair hearing; keeping their minds receptive and their hearts open to receive what joys could be brought forth from creativity. He dominated his players without any conscious effort, coaxing and wheedling, entrancing through half-closed eyes, humming the while and sometimes singing aloud so that the Orchestra could hear him. When asked how he got his marvellous effects the reply would come back, 'I just let 'em play. I let them have their heads and at the finish I might nod approvingly—or say, 'That's delightful—and if you play it again it'll be more than delightful, it'll be even a *little* better.' Never throughout a long career could he be said to have 'taken it out' on any individual musician, or even a section in any of the world famous orchestras he conducted. He loathed small and petty talk and any sort of malicious 'shop' that so many musicians have been known to indulge in at the expense of others behind their backs, where little coteries all too often develop into fractious and mean-spirited factions.

Barbirolli, like many top-notch conductors, has had his detractors, but there have been none among them who have labelled him 'tyrant' in the way that they have occasionally labelled both Beecham and Toscanini.

If there has been a revolution in conducting it has happened gradually—some modern conductors, Norman Del Mar included, think it has been going on for a period not far short of thirty years. The orchestral player has been encouraged in many cases to become enormously knowledgeable, cultured and, occasionally, as much a dominating personality as the conductor. This democratization in music is in no small measure due to Barbirolli.

His total absorption by the music he played communicated itself to others. Some very energetic persons make subordinates tired, but he imparted an inspired energy. In a conductor the face and eyes are very important, as much as any stick technique. He had very compelling eyes, which drew an irresistible response when he looked at people.

J.B. stood up to tours wonderfully, despite failing health in later years, spurred on by his love of music. His only problem seemed to be his sensitivity to light: his reason for liking the Verdi hat, which he would wear in all kinds of climates.

On one of his final Hallé tours abroad he got weary of sight-seeing and sat down on some steps for a brief rest, took off his familiar hat, and left it on the ground. He always wore dark glasses in sunny weather and he may have looked like a blind man! Passers-by dropped money into his hat and he was far too considerate and polite to stop them. Members of the orchestra joined in and a few minutes later John got up and said, 'What nice kind people.' With his head, when he was listening to matters that absorbed his interest, on one side and tilted upwards most of the time, the impression he gave could be one of amiable eccentricity—expectant, a trifle amused, sometimes implying that he might be in a state of wonder at all that was going on about him. Which he was—exuding curiosity, a fascination with the human condition.

He was a most attractive conductor for those who want to look as well as listen. His whole body bent and moved; his rhythmic sense electrified. Using a short-stepped walk-trot-shuffle-hop to make his way from the back of the platform, he arrived at the podium, gripping each side as he bowed long and low to the audience, and, in several further acknowledgements, to his fellow players, as he swivelled finally before he took up his baton. He used a longish, slender stick, almost always precariously poised, and after that first entrance and the air of expectancy created when he walked on to the rostrum he held up a closed left hand to the level of his shoulder. Through the sense of the dramatic that brought such dignity to the task before him, we felt that serious business was about to begin.

C. B. Rees, a close personal friend of John, who broadcast many an interview discussing music with the conductor, and himself a musicologist of note wrote in *100 Years of the Hallé* a vivid wartime memory of J.B.:

> Of seeing him one morning walking alone looking sadly (and bitterly) at the ruins left by the raids. I caught up with him just outside Pagani's Italian restaurant,* one of the Luftwaffe's victims, haunt of many musicians for many years. 'I was born near here,' he said to me. 'I love London . . . and all this horror has had to happen to it.'

*Where he and Evelyn had their wedding reception.

Bernard Shore, one-time leader of the violas in the BBC Symphony Orchestra, said of Barbirolli in his *The Orchestra Speaks*:

> His youthful and fresh looking face with his shock of dark hair belies his great experience . . . he is a tremendously hard worker and his deep knowledge will always be equal to the demands made of it. The orchestra has a vivid impression of his personality. A mature head full of experience and confidence, set on young shoulders.

He was clearly a man not easily forgotten . . .

Twelve years after his death his successor James Loughran was the castaway on BBC Radio 4's 'Desert Island Discs' (in September 1982) to mark the 125th anniversary of the founding of the Hallé Orchestra. In his view he was lucky to have followed Sir John Barbirolli as Principal Conductor because of the good state the Orchestra was in, its splendour and sense of style, and—more importantly—because J.B. had been so unanimously beloved by both audiences and orchestra.

And in the same month Philip Radcliffe wrote in the *Artful Reporter*, (the arts magazine for the North West):

> Hallé permanent conductors are a bit special. Hans Richter . . . Sir Thomas Beecham nursed the job for a year or two . . . Sir Hamilton Harty . . . Bruno Walter—another name to conjure with—was approached to succeed him, though refused—and Sir Malcolm Sargent held the fort.
>
> These were big names in the Who's Who of music. Then came the coup to end them all when John Barbirolli, the Italian Cockney who had succeeded the legendary Toscanini as Chief Conductor of the New York Philharmonic, was tempted back to England during the 1939–45 war to re-establish the Orchestra. His reign was to last nearly 30 years and to put the Hallé and himself on the world map. A great musician, a great showman, quirky and querulous, humorous and autocratic, altogether larger than life, admired by all who had the good fortune to come under his spell in any way,

Sir John Barbirolli, 'J.B.', was the hardest of all acts to follow.

24 *Man of Many Moods*

John could be a very entertaining companion and a first-class conversationalist, as Evelyn would be the first to testify. His discussions with late stayers after supper parties at both Appleby and then Walton Lodge would sometimes continue long after Evelyn had retired in the early hours of the morning when all the other guests except one or two had gone home to bed. And it would be John's voice, talking to his friends, that Evelyn would hear from the bedroom until she dropped off to sleep.

He would talk (when he wasn't discussing music) about great men and women; literature, because of his penchant for biography; Shakespeare, who was music to his ear; medicine; law; antique glass; travel abroad; days long past, and the London he'd been fascinated by ever since childhood. He loved a discussion about statesmen, composers, cricketers, doctors, actors, lawyers, literary figures. Or about popular composers who were dismissed for being too easily understood, or about singers such as John McCormack. Or about someone such as Herbert Walenn, who had left his mark on J.B. for life. The cellist had been his teacher and mentor, and John never allowed himself to forget him. The bond between the two had been spontaneous, and the mutual respect and admiration matured into a rare devotion. A lifetime's friendship finally ended in 1953 when Walenn died. Afterwards John wrote:

> Until two days before his death we remained in constant and close touch. During my fleeting visits to London, going to see him was always my first port of call . . . not because I thought I was fulfilling a duty but because I felt peaceful moments in the air of his serene and kindly wisdom.

Walenn's degree of affection for both John and Evelyn can be judged from the short, obviously hasty, but very warm note of congratulation he wrote on 28 April 1939 after hearing of their forthcoming marriage:

> *My dear Tito*
> Evelyn came to see me a few days ago & told me the news—*I am very glad* to know it & may everything go well so that you will have your happiness, so long delayed, *soon*—that is on your return here.
> Ever affectionately, my *Very*! dear Tito
> HERBERT WALENN

In conversation John rarely adopted Anglo-Saxon restraint and understatement, rather reinforcing and recapitulating his conversation by violent physical gesticulation. He would raise first his left and then his right hand, sometimes holding them both together at shoulder level, after he had got into his stride, using voice alone. He would frequently chase around for the right word in his mind to fit a sentence that was more often than not beautifully phrased. His tempo increased, and then came the pregnant pauses, while he was moulding the apt word—the *only* word to do the rest of his sentence justice, if the topic was one that he knew a good deal about. If he grew heated, wildly enthusiastic, grimly disparaging of the pretentious, his voice would ascend to a 'Friends, Romans, countrymen' level as he leaned forward on to the supper table. He not only excelled as a raconteur in private company, and as a teller of after-dinner stories, but he also wrote letters good enough to warrant preserving. And he had developed a habit of pencilling in the margins of books copious notes in which he expressed his views on the book, its author and some of the people who figured in its pages.

In *My Sentimental Self* by Mrs Aria, one of the books given by John to Peter Cotes—a study of the Edwardian age by an eminent London hostess and confidante of such as Sir Arthur Pinero, H. G. Wells, Arnold Bennett, Hugh Walpole, Robert Louis Stevenson and George Meredith—there are pencilled marginal notes in which the guests are dissected in a manner little short of devastating. On page 106 of this biography, however, J.B. comes to the rescue of Sir Henry Irving. Mrs Aria says:

> Irving had often said that life had taught him patience but it was not true. He never had any, either to listen to counsel, or to change any determination he made; there was no power behind his throne; he occupied it and surrounded it himself.

To which J.B. wrote in his characteristic hand, clearly boiling over at these sentiments expressed so publicly about one of his idols:

> Nevertheless, he seemed to have unlimited patience at rehearsals. Indeed he must have had patience or he would never have produced anything.

And when Mrs Aria went on to tone down her criticism by seeing both sides of her friend's character:

> He had always a keen sense of proportion, never being overwhelmed by a commendation, nor for that matter a criticism, appraising both with equal acumen,

John's marginal note directly underneath was '*Balls*'—and he went on:

> Completely untrue this . . . I have heard Toscanini mutter this too, when there were many 'calls'; bitterly insulting to the audience if there were only two or three (calls).

The conductor goes on to praise the actor, with a gigantic '*Bless him*!!!' after reading that Irving disliked a prolonged holiday and only took one himself through the exigencies of work or for the good of his company. Mrs Aria claimed that he could not endure inactivity for longer than a week—and after that he would count the hours wasted unless he rehearsed or was actually appearing. J.B. could see his own reflection in the likes and dislikes of Irving, being pleased to feel a kinship.

John was fascinated by great talent. On the wall of his study was displayed the original of a letter to his grandfather from Rossini and there was a letter from the Italian tragedienne Eleonora Duse who had been a friend of the Barbirolli family.

He treasured letters from Elgar and Delius. In 1928 (only two years after John had started to conduct) Delius had written to him from France on 7 January after hearing him conduct a broadcast of his *Summer Night on the River*:

> Your tempi were perfect, just as I want them, and I felt you were in entire sympathy with the music, for which I thank you heartily.

As a letter-writer himself he shone in his occasional letters to the Press. He would never contradict a musical critic; he often said that public performers must 'take it' as part of their lives, but he would put things right for the sake of musical accuracy. Two typical examples are those reprinted below:

> To the Editor of *The Times* 29 November 1955
> Sir,—In his generous notice of the Hallé performance of Mahler's First Symphony, which appeared in your issue of November 23, your Music Critic includes the following: 'and it was not really necessary for Sir John Barbirolli to ask his horn players to stand up, like jazz musicians, when playing the triumphant chorale at the end'. Might I be allowed gently to point out to him that the standing up for the horn players for the triumphant final statement of the chorale at the end of the symphony, far from being an unwarranted act of vulgarity on my part, arose simply from what is by now, I hope, my well-known passion for precise detail, and fidelity to the composer's intentions. If your writer will kindly refer to a full score of the Mahler First, he will find quite elaborate instructions for the precise moment at which the horn players are to stand. My knowledge of German being, to say the leaast, rather sketchy, I took the precaution of asking an eminent Viennese colleague to translate the pertinent paragraph for me.
> Yours &c.
>
> JOHN BARBIROLLI

> To the Editor of the *Guardian* 9 December 1959
> Sir,—One rejoices to read in the criticism of last week's concert of the Sinfonia Orchestra of Newcastle that the

new orchestra is commanding popular support in its native city. Your critic 'T.B.', in his remarks on the performance of Beethoven's 'Emperor' Concerto, points to one weakness, however. He says that (Dennis Matthews's) 'technical brilliance was unfortunately not given the necessary support from the orchestra, which lacked the balance and strength of a larger wind section—*especially* '*trombones*'' (my italics). Your critic also brings into his review the question of 'the struggle for survival' of British orchestras. Your public could gain the impression that financial stringency has prevented the new orchestra from using trombones in Beethoven's 'Emperor'. There is much evidence for this. And I must confess with shame that the Hallé Orchestra, always concerned with economics, also has been giving performances of the 'Emperor' without trombones. In actual fact the Hallé has been committing the crime for over one hundred years, and some research shows that all the world's greatest orchestras—from Boston to Vienna—have been doing the same. The question comes—and your readers are surely entitled to an answer—why should orchestras economise on Beethoven's 'Emperor'? I have a theory which you may care to check. Could it possibly be that Beethoven never included trombones in the score of his piano concertos?

Yours &c.

JOHN BARBIROLLI
Manchester

But while conversation, conviviality and wit came easily to John at times, there was another quieter side to his personality. He genuinely preferred to avoid pomp—when he was offered a knighthood he had wanted to be quite certain that he would not be expected henceforth to change his way of life.

In Edinburgh he always used to stay in digs with a Mrs McNab (no five-star hotel for him!), and when the knighthood was announced in the Scottish papers Mrs McNab cooked Evelyn and John a fish and chip supper after the concert as a celebration.

He was a recluse in many respects, a public figure with an inner self. His favourite place away from the 'madding crowd' was the little-known seaside resort, Seaford in his beloved East Sussex. He wanted anonymity even at the bank; D. W. Lander, who worked there, recalled:

> After my demob from the Army in 1947, I spent a year at the Midland Bank in Seaford, as a cashier. Sir John was one of my customers.
>
> His main object was to get away from the spotlight and . . . it was quite easy for him to come to a place like Seaford and walk about the little town without being recognized by the passers-by, or even the shopkeepers.
>
> When he visited the bank he did not wish his name to be mentioned, so I always addressed him as 'Mr Russell', which he appreciated very much . . .
>
> I remember meeting him in the town one lunch hour and he was quite perturbed, as he had been to the bank and seen a face other than my own at the counter—a deputy standing in for me as I was at lunch—and he thought his identity might have been revealed in front of other customers, so he left and told me he would only return during the afternoon when I was back again from my meal.

He was a creature of moods, sometimes overwhelmed by a sense of melancholia—a state of depression that had been nurtured by his strong sense of history and his memories of that London of pre-1914 that was never to return but was part of his lifetime and so would remain with him for ever.

John confessed that even at early morning rehearsals the closing of Elgar's Second Symphony would never fail to bring tears to his eyes; and the nostalgia induced by the tuneful melodies of the past, compositions by Edward German, Lehàr and Johann Strauss would always evoke the Italian side of his childhood. (Some idea of what it was like is given in the Mrs Robert Henrey's *Bloomsbury Fair* which features the Barbirolli family prominently.) Sir Henry Irving's *Life* and the theatre of his day were also irresistible attractions to John, as was the smell of an empty stage or of the dressing rooms themselves. He loved the green rooms and their adjoining workshops where the smell of size, used in scenery construction, pervaded the atmosphere. The nostalgia he felt for days that could never return is evoked by Michael Kennedy in his *Barbirolli*:

> Childhood memories for Barbirolli meant not only the Lincoln's Inn bandstand but the tale of how his father's violin was smashed in the excitement of Mafeking night at the Lyric Club, of wonderful Christmases, with Lorenzo returning home in a hansom cab laden with gifts for the family from the Queen's Hotel, Leicester Square, where he conducted the orchestra, the building of the London Opera House in Kingsway, bank holidays on Hampstead Heath, a visit to Paris exploring the old streets and buildings and listening to sermons on Sunday mornings at Notre Dame, and summer holidays at Brighton, a town he always loved, remembering the elegance of the piers and the church parades.

It is paradoxical that at such times, *holiday* periods, he would grow sad. His fits of depression even manifested themselves (and he associated the hated word 'rest' with the same state) when he was not working. His old friend, the pianist Sir Clifford Curzon, told us only a short time before his own death in September 1982:

> J.B. didn't like holidays. He felt edgy, displaced, discontented and in a hurry to get back to his extremely enjoyable musical life. A few short, sharp interludes, maybe, were necessary. But weeks of it? No. He'd much rather be at work.

Only by taking his scores with him, when away from London on those holidays he hated, could John maintain a state that did not border on advanced melancholia. He was steeped in music from the start; playing and listening to it was his sole antidote to those moods that had haunted him (and other men and women of talent) down the years.

Humphrey Brooke for many years acted as Secretary of the Royal Academy of Arts. Himself a manic depressive, yet able to write about his condition with a great objectivity, he is of the opinion that such people—'with their black dogs of depression'—tend to arouse strong feelings, one way or the other, being verbose, opinionated and egotistical, all at the same time. They tend to make superhuman demands upon their husbands or wives, who need to be exceptionally intelligent and sympathetic when dealing with the 'state' when the mood is at its worst. Brooke contends that manic depressives are often of high education and intelligence and he goes on to quote that eminent psychiatrist, Dr William Sargent, who had placed on record his opinion: 'Everything that is called genius—from Shakespeare to Churchill—is manic depressive in its most non-depressive phase.' Dr Sargent, an authority on music, contends that Wagner, Mahler, Schumann, Elgar and Rachmaninov: should be included among the composers he would diagnose as manic depressives, and that the conductor Otto Klemperer had suffered from this condition for some years before he died. Emerging from a depressive phase, Rachmaninov wrote his Second Piano Concerto, arguably his greatest work, in less than a week.

From what has been written and said about John's intense melancholia throughout his life, both during adversity and whilst enjoying unprecedented success, one is perhaps justified in asking whether he too was *a manic* depressive.

There are those like Humphrey Brooke, who regard manic-depression as not a disadvantage at all. On the contrary, he regards it as 'an enormous advantage'. In his view it is a peculiar anomaly:

> One cannot say the person who has it *suffers* from it. I don't think that's correct. The person who has it alternates between moods in which the cerebral processes are totally paralysed, which is called depression, and periods in which these cerebral processes are magnified at least ten times.

Audrey Napier-Smith has cited Bertrand Russell:

> The power to produce great art is often, though by no means always, associated with a temperamental unhappiness so great that, but for the joy which the artist derives from his work, he would be driven to suicide.

as her specific authority for holding this opinion on one aspect of her friend's character:

> To my mind J.B. was a typical example of this, which may account somewhat for the deep depressions he so often suffered, and for his insecurity. However high he stood in music, however internationally famous, with honours, family, friends, money, he still worried before every concert* that he would not reach his best standard in his music—and if he did (in a very important event) he would possibly be very depressed the next day. Like many insecure people, artists especially, he needed to be constantly reassured, and his best reassurance would be the feeling that his work—and himself—were loved. Being warm-hearted and openly emotional, he gave out so much affection and felt always a great need to receive even more back. His bitterest unhappiness was when he felt 'let down' by a friend—as in the Crickmore business. He would be very loyal to those who loved him and were loyal to him, but this made him an easy victim to flatterers. He knew this in his heart, but very seldom recognized it when it actually happened. After he was knighted he said to Norah Sandeman, a cellist in the Hallé and a very old friend of Evelyn's and his: 'Now I won't know who my friends are.'
>
> Evelyn to my mind provided all the stability he lacked, and was independent from (though naturally appreciative of) the affection of friends and loved ones. I felt that he relied on her, feeling secure by knowing she was 'there'. When he told me, at times, of his troubles and difficulties, I noted that the greater the problem the more often the words 'Evelyn says . . .' crept into the conversation. In their own home atmosphere he must have been very unpredictable—impatient and intolerant over something apparently unimportant—and patient when one would expect the fur to fly. I remember him at home once, in the kitchen with me, opening the wine for

*Before each visit to Berlin, where he was adored by orchestra, audiences and even critics, he was terrified and felt always that this joy and success could not possibly happen yet again.

> my father. The cork, for some reason, suddenly shot out and the red wine soaked his face, his hair, his white shirtfront—not to mention the wall! He never moved an inch, he was not disturbed in any way, not even a mild annoyance.'

Many years earlier, in 1944, with the Hallé, he was already troubled by depression. Writing to Evelyn he confesses, 'I have no excuse to offer, just this load of depression which seems to have descended on me. Tho' it seems some years since I have had such an unrelieved bout. I know myself of old, and *please* don't think me obstinate, but to keep myself occupied working is the only remedy. God knows, I have few other excuses, and this one I am afraid I must ask you to bear with a little longer.'

In 1966 his depressions—now recognized in medicine as an illness—grew progressively worse.

It was in Cyprus in 1968, according to Clive Smart, who was travelling with the Hallé at the time, that he witnessed one of J.B.'s worst tantrums—doubtless from having the 'black dog' sitting too heavily on his shoulders:

> We were playing on an open-air stage (the conductor's room was like a dungeon), and after the two-hour concert he walked back slowly and flopped down on the first seat. This was quite usual but here the whole audience thought he had had it. So they stopped applauding and didn't even want him to walk back again to the front of the stage. The applause died to nothing—he seemed so tired that it seemed a shame to bring him back.
>
> He came into the ten-foot square dungeon and I've never seen him 'blow his top' as he did then. Walking-stick and baton flew round the room and it was 'I came all this bloody way . . . etc'. We managed to calm him and convince him that they were just concerned about his health.

Another account said that he would customarily 'collapse' into a chair at the side of the platform in half-view of the audience until an ovation brought him back. But at Cyprus they considerately remained silent and tiptoed out.

In his book, *Barbirolli*, his friend Michael Kennedy quotes him as saying 'When one of these clouds is over me, all I can think of is the dark tunnel I'm in and all I can do is to work because if I didn't I might do something irrevocable.' And he also points out that Barbirolli underlined a sentence of Churchill's in a book about him written by his physician, Lord Moran: 'Death is the greatest gift God has made to us.' This underlined sentence is left without comment, with none of his customary marginal pencillings.

25 *Evelyn: Woman Alone*

Evelyn had almost abandoned her own career during the last years of John's life in an effort to 'postpone the event', to ease his way, take all possible strain from him so that this extraordinary spirit, with whom at times there was little of the physical left, might continue to the very last to make his great contribution to the world of music.

In the first six months after his death the void seemed unbearable. Much more than half of life was gone. In spite of her own high reputation, John had always come first—not only had their love and respect and complete trust in each other made his continuing to live imperative to her, but his reliance on her was implicit in all musical matters where her judgement was sought, her advice invited. She helped him sometimes to mark the parts they played, together and separately. Additional to the loyalty he received from his orchestras—particularly the Hallé—was her outgiving friendship; a care for the people with whom they worked. Her quiet generosity went unpublicized. She had never inspired jealousy: generally acknowledged to be one of our foremost oboists, she had always been content to stand aside, sharing the battles but watching from the wings as the fiercer light shone on him (though he had always encouraged her as an artist to learn and perfect the most difficult oboe pieces). Her repose and outer self-command hid a highly nervous being. Martin Milner saw them both from a professional's point of view:

J.B. needed a marvellous wife to understand him and in Evelyn he had one who could cope with his demanding mentality. It was Evelyn, the one nearest and dearest, who most understood him and could help him in his own interests. In spite of his sweetness and charm he could be completely illogical. In front of the orchestra he could, and would, say 'black's white' and nobody dared contradict him. Although I could speak frankly with him man-to-man, if he had made his mind up there could be no point in arguing with him!

He must have been a difficult person to live with. This is where I admired Evelyn so much in her role as wife. As in her playing, so in her public life with J.B., she was highly professional. In this capacity one could not help but admire her for the manner in which she fended off other people, those welcome and unwelcome visitors to the Green Room.

As a player, Evelyn is an extremely professional musician, and the oboe suits her. It was her musicianship that was the strongest feature of her playing at all times—that and her character combined. Personally, I found this self-effacement that she is generally supposed to have to be more at her insistence; reserving a right to keep her private person private and not make it public unless *she* wants it that way. My experience is that she's not a shy person. She stands for what's right in her own eyes. It's a mark of her integrity. That was something they shared to the hilt.

Without doubt, Evelyn is acutely conscious of the human condition and predicament—for example, the price that has to be paid for having a heightened degree of sensibility. But while this brings one into tune with the glories of nature and of art it also renders one particularly susceptible to the effects of the 'slings and arrows of outrageous fortune' to such a painful degree as to be beyond the comprehension of those not so affected.

Evelyn's life with John tested, indeed developed, her compassion and her own sensibility. The public picture of this charismatic couple was, of course, only part of the story. To share one's life with a partner is, ineluctably, to share joys and sorrows to such a degree as to form a separate dimension to life itself. For Evelyn, John's depressions were an undoubted burden—just as her deep understanding of them must have been of inestimable value to John. Even before the last few years, her anxiety had been detected throughout the Fifties and Sixties. When writing to their friend, Audrey Napier-Smith, mention of his health runs through every letter. Back in 1957 she wrote from Oslo:

> John is (I hope) asleep upstairs after a very bad night, poor love . . . I am worried that John is so tired. He *is* enjoying the trip really, and finds the enormously successful concerts stimulating, but this whipping up of strange orchestras in limited rehearsal time is very wearing, no matter how willing and eager they are (and they *really* are, too!) He gets out quite a bit, which is good, and is eating well too.

Later the same year she wrote from Rovigo, near Padua (where he was visiting Italian cousins):

> John, poor darling, is still terribly depressed. He is pretty good physically now, and doesn't get tired abnormally; insides work well without aids now, and he doesn't sleep *too* badly. He tries to eat, but this kind of depression makes him disinterested in everything, including food and beautiful places and climate.
>
> We both hope and pray daily that this melancholia will pass and that he will stick out this time in Italy. He really does try hard, but, at present, work is the only thing which helps.

Later in the same letter she apologizes:

> Dear Audrey, this is a dull letter—I think I may be slightly depressed mentally, too, in sympathy! though what a lovely country it is, and *how* grateful I am to be here. I only wish John could enjoy it and then my pleasure would be quadrupled!

Even when she herself was laid low, in Houston seven years

later, she seemed more concerned for the extra strain on John than for herself:

> John has been so sweet about looking after me, as you can imagine, and I feel sad that it has put just that much more on him to have to arrange people to drive him to shop, etc. and then prepare it all.

She sounds the same note three years later, writing from a hotel on the Opera Ring in Vienna, and recalling their recent tour in Italy:

> Damn it—I chose those days to have a violent cold with a temperature high enough to force me to stay in bed—did the Marcello though! Nearly gone now, though, and I pray J. will escape the bug.

But, she remembers happily:

> He really was in the 'brodo' (you will know his Venetian expression 'in a broth of violets') talking Venetian in his beloved Padova, and even ate a bit more than usual!

While the precise cause of John's depressions is unknown, we do know that for him they were painfully real. Our researches revealed a sense of insecurity, despite his undoubted recognition as a highly distinguished musician. Without our presuming to analyse this sense of insecurity, its existence has been acknowledged, and so has the burden it placed on Evelyn, who played such a vital supportive role in John's triumphs. But she has been able to use this vicarious experience of depression. The wife of Sidney Rothwell suffered from depressions so severe that she eventually killed herself. Rothwell says that Evelyn wrote him a letter 'of such supreme humanity and understanding' that he repeatedly drew 'comfort and spiritual sustenance' from it.

> The deep humanity of Evelyn assumed its finest flowering in a letter she wrote to me following the death of my dear wife, Marianne—who committed suicide on 20th May, 1979. The event itself was deeply grievous, but

> was in fact the culmination of a long, traumatic experience deriving in the main from the Holocaust (Marianne was Jewish, was born in Berlin and came to this country at the age of fifteen—later to learn of the loss of her parents in Auschwitz). Of the vast number of letters I received, that from Evelyn was pre-eminent in its deep understanding of the enormity of the tragedy and of my consequent bereavement. Having herself known the pain of bereavement, Evelyn was able to write—directly from the heart—a letter of such understanding (albeit in no way minimizing the degree of sorrow that must inevitably be my lot) as to be a potent source of comfort and reassurance on many occasions since Marianne's death.

That quality of kindness of spirit, coupled with practical generosity, has endeared Evelyn to many. Brenda Bracewell, who worked for the Barbirollis, always felt that she was a trusted friend:

> Too much cannot be said about her generosity. I personally found it difficult to believe that she insisted on my using her car, just after I had commenced working for them . . . In addition, she made Huntsworth Mews available to me if I wanted a break in London whenever they were both away, leaving me helpful lists of local shops etc. . . . and the making of such lists consumed her precious time.
>
> Whenever they went on their travels, she never failed to bring me something back, always carefully and thoughtfully chosen.
>
> And there was the occasion when I had fallen downstairs and badly hurt my back. I eventually arrived at Walton Lodge mid-morning; she immediately stopped work and bundled me down to the centre of Manchester, to her osteopath, waited for the treatment to be finished and then drove me all the way home. All this at great physical cost to herself and a wonderfully practical gesture, during what I knew was a frantically busy period in her life.

During the initial period after John's death, alone after thirty years of a remarkable marriage, memories came crowding in. She remembered their courting while they were with the Scottish Orchestra in Glasgow—how, when they were free, they would take the tram to Loch Lomond and go for long walks, rounding off the day with those steak and claret dinners. She was then 'the tall lassie with the wee mon' . . .

In the Forties, as a break from the New York Philharmonic engagement, she and John used to take a house in Vancouver during the early summer and move to the Hollywood Bowl concerts with the Los Angeles Philharmonic. Then, surrounded by such musical kindred spirits as Horowitz, José Iturbi, Francescatti and others—one of the others was the film star Edward G. Robinson, who delighted in turning the pages of J.B.'s cello parts—Evelyn and John revelled in playing and hearing chamber music privately 'for fun' in the houses of the many famous musicians there for the summer. This had proved a sedative at the time, and a recording of one of these purely private musical 'get-togethers' with Dorothy Kennedy playing piano, Evelyn oboe, and John cello brought back many happy memories. (If the collector of rare recordings is lucky this can be found through the Barbirolli Society, and other useful additions from such private music sessions, made together, or separately, can be heard with J.B. playing the cello for the Music Society String Quartet in the early Twenties.)

She was glad that his old mother had died before her son. Mémé saw fulfilled most of her hopes, never having to endure the great grief of losing any of her closely-knit, intensely loyal family. Evelyn remembered the great days, the heroic times when Mémé's little boy had emerged as a musical giant. She reflected on those occasions when he'd attracted the jealousy of other artists. But these were isolated cases. He was star quality, as artist and as man, though his problems had not always been as easy of solution as the world thought. His path, for the most part, had been upwards but the battles had left their scars.

In remaking her own life Evelyn was fortunate in having a musical reputation which enabled her to take up her professional career; and she was soon intensely busy playing concerts. She has many good friends, and is very fond of her own family and of John's. She goes as often as she can to the home of her younger brother in the country, where she is 'spoilt' by her sister-in-law and family, and she keeps in close touch with John's family in London.

A great joy has been travelling abroad with Kay Green, a good friend. During the past few years they have been to Turkey, Persia, Syria, Jordan, Tunisia, Greece, Sicily, Crete, France, Egypt, Italy, and Oberammagau, visiting some of these places more than once. She has also been three times to the USA for concerts and Master Classes. Being a born traveller she loves to see—and to photograph—new places.

Her handling of public and domestic matters, following John's death, proved reassuring to the warmly emotional family of which she had become such an integral part. She decided to move her main home to London soon after John died. Both their families lived in the south. She came up from Manchester several times to look for a house, staying in the tiny cottage in Huntsworth Mews, which unfortunately was far too small to take all their precious furniture and possessions. On the last of her house-hunting expeditions she saw a property with a 'For sale' board, which had not been there the night before. Although it had been an ironmonger's shop, it was in the district she wanted and seemed right, so she finalized the deal as soon as possible. It is a corner structure that spills into a side street and has its main entrance in a narrow little row of houses with a semi-old-fashioned pub almost opposite her front door that does nothing to disturb the tranquillity of the quiet neighbourhood.

Since its renovation, she has installed a kitchen in the basement, along with an outside garden covered with wire netting (to keep out the cats), where her plants are a solace and pride, numerous, varied and lovely, and a beauty to behold for all those permitted to visit the 'lady with the green fingers', as she's frequently called by her neighbours in the short, narrow, rustic street. Upstairs—where once an ironmonger did his accounts and slumbered after days of toil—can be found her bedroom, and there's a boxroom for files and so on as well as her music room.

It is here that this woman alone is rarely ever alone. Apart from her daily practice, she takes the few favoured pupils in whom she sees genuine promise and for whose benefit she will encourage, criticize constructively and gently communicate her own vast storehouse of knowledge to guide on their way, in the gruelling time ahead, aspiring young musicians in the modern world. She is often away from London—playing, lecturing, adjudicating, giving master classes and travelling for pleasure. She has recently revised her early publication *Oboe Technique*, and the later publication *The Oboist's Companion* in three volumes is a definitive work on that instrument.

Evelyn is much stronger than the average person; to call her larger than life is to do her an injustice. She possesses a virtue all too often absent from most of her fellows: patience. However much she may blaze away inside, she has always managed to look at all those she encounters with a thoughtful understanding—something that never smacks of insincerity, because she is genuinely interested in the problems that beset anyone who goes to her for help. She is ready with advice of a practical and constructive nature, never permitting herself, it seems to lose patience with the ringing phone or bemoan the fact that no letter has arrived as promised. She can look out to a world away from bleak, wet and noisy streets, cities no longer beautiful up to the stars in their heavens. She manages to see past the rooftops of her present life to that other world where the patient ones may take their own reward.

Evelyn is often talked about as a musician who actually enjoys 'doing her own thing'. Actors, ballet dancers, writers and painters are never, when together, as steeped in their respective pursuits as are those musicians in the Barbirolli circle of fellow players; something that was started by him (perpetuated by her) with his free talk, so amusingly delivered, without a trace of envy, malice or self-love—only devotion to music. He could hardly have been said to have hobbies—music was, above all, his life and is Evelyn's too (though she enjoys gardening and photography). But they had had more in common than music, strong bond though that was. For instance, their interest in antique glass, formed even before meeting each other. Evelyn had one or two, and John had a few glasses which he prized. When, together, they both became more and more interested and particularly when they returned from America after the war, glass was then very cheap. They bought a lot when they first got back, and continued to buy it through the years. Today Evelyn buys very rarely. 'The prices have got very high and I've no room anyway.' They loved the look of glass and the shapes and engravings. 'The only one I've ever broken, when washing it, was the one that John liked best. My friend, the glass expert Howard Phillips, had it repaired.' John was also particularly fond of a very rare piece, the only known portrait on glass of Nelson.

Ursula Vaughan Williams is appreciative of what Evelyn has achieved on her own:

> Evelyn has become a very talented and inventive gardener. With almost no space at her command in the tiny area of her London house she has conjured a mass of flowers from the narrow, raised flower bed she had built. When you reach the house you look down on a carpet of colour, scented air wafts round the door, and her roses flourish rising from an undercarpet of annuals. This seems emblematic of her life—wherever she goes welcome and pleasure spring up, her company is as enchanting as her garden, and her house too is filled with pleasure. Everything is arranged to be a delight to the eye, the kitchen suggests the groups a painter would enjoy turning into a still life—but the real life flows on, in delectable meals, conversation, and of course music.

Nowadays, Evelyn can pursue her many interests and live her life to the full. She does it alone. But still that nervous energy John communicated to her, that she was left as legacy, is for ever on the move. It is John—always John—the man and the artist she is obsessed by, and on her return from a trip to Greece, she wrote to a Continental recording company asking them to reissue some of the discs that are now deleted, or had never been recorded commercially by John.

> On return from a brief stay in Europe I have heard from the Barbirolli Society that they have been in communication with you re the possibility of your releasing the recordings you have of Vaughan Williams Symph. No. 6 and of the Partita of William Walton. May I add to their

pleas my own, which comes to you not only from the purely musical angle but also from a more personal one. The recordings in question were made only a very short time before my husband's death in July 1970. In fact it was in Munich, after making these recordings, that he suffered the first of many heart attacks. As you will know from other correspondence, EMI are deleting more and more of my husband's commercial recordings so that now, only seven years after his death, he is not at all well represented on discs. However, the particular reason for wishing a greater public to hear the recordings under discussion with you, is that the composers felt so strongly that my husband had a great understanding of their works. Vaughan Williams relied greatly on his judgement and feeling for his music and even altered some metronome tempi on my husband's advice. It is sad that my husband never recorded this 6th Symph. commercially. It seems vital that this interpretation should be available to the record buying public, and by making these two works available to the Barbirolli Society.

She fills every scrap of her day—gets up early, does the shopping. With a daily diary chock-full, she always makes time to receive those who need encouragement and practical help. She is for ever available to old friends from scores of years earlier. She makes people feel important. There is nothing premeditated about her good deeds. Without calculating profit or loss she makes no difference, once she decides that one is her friend.

Mrs Irene Quinn, Evelyn's housekeeper, is in her mid-sixties and comes in to look after Evelyn's house twice a week.

She works so hard. She goes away on recitals and abroad to lecture and adjudicate. Then she comes back and starts all over again. She doesn't permit herself any rest and has so many engagements that sometimes looking at her, and listening to her talking on the phone that is rarely silent, one would think her to be another teenager instead of a mature woman who is such a tried—and often *tired*—artist. There's little chance of her getting rest when in Town. When she's not playing or adjudicating, she's teaching. As a person she doesn't spare herself—she's overkind.

She worries about the young and the old; her in-laws and her own brothers and their families. All of them keep in touch with her. She does all her own shopping, all her own cooking, all her own laundry, as well as rehearsing and teaching; pupils come here and she attends the Academy, she types all her own correspondence—hundreds of letters each week, sometimes, and she has no secretary—every letter is read by her and replied to personally—she does all her own filing too. But I don't know how anybody half, or even a quarter, her age, would get through each day what she gets through.

Evelyn was President of the Incorporated Society of Musicians for a year, and is always much in demand in various capacities connected with music. With Ronald Kinloch Anderson, she was one of those behind the creation of the 'Barbirolli Room' at the Royal Academy of Music, recently opened and filled with Barbirolliana. Her success in varied projects undertaken has been largely due to her warmth, a unique sense of humour and fun. As a chairman she can preside over a public meeting; she can make a witty after-dinner speech or give interviews on television or radio and makes all such occasions entertaining and pleasurable. She can get on with most people, the least likely responding to her charm and lack of any sort of affectation; a critical but constructive judgement is always there to ensure that her natural generosity of spirit does not often get out of hand.

Evelyn was invited as guest of honour on Ladies' Night to the Savage Club on 8 May 1981. Thirty-five years earlier John, a distinguished member, had chaired the annual dinner at this club (on 7 December 1946) with Sir Arnold Bax the composer and Sir Alexander Fleming the discoverer of penicillin as guests of honour, and that occasion was recalled as one of the best and most amusing of all Savage banquets.

The Club turned out in force again for the Barbirolli name, as well as to honour a distinguished artist, but few members had expected to be treated to so many cracks, digs and jokes in what turned out to be a witty and highly informative reply by the latest guest of honour. Evelyn showed herself at her ripest that night, recalls Peter Cotes (himself a Brother Savage); 'In the Lady Violet Bonham Carter class,' murmured another who was present.

Her own background, education and standards were an enormous help to her after John's death. She soon re-established herself as a sought-after artist in her own right—not just as John's widow. One thing still came first—John. His name must be kept alive. She decided no longer to be known as Evelyn Rothwell, but Evelyn Barbirolli—that was her first step.

John is always there—whatever else she may be doing—and now with her own name to perpetuate his own; the Barbirolli Foundation; the memorial tree in Russell Square that stands a permanent reminder of the heart of oak that was born less than 400 yards away above a baker's shop in Southampton Row . . .

Although John and his needs had always come first, there had been times (not so many towards the end, naturally), and it had actually been good for their marriage, when she felt she was not needed and could go off, independently of John, to play in various orchestras as a soloist, or do recitals with her duo pianist, Iris Loveridge, or harpsichordist Valda Aveling. She had been sensible and intelligent in the way in which she had combined being the perfect wife and the independent artist. So her position in the world of music held, even in that last, less fruitful, decade. And the many years of working together with John could only give her strength after he had finally left her. But we may gain an inkling of the loss she must have felt if we consider how John's death affected Sidney Rothwell:

> In a sense, the most sincere tribute I can pay to Evelyn is to point to the fact that I have been privileged to enjoy her friendship for nearly forty years. Our formal relationship (when I was, successively, a member of staff of the Hallé Concerts Society and then John's private secretary) lasted a mere four years, but this formed the basis of a lasting friendship with both John and Evelyn. With the passage of years, I now find in Evelyn one of a diminishing band of that select few with whom one can

communicate, at what I can only describe—without, I hope, sounding sententious—on a deeply spiritual level.

The impact on my personal life of my relationship with John and Evelyn was movingly illustrated on the day that John's death was announced in the Press. Together with my family, I was in Berlin on 30th July 1970. It was my wife's practice to collect that day's copy of *Die Welt* on her way to breakfast. On that particular morning—with John's death making front page news—she carefully hid the newspaper until breakfast was finished. Then, clearly obeying instructions from their mother, our sons disappeared from the dining room and Marianne—with infinite solicitude—showed me the front page of the newspaper.

26 Coda

In her early seventies today, Evelyn still goes on, playing at home and abroad, cheering, coaxing, constructively criticizing and, among many other calls upon her time and energies, delighting in the business of adjudicating at music festivals. Indeed, she gives as much to a class of half-a-dozen students when adjudicating in a village hall as she does to a jury of distinguished fellow musicians in competitions such as the BBC 'Young Musician of the Year' or the famous international ones in Munich or Prague.

A fine musician does not necessarily make a good teacher or a good judge. But Evelyn is at once judge, teacher, adjudicator, understanding aunt and mother confessor. The clever one has little time for the fool, although a wise one who is not merely clever can spare time. Evelyn has time to spare, patience in abundance, a wish to go on and on and get things right, to make the talentless as well as the talented see a way through a maze of technical and musical difficulties.

Her patience with stupid people who try is perhaps greater than her refusal to be defeated by those clever people who refuse to be receptive—and are liable to forfeit her help.

One day we witnessed her adjudicating at a small competitive festival, from five pm until after ten at night. By the time the finals had been arrived at, she had heard all sorts of woodwind instruments—clarinets, oboes, recorders, flutes—and had made many helpful comments:

> I think if you go twice as fast, as the composer asks, it will help!
>
> Very good ensemble on the whole. I thought this more than promising. Well done.
>
> It was out of tune all too often.
>
> You made a bad start. Lack of control (through nerves perhaps?) But it kept going, on the whole, quite well. You must listen to the tone. It was always loud and it must be kept flowing.
>
> You had a lovely feeling for changes of mood, but you can afford to improve the tone quality; it is too edgy at the moment.
>
> A very difficult choice this, and I feel you haven't worked at it a great deal because the ensemble left much to be desired. At its best it sounded only competent. Music flagged. Tempo was slow.

So she goes on, never withholding constructive comment, refusing to cast down, trying always to elevate, but never compromising or making the kind of concession that lulls the indolent into false security and self-complacency. She herself has always worked hard, and believes that music can never be a career for those who think it can be made without strenuous effort, however apt and naturally talented the contestant.

As 'closing time' approaches and tired officials look as though they could go to sleep standing up, here she is again. 'You know'—she says this with a wide smile and is nodding her head vigorously in time to a wagging index finger stabbing at the air—'you know, I enjoyed this very much indeed. The rising phrases could have been more flowing, but the dynamics were there. So well done: I've given you 85!'

Evelyn is a tall, imposing, commanding presence on a platform. She projects without effort. Her audience of youthful aspirants, with their middle-aged and sometimes elderly relatives and friends, listens intently, never needing to crane forward to catch every syllable.

What makes her such a splendid adjudicator and fine teacher is her practical experience. Like John, she has played in many orchestras and ensembles—chamber, operatic, popular and classical. These have given her a grounding for which no theoretical knowledge can substitute. Evelyn forgets herself, and so nobody is allowed to forget her. She has a 'presence' capable of affecting all who play in festivals and musical contests. They are told, gently but firmly, about their intonation and lack of vitality, as well as, when they possess such assets, their flowing and expressive sounds.

Gerry McDonald, an ex-pupil, says:

> E.B. was always friendly and helpful to her pupils and I have a memory of how she did battle upon their behalf with the powers-that-be. She was ever-ready to defend students who could not tall for themselves, and on several occasions she would purchase oboes herself for deserving ones who didn't have the money; so that if these students who needed a better instrument found such and such an oboe to their liking, she would give it to them and they could repay her when they were in funds. She would do this for deserving people—those she could trust to work hard or those who had talent, and she automatically trusted those with integrity. I know she helped a friend of mine who is now working in one of the most important Irish orchestras: a girl who had great financial difficulties when she was at the Academy. And she was helpful over and above teaching.
>
> E.B. absolutely hates pretentious people and is always completely open and natural. On those rare occasions when she does get irritated with people—without ever losing her temper—I certainly wouldn't like to be on the

'receiving end' of her annoyance.* She was always very interested in students who were keen; not necessarily the most talented. I would have only made, at best, an adequate oboe player. She told me this to my face after my second year, because she thought I could take this information and be sensible about it, she said. And I said I'd been worrying about this myself for some time and I'd only about three weeks earlier taken up the recorder. After E. had had this talk with me about what I was going to do, I asked if I might play it for her. She said I obviously had talent on the recorder and she advised me that, in her view, my particular niche would be found in one of the baroque groups. So from then on I tended to specialize more and more in baroque playing—I bought a baroque oboe, worked at it and played it to E. at several of my lessons and after I'd been playing it for some time she thought I might play a couple of pieces for my annual exam on it. She said: 'Okay, Gerry, we've now got past the stage where we agree that you're promising and can actually *play* the thing; now you've got to play it in tune and *musically*.'

The standard form of address for Evelyn at the Academy is Lady B. Students address her like that to her face. It would be presumptuous to call her anything else.

When they get to know Evelyn well she's outgiving and projects to her students an image of great kindness and patience. But woe betide those who lag behind when they could be doing better! Evelyn drives herself mercilessly. Long regarded as one of the best oboists of her day by students, as well as by the general public, she always produces phrasing which is musical and with much colour and wide, dynamic range. She has extraordinary stamina as well. Evelyn has taught down the years a number of very fine players. Gerry McDonald again:

*'The only time I've ever seen Evelyn really angry was in a hotel car park, when the manager was very rude to her, and inhospitable. I realized then what someone had once told me: "She can be very formidable at times."' (Audrey Napier-Smith)

She has always been tremendously encouraging to *young* players, because she does a lot of Festival adjudicating and examining. I remember being told by Chris Redgate that one day he was studying the Haydn Concerto with her at Chetham's School of Music in Manchester, and she suddenly brusquely interrupted him by saying, 'Look Chris, this is an Andante, not an Adagio,' and she proceeded forthwith to get up, making great booming noises as she strode across the rehearsal room floor.

She does always try to encourage her students, never losing sight of the importance of being realistic at the same time. What endeared E. to the pupils at the colleges she's taught at is her refusal to toe the Establishment line if she thinks it unfair, or does any sort of disservice to her students. She would always be behind what she would regard as a just cause. She has always been interested in what students were doing—even after she has stopped seeing them. Once I was having 'girl-friend' trouble and she smoothed it out and ironed the creases. My old chum, Tony Robson, got married and E. (who was Tony's teacher at the Royal Academy) was unable to get to the wedding. But she remembered the date, sent a wire and lovely present to them both, and later visited them.

What makes a good music teacher? Certainly, since the time when Evelyn decided to give a large part of her life to helping others—busy though she was—she felt a duty to pass on her knowledge and experience to the up-and-coming or less fortunate members of her profession. She proved the fallacy of the widely-held notion that all teachers are frustrated performers. A point to remember when making an appraisal of this *oboe* teacher is that Evelyn is highly skilled at making reeds, and one of her books deals with most of the problems that one can encounter in this field. Her three-volume tutor *The Oboist's Companion* is 'required reading' for students during their first year at the Royal Academy. There are few who have not been helped by its sound common-sense and constructive advice. The work typifies Evelyn the woman, as well as the artist, for it's a 'no-nonsense' book that comes straight to the point and is as instructive to the musical layman as it is beneficial to the student.

Nowadays, between engagements at home and abroad, she teaches advanced pupils, and sets out first of all to show her students how to communicate. She believes that one must be both perceptive and generous, be lavish with one's time and not dole out one's talents in little parcels.

In the 1982 'Young Musician of the Year' competition, televised as a musical celebration, Evelyn was one of the judges. She explained how they approach the task of finding the winner of such an event. Making all of it simple, she pointed out that judging between competitors playing widely varying works on different instruments is not as difficult as it is sometimes made to appear. In the early rounds, the eliminations are on grounds of inadequate technique or musicality, or lack of soloistic flair. By the time the semi-finals are reached the judges take basic skills for granted. Then:

> We look for performances which move us, hold our interest, give us the most musical satisfaction. In fact we look for expert instrumentalists who have the personality to project their musical interpretations.

In the past Evelyn has frequently adjudicated the preliminary rounds, which are more for basic technical ability. For the finals the judges are compelled to be harsher:

> It's necessary to look for more; those who touch you, who really give a *performance.* Sometimes we judges on the panel disagree with each other. If there *is* disagreement, marks are taken by the chairman (it might be just one person who disagrees with all the rest, or it might be half and half). More often than not we do agree. The decision normally becomes obvious when the judges are good musicians, professional in outlook.

Evelyn is not only concerned about those who are directly her pupils; she is concerned for young people and the encouragement of all musical talent. This manifests itself in the amount of adjudicating she undertakes—under such distinguished auspices as that of the Chamber Music Competition for Schools Trust, of which she is a Trustee. And her involvement with Chetham's School in Manchester (which, incidentally, produced three of the four finalists in 1982's 'Young Musician of the Year' competition) goes well beyond her formal commitment to audition potential entrants to the school and an annual internal assessment of oboists and other instrumentalists. Her interest in the pupils' welfare is well known, extending beyond each life at the school to later careers. One official of Chetham's told us, 'Evelyn knows more about the school's pupils than we do!'

Evelyn today says that she does not wish to become too involved in teaching certain types of music, although her wide and intense interests enable her to voice authoritatively comments that modern players find helpful to their studies. She is interested in many of those techniques that, once so revolutionary, are today no longer regarded as advanced. Musical revolutions are going on constantly and what was regarded as avant-garde five years ago is today traditional oboe music and playing. Evelyn has long been regarded by students as being the very 'last word' in teaching traditional techniques.

In the Seventies with John's death and many commitments to fill, committees to sit on, adjudications (away from the Academy) to give and charitable bequests to administer, her itinerary sometimes became so full and her schedule of professional engagements so overwhelming that she had occasionally to take leave from the Royal Academy. But no time away was ever contemplated, or arrangements made with the Principal, unless her students had initially been taken into consideration.

Below, an itinerary of Evelyn's, taken at random, for three months in 1982.

Monday, April 19th	Adjudicating at the RAM all day for LRAM
Tuesday, April 20th	Adjudicating at the RAM. Fly to Belfast evening
Wed 21—Sun 24th am	Adjudicating for a competition in Belfast
Sat 24th	Fly home late afternoon for Janet Craxton's Memorial concert evening
Sun 25th	Out part of day and evening
Mon 26th	Out from about 11 am until late night
Tues 27th	Teaching all day: out to dinner
Wed 28th	Teaching. Oboe faculty members for working dinner
April 29th	Teaching, then Overseas League Competition Jury Woodwind and Strings semi-finals 5 pm on

April 30th	To Tamworth
May 1st	Adjudicating in Tamworth
May 2nd, Sunday	Return to London
May 3rd and 4th	In London: teaching and generally clearing up. Out in the evening
May 5th	Overseas finals, Ensembles 5 pm on
May 6th	Day activities not fixed: but have some American musicians to dinner
May 7th	Business luncheon and out to dinner
May 8th	Teaching at home
May 9th, Sunday	To Southampton
May 10, 11, 12	Adjudicating in Southampton
May 13	Return to London
May 14, 15, 16	Away—short break with family in the country
May 17th	Teaching during day: memorial concert at RAM evening
May 18th	To Blackburn
May 19th	Adjudicating and Master Class, Blackburn
May 20th	Return to London
May 21st	Master Class in Chigwell, Essex

Thereafter I am fairly free except for lecturing, adjudicating, radio and TV interviews up North on intermittent dates, returning on June 10th

June 11th	To Bishop Auckland for Master Class evening
June 12th	Bishop Auckland adjudicating
June 13th	Return London
June 14th	Overseas League Finals QEH evening. Leave 5.30 pm
June 15th—18th	Free at present for music practice, etc!
June 19th	Whitstable Concert
June 20th	Return London
June 21, 22, 23, 24	RAM end of term examining
June 25	Great joy! Go to Glyndebourne dress rehearsal of *Orfeo* courtesy of Janet Baker

Then I'm free till I go away 1st or 2nd, and on to Bournemouth Festival 4th to 10th.

Full days indeed! Evelyn and John had always led rich full lives, working to satisfy their sense of perfection—her standards as an artist were so high that she never approached a performance with complete self-confidence. Yet she has played the great oboe concertos many times and still gives recitals covering a wide repertory with her friend, the pianist Iris Loveridge. Some musicians on tour are content with meeting professionally on the concert platform, but the two members of the Barbirolli Duo have a genuine affection for each other. According to Iris Loveridge:

> We seem to live in each other's pockets, and are very attached. In fact we so enjoy working together that afterwards people will come round, or even write later on,

to say that happily we've communicated our sense of enjoyment to them.

E., is much deeper than many people—even those who admire her a great deal—realize. She is more basic than people think when meeting her for the first time. She's witty of tongue, and great fun as a character.

It was only about eight years ago, when she had moved to her present home in London, that Harry (my husband—himself a keen gardener) introduced her to gardening. And, like everything she goes in for, she does it with a vengeance—nowadays seldom passing a garden centre without stopping to look around, sometimes to buy, to take away with her most lovingly. She once told us that she felt in planting and tending she was 'creating'—music, gardening, teaching, all have the sense of creativity so much part of her big-hearted self.

In the spring of 1983 we had a large tour—a crowded diary—for Scotland. She loves Scotland which of course is where it all first really started with John. What makes it fun with us is that Harry's a Scot, too, and I think that John (who was so many things) was called as well as Glorious John and Cockney Johnnie, 'John O'Scotland', also. All very interesting in the land of Burns and Scott! . . . But this was also the land of the National Scottish, where Evelyn and John first grew to know each other when they'd left London and went a-courting to Loch Lomond, as E. has so often told me.

Nowadays she often asks me whether she should retire. Her standards are high and, being a perfectionist, she doesn't want to lose her flair and verve—her mental agility or her physical energy. However, I say, 'No, you must go on—and on.' For really, she's as good as ever . . . Yes, we love playing together and she still makes such beautiful sounds. That real Barbirolli 'sound', that musicians talk about with admiration everywhere.

I'm very fond of Evelyn. It's a great joy to work with her, and I'm glad she enjoys working with me. I'm convinced that's the best way of working—admiring and respecting each other's work and having a warm affection one for the other.

Tully Potter, who is currently writing a biography of Adolf Busch the violinist, first heard Evelyn's playing in the mid-Sixties:

> Busch had great admiration for Evelyn Rothwell, as did his conductor brother Fritz, who gave her a photograph at Glyndebourne inscribed 'The best of all oboe players'.
>
> I last heard her play in 1980, and I remember thinking how superb her breath control still was . . . and she hadn't lost anything in tonal mastery, to my ears.

While Potter felt that Evelyn's introductions to her music, as well as her actual playing, reflected a relaxed and sunny character, Martin Milner had a slightly different view, as he explained in the interview quoted on page 207. As he said, she is an extremely *professional* musician.

John had set much store on her musical judgement. Had trusted her ear implicitly. When they were working in an unfamiliar auditorium they rehearsed together as one, to make sure that the famous Sound was exactly what he was demanding. Pauline Pickering, who formed the Barbirolli Society after his death, had the privilege of watching rehearsals in a wide variety of halls. She recalls Evelyn's activity: at both sides of each hall, standing way back, sitting in the middle; at all acoustic points, making sure that the balance was right; anticipating what John might want without worrying him about it, always unobtrusive, quietly determined to get things right. When John was recording he always liked Evelyn to be in the control-box: he trusted her above all others.

Working with musicians, one becomes aware of a variety of attitudes to their art (or craft)—ranging from the downright cynical to the idealistic. There can be no doubt about Evelyn's attitude. This was forcibly illustrated on one occasion when John and Evelyn's return from abroad was immediately followed by preparations for a major musical event at home. The event was *The Dream of Gerontius* to be given in the Royal Albert Hall. The rehearsals—with the BBC Symphony Orchestra and soloists—were at the BBC's Maida Vale studios and Sidney Rothwell remembers going through some accumulated correspondence just before the start on the first day.

> The music started and, after a time, Evelyn suddenly called a halt—'I must listen to this,' she said. Although deeply involved in business affairs she was, at the same time, acutely conscious of the point John had reached with the orchestra at the singing of 'Go forth upon thy journey, Christian soul!' This was my first experience of *The Dream of Gerontius* and I shall never ever forget the tremendous power—musical and spiritual—of the words that came from the towering figure of David Franklyn. Equally moving was to share this experience with Evelyn, whose identification with the music was quite palpable.

Some people take from other people and drain them. Evelyn is the opposite; she gives of herself and, although she has not the time always to suffer fools gladly, she 'builds' people: making them more. So much of John's energy has been transferred to her; an energetic player and in great demand today, she is a mixture of them both, in a world of music that rarely stops.

Possessed of a nervous energy, a sense of melancholia, and the zest and optimism of all exceptional human beings, John Barbirolli got on with what needed doing, letting the world judge his efforts if it felt so inclined. He always had time for others—he was more concerned about others than himself. His orchestral 'Sound' seemed magical. He willed it from apparently nowhere, from orchestras of all classes and capabilities, as if there'd been no pain, no creative struggle, no personal loss.

And today Evelyn perpetuates the spirit *and* the action. Her life could never again be the same after his death, but she managed to give the lens a twist and brought life again into focus. Like John, she has a sense of values which decrees that some things are worthless and others must be virtually beyond betrayal. Their instinctive sense of decency was always just below the surface, and with Evelyn it still remains: one of her shining attributes. They shared a feeling for life, but it is as though the impish sense of humour, once peculiarly his, has now been transferred to her, along with that receptiveness to new experience, and whatever else comes rolling along.

The date of 5 July has had, for many years past, a dual significance for Evelyn. They were married on that date in 1939, and John made his debut with his newly-formed Hallé on the same date in 1943. But she manages still to make every day for J.B. She feels his presence in some ways as much as when he was in life. A sense of him is there whether she's playing, teaching, adjudicating—or just living. The two of them are combined, as if whatever she does should—must—be worthy of him. It's the most important achievement for Evelyn to realize, and to make quite certain, that John's creativity, his warmth and his humanity live on through her.

Acknowledgements

In writing this book, beside making use of a sixty-years accumulation of Press cuttings, many interviews and tape-recordings, countless 'Did you hear this one?' conversations, a mound of correspondence, old programmes and concert hall bills, Evelyn's and John's own writings and certain books listed in the bibliography, we have helped ourselves occasionally to the writings of others who have known our subjects on and off the platform, quoting such contents as seemed helpful in producing the characters of the two people.

Particularly we have referred to previous biographies of Sir John Barbirolli. A great debt is owed to Sidney Rothwell, one-time secretary to Sir John, for reminding us of many incidents and anecdotes for re-telling here; to Ursula Vaughan Williams, for permitting publication of selected correspondence of her late husband and herself with the Barbirollis. Also to Nigel M. Anderson; Valda Aveling; Peter and Pat Barbirolli; the Barbirolli Society (and its Chairman, Pauline Pickering, and Vice-Chairman, Paul Brooks); Deirdre Jane Barrington-Cox; Pamela Bowden; T. E. Bean, for many personal reminiscences, articles and Hallé Magazines; Brenda Bracewell-Coupe; Ernest Bradbury; Humphrey Brooke; Christopher Brunel; Archibald Buchanan, for kind research in Glasgow libraries; Alan Civil; Lore Cowan; Charles Cracknell; Wayne Crouse; Michael Davis; Muriel, The Lady Dowding; Myra Fogarty; Denham V. Ford, (Hon. Chairman of the Sir Thomas Beecham Society); Margaret Furtwängler; G. Walter George; Tina Gibilaro; Elizabeth Godlee; Rachel Godlee; Richard Godlee; Zenovia Goonan; Polly Gray (BBC Archives); Edward Greenhalgh, Barrie Hall; Beatrice Hancock; Eric Hancock; the Rt Hon. Edward Heath, MP; Annette Hewitt; Rex Hillson (Chairman of the Hallé Concerts Society); Cecilia Jaggard; Natalie James; Patricia Johnson; Tom and Kathleen Johnson; Edward Kilfoyle; Ronald Kinloch Anderson; Fredell Lack; D. W. Lander; Ivor Lester; Lesley Lewis; Iris Loveridge; Gerald McDonald; Harry Nightingale; Sam and Annie Oddy; Alexander O'Reilly; Gladys Parr; Thomas Pitfield; Tully Potter; Reginald Pound; Neville Roberts; Franz Roehn; Helen Rosenauer; Harold Rosenthal (editor of *Opera*); G. F. (Peter)

Rothwell; Stuart Scott, for the loan of his valuable Press archives; Clive Smart (Secretary and General Manager, the Hallé Concerts Society); Wolfgang Stresemann; Frau Friedrike von Wedelstaedt; Roy Watson; Helen Wilcoxson; John Wilding; Judith Windsor, for help with translations; Linda Wood (British Film Institute), for her painstaking research and likewise to Barry Mann (archivist of the Savage Club), D. Phillips and Eric Wooliscroft. We made valuable use of the British Library, the Newspaper Library at Colindale and the City of Westminster Music Library. Our thanks for re-typing the manuscript to Mrs M. Cummings, Eleanour Harvey and Annette Scott; with thanks to Audrey Napier-Smith for reading the manuscript and making so many constructive suggestions.

Thanks also to the following for permission to quote from copyright material: *Artful Reporter* for the extract from Philip Radcliffe's article; the *Daily Mail* for a review from the *News Chronicle* and a review by Peter Black; Granada Publishing for quotations from *Barbirolli* by Michael Kennedy and from *100 Years of the Hallé* by C. B. Rees; the *Guardian* for quotations from the *Manchester Guardian* and from the *Guardian*; Hamish Hamilton Limited for extracts from *John Barbirolli* by Charles Reid; The *Observer* and Humphrey Brooke for the quotation from 'Extremes of Mind'; the *Radio Times* and Neville Cardus for a quotation from an article; and Bernard Shore for the extract from his book *The Orchestra Speaks.*

We would wish to thank the Arts Council of Great Britain for making available information from their archives and for permission to reproduce certain material. The Council's Associate Music Director (Mr Eric Thompson, OBE—to whom we are similarly grateful) has administered the Guilhermina Suggia Gift for the 'Cello for many years, and his researches for us resulted in some unexpected but valuable new source material.

More than a word of appreciation is also due to our wives, Lily Atkins and Joan Miller, whose unfailing and sympathetic help has proved so beneficial to our collaboration. Most of all, our gratitude to Lady Barbirolli for her wholehearted co-operation and for making available her unique collection of professional and personal photographs.

Select Bibliography

Aria, Eliza *My Sentimental Self*. Chapman and Hall, 1922

Arundel, Dennis *The Story of Sadler's Wells*. Hamish Hamilton, 1965

Atkins, Harold and Newman, Archie. *Beecham Stories*. Robson Books, 1978.

Bean, T. Ernest. Articles in 'Manchester Guardian' and the 'Times' December 1944 and January, 1945.

Blankopf, Kurt *Great Conductors*. Arco, 1955.

Brook, Donald *Conductors' Gallery*. Rockliff, 1946.

Brook, Donald. *International Conductors' Gallery*. Rockliff, 1951

Cardus, Neville (editor). *Kathleen Ferrier: a Memoir*. Hamish Hamilton, 1954.

Cardus, Neville *Talking of Music*. Collins, 1957.

Coates, Eric *Suite in Four Movements*. Heinemann, 1953.

Cotes, Peter *No Star Nonsense*. Rockliff, 1949.

Daniels, Robin *Conversations with Cardus*. Gollancz, 1976.

Elkin, Robert *Royal Philharmonic*. Rider, 1946.

Erskine, John *The Philharmonic Society of New York: Its First Hundred Years*. Macmillan, 1943.

Ewen, David *Dictators of the Baton*. Ziff-Davis, 1943.

Ewen, David *Musicians Since 1900—Performers in Concert and Opera*. Wilson, 1978.

Ferrier, Winifred. *The Life of Kathleen Ferrier*. Hamish Hamilton, 1954.

Gelatt, Roland *The Fabulous Phonograph*. Cassell. 1956.

Grove, Sir George *Dictionary of Music and Musicians*. Fifth Edition, edited Eric Blom. Macmillan, 1954, reprinted 1975.

Hallé Magazine, from 1943.

Heath, Edward *Music: A Joy for Life*. Sidgwick and Jackson, 1976.

Henrey, Mrs Robert *Bloomsbury Square*. Dent, 1955.

Holmes, J. L. *Conductors on Record*. Gollancz, 1982.

Kennedy, Michael *The Hallé Tradition*. Manchester University Press, 1960.

Kennedy, Michael *Barbirolli Conductor Laureate*. MacGibbon and Kee, 1971.

May, Robin *A Companion to the Opera*. Lutterworth Press, 1977.

Mueller, John H. *The American Symphony Orchestra: A Social History of Musican Taste*. John Calder, 1958.

New Grove Dictionary of Music and Musicians, ed. Stanley Sadie. Macmillan, 1980.

Oxford Companion to Music, ed. Percy A. Scholes. Tenth Edition. Oxford University Press, 1970.

Rees, C. B. *100 Years of the Hallé*. MacGibbon and Kee, 1957.

Reid, Charles *John Barbirolli*. Hamish Hamilton, 1971.

Rigby, Charles *John Barbirolli*. Sherratt and Son, 1948.

Rigby, Charles *Philip Godlee and His Friends*. Dolphin Press, Sale, 1954.

Rigby, Charles *Kathleen Ferrier*. Robert Hale, 1955.

Rosenthal, Harold *Opera at Covent Garden: A Short History*. Gollancz, 1967.

Rothwell, Evelyn *Oboe Technique*. Oxford University Press, 1952, revised 1982.

Rothwell, Evelyn *The Oboist's Companion*. Oxford University Press, 1978.

Schonberg, Harold C. *The Great Conductors*. Gollancz, 1968.

Shore, Bernard *The Orchestra Speaks*. Longman's Green, 1938.

Tillis, Malcolm *Chords and Discords*. Phoenix, 1960.

Vaughan Williams, Ursula *R. V. W.* Oxford University Press, 1964.

Williamson, Audrey *Theatre of Two Decades*. Rockliff, 1951.

Wood, Sir Henry J. *My Life of Music*. Gollancz, 1938.

Wooldridge, David *Conductor's World*. Barrie and Rockliff, 1970.

Index